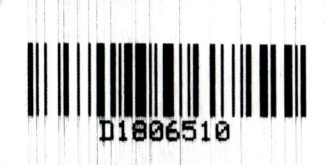

AN EYE ON IRELAND

Justine McCarthy is an prize-winning journalist, with over a dozen awards to her name. In a career spanning more than thirty years she has worked for many major Irish publications including the *Irish Independent*, the *Sunday Tribune* and *The Sunday Times*. She has been an adjunct professor of journalism at the University of Limerick and is the author of two books: *Mary McAleese: The Outsider* (1999), an unauthorised biography of the former President of Ireland published by Blackwater Press, and *Deep Deception* (2009) about the sexual abuse of young swimmers by their coaches published by O'Brien Press. She lives in Dublin and writes a weekly *Irish Times* column.

An Eye on Ireland

Writings from a Changing Nation

JUSTINE McCARTHY

HACHETTE
BOOKS
IRELAND

First published in 2023 by Hachette Books Ireland
First published in paperback in 2024

Copyright introductory essay, collection selection and
Sunday Tribune pieces © Justine McCarthy, 2023

Copyright of other selected journalism rests with publishers
as cited in the permissions acknowledgements below.

A CIP catalogue record for this title is available from the British Library.

ISBN 978 1 39972 918 5

Typeset in Sabon LT by Bookends Publishing Services, Dublin
Printed and bound in Great Britain by Clays Ltd, Elcograf S.p.A.

The publishers would like to thank the following publishers
for kind permission to reproduce the columns in book form:
Mediahuis Ireland, *The Sunday Times*, *The Irish Times*.

The publishers would like to thank Bloodaxe books for
permission to reproduce lines from the Brendan Kennelly
poem 'Old Irish' from the book *Glimpses* (2001).
www.bloodaxebooks.com

Hachette Books Ireland policy is to use papers that are
natural, renewable and recyclable products and made from
wood grown in sustainable forests. The logging and
manufacturing processes are expected to conform to
the environmental regulations of the country of origin.

Hachette Books Ireland
8 Castlecourt Centre
Castleknock
Dublin 15, Ireland

A division of Hachette UK Ltd
Carmelite House, 50 Victoria Embankment, EC4Y 0DZ
www.hachettebooksireland.ie

Contents

For Murrough, my best story

Foreword

The surprise is not that Justine McCarthy's newspaper columns are now published in book form, but that it took so long for it to happen.

Starting out in the 1980s, it was enough for women just to be there – observing, reporting, questioning, challenging. And Justine, well, she instinctively knew a story and she knew how to tell it.

A journalist, doing her job.

Back then in the smoky, testosterone-drenched clatter of the *Irish Independent* offices, it wasn't about building a body of work to stand as a unique and compelling record of momentous times in recent Irish history. It was about telling the story.

Through four decades of societal change – mapping the movement, moods and occasional madness of modern Ireland – Justine has done both. With laughs along the way to leaven the mix. But nearly forty years? Really?

Idealism dims, memories fade, anger recedes. It's easy to forget what life was like during that turbulent transitional period. Progress didn't come on a plate.

For those of us around from the beginning, this collection jolts like jump-leads to the complacent heart. For the many who were not, dive into these columns from an Ireland of not so long ago. It's an eye-opener.

It may be 2023 now but don't get too comfortable. We are where we are and Justine fills us in on how we got here. It's been some journey. You wouldn't believe the half of it and you won't want to believe the other half.

An Eye on Ireland opens in 1990 with Mary Robinson's watershed election as Uachtarán na hÉireann and takes us up to the present day with broadcaster Ryan Tubridy's spectacular fall from grace in RTÉ.

The President and The Presenter bookend a rich mix of political and social observation, reported with Justine's trademark clarity and a colour writer's quick eye for arresting detail.

In between, she chronicles the slowly loosening grip of the clerical hand which stifled generations. It's the likes of women like Justine McCarthy who give the patriarchy a bad name. She champions the women shamed and punished by their church and is there for women again when they are institutionally let down by a patriarchal establishment.

The waning dominance of the Catholic hierarchy is entertainingly captured in Justine's dash to New York to cover the breaking scandal of Bishop Eamonn Casey's secret child, only for her to discover that the fleeing Prince of the Church is hiding upstairs and out of bounds in First Class on the same flight.

She reminds us of the horror and heartbreak of the Troubles, with stories of ordinary lives lived and torn apart. Fascinating vignettes are offered from darker days, such as a cross-border train trip to Belfast with uneasy fans to watch the Republic of Ireland play Northern Ireland in a World Cup qualifier.

We are transported back to the Planning Tribunal and the boom-bust times of the Noughties. We marvel at the chutzpah of politician Liam 'I want to bring the same pioneering and entrepreneurial vision to Iraq that I brought to Dublin County' Lawlor and at the hypocrisy of political 'Holy Joes' pontificating about sexual morals while chasing brown envelopes stuffed with developers' cash.

The murder of Veronica Guerin. The death of Kelly Fitzgerald. The evil of George Gibney. The courage of Susie Long. The strength of Lavinia Kerwick. The bravery of the sex abuse survivors and the dissembling of the abusers and their powerful facilitators.

The struggles for hard-won and hard-fought referendums.

It's all there, so we never forget.

Along with rollicking episodes like the curious case of Ben Dunne, Charlie Haughey and the bri-nylon shirts; an EU tourism ministers' summit meeting in the West of Ireland. the appearance by the Virgin Mary on a tree stump in Limerick and the glory days of The Boys in Green.

Justine, my colleague and friend, prefaces her collection with an absorbing personal essay. She calls it 'A Love Letter to Journalism'. This book is journalism's unambiguous reply: a love requited.

– Miriam Lord

A Love Letter to Journalism

As a child, everything terrified me – darkness, the thought of being left alone, old Bill Slattery's empty mansion across the road from our house. My antennae were always on the lookout for danger. The notion that this timorous mouse of a child would grow up to be a career witness to horrors and cruelties seems more fantastical than any bogey man.

After reading *Lorna Doone*, I dreamt recurrently that I was aflame in a burning building. Before succumbing to sleep at night, I tried to shrink myself smaller than a dot in my dormitory bed whenever an aeroplane roared in the sky above my school, convinced it was going to crash to earth and crush me. Little wonder that Sister Ursula pleaded with me, to no avail, not to take the honours English paper in the Leaving Cert because, she said, my imagination was 'too vivid'.

School holidays brought no relief. Our house sat amid copses of evergreens atop a slope above the Bandon-to-Clonakilty road. Below was a bend so sharp it made even slow drivers slam their brakes. Every time I heard the screech of brakes, I knew my speed-addicted mother was driving that car, that she had failed to avoid hitting the wall and that she was lying dead down there in her cherished Sunbeam Rapier with its silver bird on the bonnet. I knew it for certain, until I heard our front door thud and her car keys tinkle on the hall table downstairs, and I allowed myself to breathe again.

It was on a winter's day that one of my worst fears came true. I had been sent home from boarding school for a week, after a solitary head louse dropped ignominiously from my hair onto my copybook. My mother was at a funeral in Limerick and I was left alone. It was one of those days when the Man Above never switched on the light in the sky, foretelling a storm. I walked to town for the latest edition of *Jackie* magazine and a Mars bar in O'Farrell's shop. It was dark when I got home. I drew the curtains around me in the window seat and nestled in for a spell of reading bliss. Then the lights went out. And they stayed out. I had never known such unadulterated terror. I screamed and screamed for someone to come and rescue me but the only response was the banshee-howl of the storm. I ran for my life from the house, through the groaning wood at the bottom of the garden, down New Road, into Market Street, past the cinema, along South Main Street, passing Mister Downing's tailor dummies and the dead cows hanging in Mehigan's butcher shop window, over the bridge, beyond the Munster Arms Hotel, and into Shannon Street, until I collapsed on Jean Crowley's doorstep, a drenched and bawling fright.

Jean had lived with us until she married and made her own home on the other side of town but she continued to work in our furniture shop. Once she had got me soothed, she phoned my mother, who was, by then, in a state of near hysteria herself, having returned from the funeral to find the front door wide open, the lights on in the house, and me gone.

This tendency to catastrophic thinking was rooted in an earlier event, my father's death when I was four years old. He was only forty-four when he died of a massive heart attack on his way home from work. I can recall very little from my childhood but I vividly remember that day. I was playing dolls on the landing with Adrienne, the sister closest in age to me, when two uncles appeared. Their demeanour was so sombre it seemed to block out all the light. They carried us to the kitchen where the men who made coffins in the backyard for my father's undertaking business were silently lining the room, heads bowed. I can still see and hear myself following Birdie, who minded us, around the kitchen as she poured tea for the men, and probably something stronger from the bar on the other side of the wall. 'But what does dead mean? When is daddy coming home?' I kept asking her.

Although my mother lived to be eighty-five, she never truly recovered from her shock and grief. My oldest sister Berenice had had our father to herself for four years before Adrienne was born and everyone said she was 'the apple of his eye'. Her truncated life would be shadowed forever by his loss. Gina, the youngest, was only a year and ten months. I was the one daughter who did not inherit our mother's Spanish-hued good looks. With my fair hair and freckles, the consensus was that I was 'pure McCarthy'.

As a young teenager, I envied my sisters' resemblance to mum and felt a burden of having to carry the family's torch lit by my father. As I came to learn from strangers about the many kindnesses he did in his life, I grew proud to carry his torch.

Decades later, a civil servant I had reason to call about something I was writing mentioned that he was from Bandon too. He suggested we meet for a cup of coffee. He had an ulterior motive. He wanted to tell me that one of his siblings had died as a small child more than thirty years earlier. His parents had returned from emigration to England but times in

Ireland were hard and money was scarce. His mother had told him that, if he ever met me in Dublin, he was to tell me they were eternally grateful to my father for burying their child free of charge.

In the years after Dad's death, Mum did her best to raise her four girls alone and prepare us for life, her motto being that a woman should always be able to provide for herself. Whenever adults used to ask me what I wanted to do after leaving school, I said I might be a dancer with Legs & Co. on *Top of the Pops*. Other than the risk of a sprained ankle, it seemed an unthreatening enough occupation and, besides, the costumes spangled enticingly. My answer changed one defining day when a gentleman visitor from Dublin quizzed me about my future. It was the summer I was 16, by which time I had realised that my doing the Funky Chicken for the BBC was more impossible than it was glamorous.

'I don't know,' I admitted.

'What do you like to do?' he asked.

'I love writing.'

'Why don't you become a journalist?'

'What do they do?'

'They write articles for newspapers.'

Right so, I resolved, that is what I will do. I will write lovely, flowery articles for a living.

That winter, I got my first byline when the *Evening Echo* published a poem I wrote inspired by Leonard Cohen's 'Bird on the Wire' called 'Nowhere Land'. It may have been utter doggerel but seeing my name in the newspaper made me dizzy with joy. The following summer, the visitor from Dublin returned and my mother insisted that I read aloud for him the essay I had written on 'Why I Want to be a Journalist' as part of my application for entrance to the two-year journalism course at the College of Commerce in Rathmines. I took my usual position in the window seat and read my purple prose about the magic that words can weave. The visitor told me it was marvellous. That was the first lie I would encounter in my odyssey as a journalist.

Soon, however, I was on my way with my mother driving along by the canal in Dublin, heading towards Rathmines for the aptitude test and interview to gain admission to the college course. My heart was pounding and my stomach was lurching in a malady of nerves. Mum stopped the car, broke in half one of the little blue tranquilisers she was prescribed forever after my father's death, and handed me one half. 'It'll keep you calm,' she said.

Had I not swallowed it, I might have bolted from the college as soon as I set foot in it. Everything about the place was intimidating, not least the other applicants. As we waited our turn on a bench outside the interview room, the boy beside me wore a pinstriped suit as unselfconsciously as if he had been born in it. The girl on my other side had the sort of glossy hair cut in a bob that spelled out self-assurance with every toss of her head. Eleven years in a convent boarding school had ill-prepared me for this introduction to Dubliners' cosmopolitanism.

Nor had anything prepared me for the interview panel of four men and one woman, featuring Tim Pat Coogan, the already famous editor of *The Irish Press*, and Seán Egan, the course director who presented a regular Sunday-night religion programme on RTÉ television. It was the woman, a psychologist with the Vocational Education Committee, who asked the only question I remember.

'If your boyfriend was playing a match, would you shout and jump up and down on the sidelines to support him?'

The picture she painted was so foreign to me it left me flummoxed. 'I'd be more likely to be the one playing the match,' I blurted. On the long drive home, I consoled myself it was a good answer because, not only had it asserted that I had a sporting existence of my own, thank you very much, but it dodged the embarrassing admission that I had never had a boyfriend.

The letter came at the end of August. 'Thank you for your application, but ...' They say you can't miss what you've never had. It's not true. My dream of becoming a journalist was so deeply planted in me that in my mind, by the time the letter arrived, I already was one in all but qualification. Rathmines was the only academic institution in Ireland where you could study journalism in those days and so the rejection was tantamount to a death sentence. I cried for days on end. My tears could have filled the river Bandon and all its tributaries. Unable to bear my anguish a moment longer, my wonderful mother dug out the Dublin telephone directory from the cupboard under the stairs, found Seán Egan's home number and rang him. I listened as she implored him to give me a chance. She told him she was a widow with four daughters and that I, her second youngest, was distraught because the only thing I wanted to be was a journalist. The kind man relented.

On the first morning of the course, he enumerated the realities of the life we had chosen. Ahead of us lay low social status with commensurately low pay, plus a disproportionately high incidence of alcoholism and the likelihood that we would die several years younger than the average person. 'Do you still want to be journalists?' he asked, as twenty-four young heads bobbed eagerly.

We were given our book list for classes in newspaper law, sub-editing, the New Journalism writings of Tom Wolfe, Norman Mailer and Truman Capote, statistics and shorthand, and got the afternoon off to go and buy them. While searching for Hanna's bookshop, I shyly approached a woman in Dawson Street and asked her where Nausea Street was, mispronouncing its address. The stranger, who said she was from Mayo, took pity on me and invited me to Switzer's café in Grafton Street for tea. She then escorted me to Hanna's door. I never saw her again; never got to tell her how her kindness had steadied me that day when my overwhelming urge had been to flee back home.

For I was constantly afraid of being unmasked as a fraud. I have never suffered from imposter syndrome because I have always known I am an imposter. I told no one in college that I had failed the entrance interview and that only for the grace of my mother I would still be back in Bandon nursing my crushed dream while they were poring over Woodward and Bernstein's *All the President's Men* and learning the inverted pyramid style of news reporting. When classmates from Dublin chatted about seminal programmes they had seen on British TV or articles they had read through the years in *The Guardian* and *The Observer*, I acted as though it was normal, whereas my normality had been single-channel television – even RTÉ2 was inaccessible where we lived – and *The Cork Examiner*, or 'De Paper' as Corkonians called it.

If I had any talent for journalism it was the ability to fake composure. It is a trait that sustained me in Belfast while keeping pace with a running riot from City Hall to the Falls Road after Gerry Adams's election as a Westminster MP; bunking down with Irish soldiers in Lebanon as the bellows of a nearby gun battle blared outside Camp Shamrock; alone in a building on the Shankill Road while interviewing a loyalist paramilitary who had murdered a Catholic woman just because she was a Catholic; skidding to a halt within inches of accidentally ramming an armed police checkpoint on a lonely road in County Tyrone during a snowstorm, having spent the day with the IRA commander Martin McGuinness. The night before interviewing him, I sat with a family I had never met before while they ate their dinner from plates perched on their laps in the sitting room of their Derry city home.

The RTÉ evening news was on the television, the news-reader's words drawing a stream of vitriol about the Free State from the family in between mouthfuls of fried egg and chips. McGuinness's people had given me the address of this house and told me to wait there until they would contact me. The news was still droning on when a pair of taciturn men arrived and drove me to a dingy flat – an IRA safe house, I presumed – in the Bogside. They drew the curtains on the window, put a cassette of rebel songs on a tape recorder and, to the anthemic lyrics of 'The Men Behind the Wire', they proceeded to interrogate me. Why did I want to interview Martin? they wanted to know. How could somebody from Cork have any understanding of what was going on in the North? Was the thunderously anti-Sinn Féin/IRA newspaper I worked for planning to do a hatchet job?

At such times, the scared mouse was still squealing inside me. She never left. She was there the night the *Irish Independent* sent me to scour the Louth–Armagh borderlands to bag an interview with the wife of the INLA terrorist Dessie O'Hare, known as the Border Fox, as he led gardaí on a countrywide chase with his kidnap victim John O'Grady while cutting off bits of the dentist's dexterous fingers to accompany the ransom note. On that occasion, the photographer I was working with refused to budge from the car to accompany me up unlit lanes to isolated houses because, he said, he was near retirement and had every intention of surviving to enjoy it.

I'd begun having panic attacks in my early twenties. The first one was on a crowded bus crawling through O'Connell Street. I thought I could not breathe; I thought my heart was beating so fast it would give out. The attacks grew frequent and intense. At three o'clock one morning, Mum called the GP when she found me on the bathroom floor and I cried out with total conviction that I was dying.

After my son Murrough was born, the panic became linked with phobias. I became terrified of flying. When my editor told me I was going to Egypt to cover what was expected to be the final foreign trip by the globetrotting but now ailing Pope John Paul II, I booked an emergency appointment with the Aer Lingus Fearless Flying School at Dublin Airport the day before departing. I followed the advice to request an aisle seat, to concentrate on my breathing, and to keep rubbing my wrists with ice cubes to control my body temperature but every moment of the journey to Cairo and back was hellish.

Another time, I paid €300 to a neurolinguistic programming

therapist who promised, in his splendid penthouse overlooking the Liffey, that he would cure me. Nothing worked. So, eventually, I stopped flying altogether, and using elevators, and made sure to arrange that any interviews I had to do would take place at ground level.

Five months after 2,753 people were killed in New York when terrorists deliberately crashed two airliners full of passengers into the World Trade Center, Vinnie Doyle, the pioneering *Irish Independent* editor, told me to drop everything and get to Baltimore, Maryland as quickly as possible. Naturally my fear of flying was intensified by the 9/11 events and flying to the States seemed completely terrifying to me.

News was breaking of a suspected $750m fraud at Allfirst Bank, a subsidiary of the Allied Irish Bank Group, and that an American employee, a foreign exchange trader called John Rusnak, had gone missing. I told Vinnie I couldn't go and, for the first time, confessed that I was scared of flying. His response was to offer me 'unlimited expenses to fill yourself with gin – just get on that plane and go'. In the split second when I decided I had no choice but to high-tail it to Baltimore, the adrenaline started pumping and I knew there was no other job I could love more, despite the fear. Journalism had made me dare to live. It kept shooting me out of my comfort zone.

As I was leaving the newsroom, I spotted a parcel in my postal pigeon-hole. I grabbed it and ran for a taxi, not thinking to open it until I reached the departure gate at the airport. Inside was a cover note from a publicist attached to a newly published book about overcoming the fear of flying. Each chapter addressed a specific scenario. So you think the engine will fail. Or the oxygen supply will run out. Or the plane will experience a sudden loss of altitude. When I reached the chapter that went 'so you think hijackers will take over the plane and crash it', I flung the book in the nearest bin, boarded the plane and begged the air steward for a large gin before takeoff.

My condition was eventually diagnosed at the Dublin Stress Clinic in St John of God's as agoraphobia, which, to my lay-woman understanding, means being bloody scared of everything. I had a couple of treatment sessions in St John of God's but never went back after I was made to stand in an unmoving elevator with the door open. Even that led to panic, at which stage I deemed myself beyond help. From early in life, I had perfected strategies to conceal the mouse inside me. Mostly, they involved bottling up my fears and feigning composure. I became so adept at this that my brilliant features editor in the *Irish Independent*, Jim Farrelly, extolled my 'courage' in covering the Troubles in Northern Ireland when he nominated me for a journalism award. No award could have provided a bigger confidence boost than that commendation.

During my first year in Rathmines, RTÉ had begun broadcasting a weekly CBS drama called *Lou Grant*. The eponymous Lou, played by Ed Asner, was the gruff but soft-hearted city editor of a Los Angeles daily newspaper. One of the newsroom staff was Billie Newman, a curly-haired reporter who shared her first name with my father and wrote stories about injustices that demanded action from the authorities.

In my imagination, I was Billie Newman. We shared more than a shock of curls. For as long as I can remember, injustice – or what I called 'unfairness' – enraged me and, contrary to my timorous nature, I impulsively railed against it. One of my most vivid childhood memories was of a Sunday night in school. My classmates and I were in the music hall, a cavern divided into 10 individual practice cells each furnished with an upright piano, a stool and a metronome, when a pair of white-faced nuns gathered us girls together to tell us that Catholic civilians peacefully marching in Derry that afternoon had been massacred by British soldiers. My instant reaction was not one of sorrow. It was fury. I was consumed by shocked rage that people walking the streets of their own city could be shot to death by their – purported – own army.

Years later, watching Billie Newman expose the inhumane conditions of homeless people and drug addicts in Los Angeles, I had an epiphany. What became clear to me was that writing for writing's sake was a futile exercise. Writing must have a purpose and, though it smacks of a beauty queen cliché, the best purpose was to make a difference and, maybe, help make the world a better place. Fortunately, even my vivid imagination could not conceive how desperately our country needed improving.

I grew up in a political family. My grandfather had been a prisoner in the notorious Ballykinlar internment camp in County Down during the War of Independence and was subsequently elected an independent member of Cork County Council. His second son, my father, became a Fianna Fáil councillor and, at the time of his death, he had been expected to stand in the next Dáil elections. The party's cumann meetings were held in a backroom of the public house on South Main Street that we lived above until he died. More than a decade afterwards, a Fianna Fáil delegation visited my mother and asked her to contest the local elections. I pestered her to acquiesce, until she did and, though she took to her bed from the outset of the campaign with a mysterious, symptom-free illness that might be classified as Second-Thoughts Syndrome, she came close to taking a seat.

Mum was the first feminist I met, not that it would have been evident to strangers, or even to her. She was a creature of remarkable beauty who knew how to maximise her impact. She had a custom of hitching her hemline higher when seated to show off her phenomenal legs. Mum often said I ought to write a book about her life. Born Bridget Mary McGrath into a farm family in Carrigtwohill, east of Cork city, she likened the ecstasy of her first kiss with our father to 'being hit by a combine harvester'. She handed back the engagement ring another man had given her and my parents were married within four months of first setting eyes on each other. She was only thirty-nine when the husband she adored dropped dead without warning, making her a widow with four daughters aged from ten down to a year old. She told us the reason she decided to go on living was because we needed her. She made it her mission thereafter to ensure that none of us would repeat her mistake by ever allowing ourselves to be dependent on a man to look after us. 'I couldn't change a light bulb when Billy died,' was her refrain when drumming into us the imperative that we should be self-reliant.

Mary Taaffe was Mum's best friend. Her husband had died when she was still in her twenties, leaving her with three sons to rear in an era when married women, including widows, were officially prohibited from working in the public service and, unofficially, in much of the private sector too. The two women were each other's bulwark. It was straight to Mary's house in Bandon that Bride – as she was known to her friends – drove, still shaking, from a scheduled meeting in the Department of Finance in Dublin. She had been endeavouring to resolve an astronomical tax bill for several years after my father's death. There were many days when my sisters and I would wait in the car on the South Mall in Cork for what felt like hours while she attended meetings with her accountant, returning red-eyed to us for the subdued journey home.

In desperation, she turned for help to her husband's political party and to a colleague she had often met with him socially. By then Charles Haughey was the Minister for Finance and poised to become one of Ireland's most loved and most loathed politicians. When the raven-haired and sallow-skinned Bride walked into his office that day, what the government minister saw was not a widow with a plight but an exquisite opportunity. He proceeded to pursue her around his desk until she fled, traumatised. Two decades later, I would be assigned to write a colour piece for the *Irish Independent* about the Taoiseach's attendance at the annual Phoenix Park motor races one September Sunday which coincided with his birthday. Haughey, or The Boss, as the party cravenly called him, was seated imperiously at the top table in a marquee reserved for VIPs. Before him sat the sycophantic ranks of his acolytes. Rubens might have sketched the scene as his template for *The Feast of Herod*. When I approached Haughey with my notebook, the acolytes began a slow hand-clap, demanding that I 'give him a kiss' for his birthday. I scribbled a couple of quotes from him and, like my mother before me, I fled.

Mary Taaffe was a poultry instructress with a wardrobe of

shapeless slacks and the gravelled voice of a smoker. She and Mum drank gallons of tea, puffed their cigarettes as productively as a pair of smoke machines – menthol Consulate for Mum, Carrolls Number 1 for Mary – and picked at the cold carcass of a roast chicken while debating politics and current affairs into the small hours. They encouraged us to pitch in too. Those nights were my finest education. Two young widows with seven children between them, one selling beds, carpets, wallpaper and settees, the other – restored to paid employment after the marriage bar was lifted in 1973 – schooling farmers in how to manage their chickens and eggs, taught me the rudiments of women's struggles. Perhaps it is no coincidence that the first article I had published in a national newspaper was a freelance feature for *The Irish Times* concerning discrimination against women in Trinity College's rowing club.

On one of those chicken-and-fag nights I thought I would explode with anger when Mum recounted the following tale.

After the first of us, Berenice, was born, the parish priest had required my parents to present themselves in St Patrick's, the Catholic church high on the hill looking down on all the other churches in town. My father was directed to a seat in the centre aisle while my mother was brought to kneel at a side altar for a 'churching' ceremony to purify her after the sordid exertions of childbirth – or child conception, more like – before being despatched doctrine-bound to do it again and again, as often as God's desire.

My parents left the church that day vowing to never participate in the demeaning stunt again. By the time our baby sister, Gina, came along, Mum must have been as irredeemable as Mary Magdalene before Jesus Christ rid her of her seven demons. Yet she never stopped attending church and, for a while in her declining years, she became a daily communicant. That too stopped after the early media reports that the Church had been covering up child sexual abuse by priests caused her to confide to a priest in confession that the revelations had shaken her faith. 'If that's how you feel,' the holy man retorted, 'maybe you should go and join another church.'

I left Rathmines after two years with a 180-words-a-minute proficiency in Gregg shorthand, an adequate typewriting speed and four staunch friends. We were all country girls who recognised ourselves in each other. Marese from County Sligo would go on to work for the *Irish Independent* and *The Irish Times*, Mary from County Tipperary went to RTÉ, Bernie from Connemara to the *Connacht Tribune*, and Anne from Ennis joined *The Irish Press*. Journalism was the umbilical cord that united us and the good hearts of those women have rendered that cord indestructible ever since. It is fashionable, especially in these days of misinformation when everyone fancies themselves as a 'citizen journalist', to demonise professional journalists as lazy mouthpieces for the establishment and, of course, there will always be some, but most of the ones I know are not cynical. On the contrary, they remain idealistic against the odds. In Rathmines, we had been taught that scepticism was essential in a journalist, echoing George Bernard Shaw's observation that 'the happiness of credulity is a cheap and dangerous quality'. Cynicism, on the other hand, was to be avoided.

It seems inconceivable that journalists given privileged insights into the hard lives of strangers who place their trust in us to tell their stories could remain indifferent or devoid of compassion. This sense of fraternity explains to me why many of my favourite people are journalists. Their veneer may be hard-bitten but, inside, they care. They care about truth and fairness and the underdog and the damage done by prejudice, deceit, deprivation and inequality. The added bonus is that they make scintillating company on a night out, fizzing with scandalous stories unfit to be told in public under Ireland's censorious libel laws.

I came to work for the *Irish Independent* after taking the long way around via a trade magazine called *Commercial Transport* in Rathcoole, Co. Dublin where the apogee of my research was test-driving a forklift truck on a disused English cricket crease in Leighton Buzzard. My arrival in the *Indo* coincided with the economic depression of the early 1980s. Ireland was a joyless country. The staple news diet consisted of dole queues snaking across the grey wastelands of Ireland's Republic and dazed blast victims stumbling among the rubble of bomb explosions north of the border.

The level of unemployment was vicious. Young people were emigrating in battalions, spawning stories about parishes so bereft of their youth they could not muster a Gaelic football team. The catchcry of the zeitgeist was 'Will the last person to leave the country please turn off the lights?' This was before independent radio and television were licensed or British newspapers started publishing Irish editions, and long before the technology age of mobile phones and their social media apps. News outlets were confined to RTÉ and *The Irish Times*, *The Irish Press* and the *Irish Independent* with their Sunday editions and evening papers, the *Sunday World*, and a plethora of provincial newspapers serving most counties. The limited choice of information sources mirrored the suffocating political system of 'two-and-a-half parties' comprising Fianna Fáil, Fine Gael and Labour. Ireland was rigidly Catholic, agricultural, poor, insular, patriarchal and deluded that it was a great place to bring up children.

Playboy magazine and *The Joy of Sex* by the appositely named Alex Comfort were banned. About ninety per cent of the population defined themselves as Catholics and just 6.2 per cent of all babies were born 'illegitimate', a status still on the statute books along with the death penalty. Over-the-counter sales of condoms were illegal. Sex between men was a criminal offence. The film censor banned *Working Girls*, which was about life in a Manhattan brothel, and one of the country's most vocal lobby groups was called the League of Decency.

Heroin addiction was killing young people in Dublin's inner city as the ravages of inter-generational poverty took hold. Divorce was illegal, forcing spouses who could no longer bear the sight of each other to stay living under the same roof behind a false façade of marital harmony. The country's religiosity turned delirious the summer it was reported that the Virgin Mary statue had started moving in Ballinspittle, near Bandon, triggering a domino effect of similar sightings around the country.

These were the pietistic years after Pope John Paul II's Irish visit in 1979, when one million people had gathered to see him in the Phoenix Park and, at a mass on a racecourse in Galway, he declared 'young people of Ireland, I love you', while flanked on the altar by the local bishop, Eamonn Casey, and Father Michael Cleary. The latter was Ireland's original pop star priest. Despite the orthodox views on sexual morality that he preached, the Dubliner, never short of a yarn or a cigarette between his nicotine-stained fingers, was regarded as the modern face of the Church, having recorded two song albums and with his own late-night phone-in radio show. After he died in 1993, the sensational truth came out that Father Cleary, the 'singing priest', had been sharing his parochial bed with his housekeeper, Phyllis, with whom he had two children.

These bleak years were also before the advent of Ryanair, when one of the rare affordable ways to get off the island was to catch a flight to Castro's Cuba on the USSR's Aeroflot planes. These antiquated aircraft regularly stopped off at Shannon, occasionally disgorging some misguided Soviet citizen seeking asylum from the communist empire.

One spring morning in the years before my fear of flying, I was woken at home on a day off by the ringing of the phone. 'Have you an American visa?' my *Indo* editor asked. When I said I had, he told me to go straight to the airport where there would be a plane ticket to New York waiting for me at the Aer Lingus information desk. In the taxi, the car radio was apoplectic with the international news story that Eamonn Casey had fathered a child by a young American woman when he was the bishop of Kerry. My assignment was to interview the woman, Annie Murphy, by appointment at her home in Connecticut the next day. The flight to the US made its compulsory stop-over at Shannon Airport, when we passengers were shepherded into the duty-free shop in the expectation of filling its tills before re-boarding and heading onward across the Atlantic.

More than 30,000 feet above the ocean, Kathy Bates was

unleashing road rage in *Fried Green Tomatoes at the Whistle Stop Café* on the in-flight movie when an announcement was made asking Justine McCarthy of the *Irish Independent* to make herself known to a member of the cabin crew. I pressed the call button and an air hostess, as they were called then, told me a message had been received in the cockpit from my office notifying me that 'the person you're interviewing is on board'. Guessing the news desk's cryptic reference was to Casey rather than to Murphy, I asked if the bishop of Galway was on the plane. The air hostess said no and walked away.

I happened to be seated among a delegation of Cork doctors who were on their way to a medical conference in San Francisco. One of them asked what the message was about. When I explained that I needed to find the fleeing bishop, they volunteered to help. And so, up and down the Boeing cabin we trooped, scrutinising every passenger without luck. The aircraft was one of those double-decker ones with the upstairs reserved for first-class passengers. As I started up the steps, my way was blocked by two crew members who informed me my steerage-class ticket did not allow me access. No, they assured me, Bishop Casey was not up there. But he was, of course, as history records.

While we passengers had been corralled at Shannon, he had been whisked to the State-owned airliner and smuggled on board. On arriving at Kennedy Airport, another car collected him from the door of the plane and magicked him straight off to New Jersey, to the chagrin of waiting American journalists who had been tipped off that the Irish prelate was winging his way to New York. When the *Sunday Tribune* tracked him down eighteen months later, the bishop triumphantly told the newspaper he had eluded an Irish journalist who had 'chased' him across the Atlantic the day he fled Ireland.

In those early years, older colleagues reminisced that when the pope came to Ireland they had made a point of not going to see him because of Catholicism's stranglehold on the country's social and sexual mores. They were the radical minority. In many ways, Ireland became even more puritanical after the papal visit, especially for women. Within two years, the Pro-Life Amendment Campaign was founded with the aim of securing the eighth amendment. The period around the referendum campaign the lobby secured, culminating in the 1983 constitutional ban on abortion, was a frightful time to be female in Ireland. 'Expert' men, who would have crossed a supermarket aisle to avoid making eye contact with a shelf of sanitary towels, pontificated on the national airwaves about uteruses, menstruation and their preferred method of contraception, otherwise known as cross-your-legs, ladies. One of the most farcical arguments advanced revolved around St Aquinas's theory that a male embryo is divinely furnished with a soul at an earlier stage of development than its female counterpart. It was mad stuff. And, if you were a fertile female, it was horrifying.

Inevitably, there were tragic consequences of the constitutional ban, as exemplified by the X Case when the State prevented a 14-year-old schoolgirl who was pregnant by rape from travelling to Britain for an abortion. The widespread trepidation caused by the case was captured by Martyn Turner's iconic *Irish Times* cartoon depicting the Ayatollah's morality police inspecting outward-bound female passengers for tell-tale tummy bumps at Dublin Airport.

The repercussions of the legal case, which went all the way to the Supreme Court, meant the female half of the population no longer had the same unfettered freedom to travel abroad as their fathers, brothers, husbands and sons, or to obtain information about abortion services in other jurisdictions – not even from their doctors. The climate became so suspicious it was proposed that British telephone directories should be confiscated from public phone boxes, causing girls and women to think twice before dialling directory inquiries for fear someone might think we were seeking the number for an abortion clinic. The Irish edition of *Cosmopolitan* magazine arrived on these shores with whole pages left blank where, in the UK editions, there were advertisements for Marie Stopes clinics and other pregnancy termination services.

In my early years in the *Indo*, we wrote our stories on golf ball typewriters that made an exhilarating clatter, using carbon paper to make 'blacks' – duplicates – which 'copy boys' then carried to the printers. Sexism was so ingrained that women reporters were not allowed down to the basement where the monster presses churned out our work in case we would distract the printers and delay the edition hitting the street.

Journalism was an unapologetic man's world. Pictures of pretty girls routinely adorned the news pages. Editors preferred to report on the annual Calor Kosangas Housewife of the Year than on the fact that, in 1989, the average female industrial wage was sixty-nine per cent of what men got. There had never been a woman editor of a national newspaper at that stage and female journalists were still stereotyped as 'lifestyle' writers.

Under Vinnie Doyle's editorship, the *Indo* had recently abandoned its 'women's page' but, as yet, there was not a single female photographer on the staff nor female editors on the news desk or in the business, farming or sport sections. There was no woman among the political, industrial affairs, health, education, religion, economics or agriculture correspondents, and all the heavyweight columnists were men. Girls with notebooks were quite the novelty for the lads. One night, I was covering an event in the city when a senior, over-rated and over-paid colleague who was there for his leisure offered to drive me back to the *Indo*. Rushing to meet a deadline, I gladly accepted. He drove me in his Mercedes car to the back door of the office in Prince's Street, reached across to grab the door handle, and insisted I kiss him.

He was a decidedly unattractive specimen and I would have sooner kissed a cactus marinated in Ian Paisley's bile but I was so utterly conditioned to be polite and to not hurt anybody's feelings that I gave him a peck on the cheek and went back to work. Another day, I was walking along a corridor in Independent House on my way to the expenses hatch when another male colleague, whom I knew only to see, opined behind me: 'Justine, you've a good figure but you've no arse.' I said nothing, just went on walking. He went on to ascend to the middle ranks of a trade union.

Vinnie Doyle and the features editor, Michael Brophy, introduced colour-writing to the *Indo*'s news pages in the mid-1980s. With the utmost patience, Michael taught Liz Ryan – a talented writer and future novelist – and me how to hone the descriptive-reporting style and despatched us to capture the atmosphere at everything from horse fairs to general election campaigns. We had a ball covering the best 'markings' (events) and getting prominent space in the paper, complete with big picture bylines that enhanced our profile with readers.

We were conscious that some colleagues resented us, and understandably so, but the counterbalance was that they were on the four-day-week payroll with a staff pension scheme, guaranteed holidays and paid sick leave whereas we, as freelancers, had no such security. We were also conscious that our being female was partly the cause of their irritation. The crux came when the *Indo* chapel of the National Union of Journalists passed a motion barring freelancers from working in Independent House. We were no longer allowed work in the building that housed our desks and typewriters. Neither were we allowed to attend the chapel meetings because we were not on the staff, even though we were union members. Liz and I never learned what exactly was said about us when the motion was passed, only that, ostensibly, the ban was imposed – and lasted for about six months before petering out – to prove to management that additional permanent jobs were needed in the newsroom.

I never did understand how forcing us to work from home and, having to physically deliver our copy into the office by deadline, could establish that case. To both our minds, the motion banning us was hostility disguised by a veil of workers' rights.

When I had first resolved to become a journalist, reporters were regarded as muckrakers lurking on street corners in upturned raincoat collars and a press pass jammed in the hatband, barely able to scrape together the price for a pint in the early-hours dockers' bars down on the quays. Being scorned by the establishment was part of the allure. Journalism had its own unique ecology, its own lingo and way of life. The smell of the newsprint and the cacophony of the newsroom were intoxicating.

In the days before LinkedIn and the Freedom of Information Act, telephone operators, postmistresses and postmasters in towns and villages dotted all over the country were primary sources of reliable information. Ours was a boisterous world filled with shouts of 'copy', 'reverse ferret' and unprintable catchphrases.

Now those corybantic rhythms have been stilled by the hush of emails, texts, computer keyboards and dodgy Wikipedia sourcing. Technology delivers information in the blink of an eye, accelerating the news cycle. In the late twentieth century, yesterday's news was deemed only fit to wrap today's fish-n-chips. Now yesterday's news is ancient history.

The arrival of Google and social media, of camera phones and roaming Wi-Fi, of online publications and newspaper apps has increased journalists' workload and the public scrutiny of the job we do. The benefit is that it has made the trade more professional, necessitating stricter ethical rules and fact-checking standards. The Press Council, the Ombudsman and the Broadcasting Authority of Ireland are all keeping a beady eye and new academic courses are providing alternative routes into journalism for some stunningly smart graduates.

All of this is good. But it has its disadvantages too. The immediacy of news has intensified the competition for sensational scoops, generated an insatiable appetite for celebrity tittle-tattle and popularised clickbait, contributing to a general dumbing-down of society. Journalism has come to be seen by some school-leavers as a stepping stone to fame and an entrée to the social whirl of movie premieres and the in-crowd. Some journalists fancy themselves as players in their chosen fields of specialism. Others expect to become television presenters or war correspondents overnight but it is those graduates with that indefinable thing in their genes that makes them just want to be journalists who tend to stay the course.

Though its razzle-dazzle had not been the attraction for me, journalism has brought me to places and to people beyond the frontiers of my dreams. When Mary Robinson made the first official visit by an Irish president to Buckingham Palace and the Irish Guards regiment played 'Amhrán na bhFiann' in the courtyard, I looked across at the Tánaiste, Dick Spring, and when I saw his chin tremble with emotion, the hairs stood up on my neck.

During the Somalian famine, while Robinson was visiting an orphanage in Baidoa, I watched as an emaciated man lay slumped beneath a tree and realised he was dying. Vincent Browne, whose passionate soapbox appearances on *The Late Late Show* years before had convinced me I was right to want to be a journalist, told me I could not help the dying man but that my job was to write about what was happening in that wretched country, with its omnipresent stench of human decay.

In Rome for the 1990 World Cup draw, when 1,100 journalists from all over the globe, except me, had their laminate press passes, I wangled a seat in the sponsors' section beside a businessman from Naples who elbowed me excitedly in the ribs every time the still-smouldering Sophia Loren mentioned his home city from the stage.

I was back in the Eternal City a few years later for the beatification of the Christian Brothers founder Edmund Rice. During our homeward-bound flight, an electrical storm rocked our plane so ferociously that the bishops up front with the politicians led the first-class passengers in a rendition of 'Nearer, My God, to Thee'. At the foot of Mount Sinai where Moses found the Ten Commandments, it rained in the desert for the first time in fifteen years, so the locals said. I had been reporting on Pope John Paul II's visit to Egypt.

In New York, I accompanied Marion Serravalli, the purchasing manager for a New Jersey paper mill, on a shopping expedition to buy kohl eyeliner for her first visit as his wife to her erstwhile pen pal, Paul Hill, having married the Belfast man, who was wrongly convicted of the Guildford pub bombings, in England's Long Lartin jail.

In Berlin, I hired a hammer and chisel from a hawker to carve a piece from the wall as it was coming down to bring home to my mother and then followed the sound of singing to a square off a side-street where about a hundred East Germans were celebrating a religious feast day in the open for the first time in their lives. Their liberation from behind the Iron Curtain wetted their cheeks as they sang hymns of praise.

In Israel, I waited out the Jewish Sabbath in a grotty hotel on the border until I could obtain a press pass to cross into Lebanon. My assignment to write a feature about Irish peace-keeping soldiers had begun ominously when my luggage failed to arrive with me on the British Airways flight to Jerusalem. My wait was interrupted by the arrival of a dashing Irish captain at the hotel, complete with a plastic carrier bag filled with toothpaste, toothbrush, deodorant, several pairs of hideous bloomers, a pair of 501 denim jeans and an oversized, shocking-pink t-shirt saying 'Don't Let the Bastards Get you Down'.

In Tenerife, an Aer Lingus executive treated me to lunch on a yacht while I tried to extract answers from him about the then State airline's 'white elephant' purchase of a banana plantation that was causing political ructions at home. In Finland, I declined an invitation to join a group taking a naked sauna followed by a roll in the snow, explaining that I was an Irish Catholic and it was against my religion.

In Belgrade, NATO-bombed buildings gnawed the skyline in the background of the daily vigils at twilight celebrating the Serbian war criminals Slobodan Milošević and Radovan Karadžić, the latter still on the run from the International Criminal Tribunal for the Former Yugoslavia. On a flight to London during the 1987 general election campaign to cover Garret FitzGerald's appearance on the BBC's *Wogan* show, the outgoing Taoiseach sipped a Buck's Fizz because it was his birthday and promptly spilled the rest of it over his stockinged feet. 'Please don't write that,' he asked. 'It's bad enough everybody knows I wear odd shoes.'

A distractingly bare-chested Pierce Brosnan consented to an impromptu interview on a blazing summer day in the Wicklow mountains before he was James Bond and during a break while he was filming *Taffin*, a movie destined to bomb at the box office. In Hollywood, I interviewed Tom Selleck, Ted Danson and Steve Guttenberg when *Three Men and a Baby* went on release in cinemas.

I met writers whose fiction I had devoured. John McGahern

showed me the spartan room in his lakeside Leitrim cottage where he wrote *That They May Face the Rising Sun*. Over tea in the Shelbourne Hotel, Belfast native Brian Moore described his new life in the Malibu sunshine, a stark contrast to the unremitting greyness suffusing *The Lonely Passion of Judith Hearne*. In Manchester, another Belfast man, the footballer George Best, sat beside his latest girlfriend on a hotel sofa and said, this time, he had found true love. I interviewed the still-handsome Seán O Faoláin in the nursing home where he lived out the end of his life and I have the late Harry Belafonte's number in my phone contacts since interviewing the singer, movie star and activist in his role as a UNICEF goodwill ambassador. In Sandymount, I interviewed Paul Durcan about his poetry and his blood connection with one of the Easter Rising leaders, John MacBride.

It wasn't lost on me that the overwhelming preponderance of politicians, artists, business representatives and famous people I interviewed were men. That's the nature of patriarchy. Yet the most transformative stories of the times were all about women and girls.

There was the High Court's upholding of Eileen Flynn's sacking from the teaching staff of a Wexford convent school over her love life with a married man. Joanne Hayes was hauled before a tribunal and proverbially stoned over her love life with Jeremiah Locke, another married man, in the landmark Kerry Babies case. Ann Lovett died at the age of fifteen after giving birth at a holy grotto to a son who never lived a day. For anyone who did not experience that Ireland, the momentousness of Mary Robinson's election in 1990 as the State's first woman president is hard to appreciate. A searingly smart lawyer who had doggedly established various rights for women in the courts, she bowed to no man. Her election slogan was 'a woman's place is in the Park' and when the count confirmed she had won that place in Áras an Uachtaráin, euphoria erupted in homes and hearts and minds where tapers of discontent had flickered for generations of women. 'The hand that rocked the cradle has rocked the system,' Robinson declared. Women celebrated and feminist men bought them red roses, both as a reflection of her Labour Party's emblem and as a gesture of 'welcome to our world'. That was the turning point.

Seeing was believing. Other women started speaking out. Christine Buckley poured out her soul on Gay Byrne's radio show about the abuse she suffered as a child in Goldenbridge orphanage. Louise O'Keeffe beat the State in the European Court of Human Rights in her quest for redress after being sexually abused when she was a child by Leo Hickey, her school principal in Dunderrow, County Cork. Teenager Lavinia Kerwick met the Minister for Justice to demand law reform after she became the first rape survivor to abandon her anonymity.

Vicky Phelan refused to sign a gagging agreement so she could warn other women with terminal cervical cancer that the authorities had withheld information about their health from them. Miss D won her case in the High Court when the Health Service Executive impeded her from going to England for an abortion after she and her boyfriend were informed that their hoped-for baby would not survive after birth. Post-symphysiotomy sufferers gave account after account of the excruciating pain they endured until the United Nations called for a criminal inquiry into the practice and the establishment of a compensation scheme. Philomena Lee helped make a movie about how her baby son was snatched from her in Roscrea's Sean Ross Abbey and exported to adoptive parents in America.

Catherine Corless was proved correct when she claimed that 796 children who died in a Tuam mother and baby home had been buried in a part of a sewerage system. Former residents of the Magdalene Laundries for 'fallen women' wept as they recalled being deprived of their names and given numbers instead and how their children were used without their consent for vaccine trials for rich pharmaceutical companies. On and on it went, girls and women telling their stories of the injustices, cruelties, abuses and violence perpetrated against them until the momentum reached a point of no return. Women's stories dragged Ireland kicking and screaming into a better future.

If an ability to fake it had been my passport to journalism, luck's intervention kept me going. One of our trade's secrets is that the best scoops happen by chance. It was one of these vagaries that led me to the young woman at the centre of the Kilkenny incest case in March 1993. As the criminal courts were packing up at the end of another day, news emerged that a forty-eight-year-old man had been sentenced to seven years' imprisonment for repeatedly raping and assaulting his daughter for fifteen years. A photographer and I were despatched from the *Indo* to go and find the woman, equipped only with the knowledge that the family resided somewhere in County Kilkenny. It was already dark when we left Dublin.

We drove from village to village but nobody knew anything.

Growing hopeless, we stopped at a roadside chipper for something to eat. I asked the girl behind the counter if, by any chance, she knew where the woman in the court case might be. 'Why do you want to know?' she asked. I said I was a journalist and I was hoping to interview her. 'Wait here,' the girl said and left the chipper. Moments later, she returned. She led me to a nondescript building and up steep stairs into a room beneath the rafters. 'Come in,' said a pale, young woman. In the gloomy light, a bundle was discernible on the bed in the corner. It was her child, swaddled in her overcoat. She told me the little boy had learned only that evening that his grandfather was his father.

I thanked the woman for talking to me and went to a nearby pub to phone in my story to the *Indo*. When I was finished, the copy-taker told me to hold on because the acting editor wanted to talk to me. He came on the phone and said I was to return to the woman and offer her money – I do not remember the specific sum he mentioned – for an exclusive interview on the record, including pictures, for Saturday's paper. I refused, arguing that it would ruin both her life and her child's. He insisted. He said it was an order. I returned to the room beneath the rafters and told the woman I had been ordered by my editor to offer her the stated sum of money for an interview which would identify her and her son. 'Now I've made you the offer,' I said, 'I'm advising you not to do it because you and your son will always be known for this.'

'I'm going to do the interview,' the woman said and my heart fell, before she added, 'but I don't want the money and I don't want to be named. Come back in the morning and we'll do it.'

I went back the next morning and she talked for nearly two hours about the savagery her father had subjected her to since she was a young child, her pregnancy and the birth, her frequent admissions to hospital with her injuries, her failed attempts to run away and how nobody in authority raised the alarm. At the door, as we were saying our goodbyes, she said: 'Do you know why I decided to talk to you?'

'No, why?' I asked.

'Because my son said you've hair like the girl in *Days of Thunder*. He loves that film.'

There is no accounting for serendipity. It struck again in February 1996. Ed O'Brien, a twenty-one-year-old IRA man with the open face of a child, blew himself up with a bomb he was carrying on the Aldwych bus in London. A posse of international media immediately set up camp outside his parents' home in Gorey, County Wexford in pursuit of an interview.

I was among them, when a local man called me aside. 'You work for the *Irish Independent*, don't you?' he said. Instead of the barracking I was braced for, he told me he was close to the O'Brien family and he would tell them they could trust me. Soon after, he reappeared and beckoned me inside the house. The dead man's parents were sitting side by side on the couch in their living room forming a tableau of grief.

They said they knew their son used to sell *An Phoblacht* in the town but they had been oblivious to how deeply involved he was in the IRA until a garda appeared on their doorstep to tell them he was dead. The couple brought out their photo albums and were recounting memory snatches of their child's life when we all heard a noise and looked up to see a Sky television sound boom poking through a small window in their front room.

The ever-quotable G.B. Shaw said that patriotism is the conviction that your country is superior to all others because you were born in it and, for me, there is a grain of truth in that. Reporting and commenting on Ireland has been a particular pleasure because I love my country. It's home. It's where I belong: that instinct to make connections with others; the scathing humour to lighten the load; those beautiful West Cork peninsulas; the richness of the spoken and written language; the all-togetherness in good times and bad.

During more than four decades as a journalist, I never stopped loving my country, nor detesting it constructively. That work of construction will never be completed. I look at the Ireland we have now and not only do I love it, I like it enormously. But there are many threats to its continuing better mood.

Peace in the North will remain on shaky ground as long as political parties can shut down Stormont on a whim. The protracted homelessness crisis and the unwieldy asylum process in the Republic have entrenched inequality and given those who spread hatred a platform for their agenda; those people who hate the Ireland we have now and want it to go back to the way we were; people who claim to be patriots and use the national flag as their chosen flag of convenience. As Banksy says, 'people who enjoy waving flags don't deserve to have one'.

In many ways, Ireland is almost unrecognisable from the place it was when I took my first tentative steps as a journalist. During the many days I spent in the National Library selecting the articles for this collection, I came to appreciate all the better how dramatically the country has changed. By opening its mind, Ireland opened itself to opportunity and journalism helped by being the conduit for the stories of the good and the brave. The dole queues have virtually vanished, along with the Troubles. The greyness has given way to a rainbow of ethnicities as emigration switched to immigration. The valleys of squinting windows and judgmentalism have been re-settled by a live-and-let-live tolerance. After one hundred years of independence, there is, at last, a sense of freedom in the Irish air.

– Justine McCarthy

The 1990s

The 1990s

The Celtic heroine is crowned in a new dawn

Hibernia stroked the strings of her harp. Justice held aloft her sword and her scales. Liberty teased as she reclined on the steps of the dais.

Irish Independent, 4 December 1990

The ladies painted by Vincenzo Valdrè 200 years ago on the ceiling of St. Patrick's Hall watched the new female symbol of Ireland walk tall and proud between the phalanx of formal suits to take her place in the land's highest office.

Seldom had the national anthem sounded so stirring. The cymbals clashed, the drums rolled and the emotion of ceremony swelled the banners of the knights. Army and naval officers stood in frozen salute. The powerful men of the nation in their stiff morning suits and silver ties were reduced to bystanders.

"I am of Ireland," she had said, "come dance with me in Ireland."

They did not dance. They applauded and, were it not for the constraints of decorum, they might have burst into raucous cheering and carried her off into the misty horizon on their shoulders. A Celtic heroine crowned in a new dawn.

Uachtarán na hÉireann, Máire Mhic Róibín, smiled briefly at her husband. In the golden 18th century hall, politicians, judges and church leaders lent their solemn presence to the occasion.

The victorious and the vanquished celebrated the dignity of the office and its new incumbent.

Brian Lenihan and Austin Currie sat side-by-side betraying nothing less than graciousness in defeat. The former President, Dr. Patrick Hillery, clapped for his successor with his hands and his heart.

The Chief Justice Tom Finlay, having presented the Presidential seal, radiated pride in the elevation of the woman from the Law Library to Áras an Uachtaráin. Like a father pinning the orchid to his debutante daughter's decolletage, it was he who guided her through the 45-minute ceremony with his frequent looks of encouragement.

"In the presence of Almighty God," she had sworn, "I, Mary Robinson, do solemnly and sincerely promise and declare that I will maintain the Constitution of Ireland and uphold its laws, that I will fulfil my duties faithfully and conscientiously in accordance with the Constitution and the law, and that I will dedicate my abilities to the service and welfare of the people of Ireland. May God direct and sustain me."

Throughout the inauguration, the sobriety of the ritual had been punctuated only by the clicking of press cameras, the whirr of their motors growing louder whenever the President looked up from the leather-bound programme she held with steady, tapering fingers.

In the restricted press corner, journalists – advised by the protocol section of Foreign Affairs to dress appropriately – tugged at their neckties and grumbled that Tony Gregory, TD, had turned up in an open-neck shirt.

The Taoiseach was the first person to address her with her new title. "A Uachtaráin," he said. She looked at him and smiled, then reached for the crystal glass on the table and sipped delicately. With her antique jewellery and amethyst watermark silk, President Robinson even outshone the hierarchs of the churches, seated on gilt chairs in their flowing ecclesiastical robes.

Under the stall plates of the knights of the Most Illustrious Order of St. Patrick, political leaders of Northern Ireland, the SDLP's John Hume, the Official Unionist, Ken Magennis and Alliance leader John Alderice sat forward to hear the President's first speech in office.

"As the elected choice of the people of this part of our island, I want to extend the hand of friendship and of love to both communities in the other part," she promised. "And I want to do this with no strings attached, no hidden agenda."

Members of the Oireachtas, Council of State, the highest ranking officers of the security forces, diplomats, newspaper editors, the chairpersons of local authority councils, the friends and family of Mary Robinson listened earnestly as she described the face of modern Ireland "… is álainn an pobal iad muintir na hÉireann."

The stifled echoes of the 21-gun salute fired from Collins Barracks permeated the 13th century battlements as the new President prepared to inspect the guard in the courtyard. In the grey noon drizzle, she walked ramrod straight past the ranks of the immobile soldiers, while a young officer wiped the lens of his Canon camera for a picture of the forces' new Supreme Commander.

As the cavalcade, escorted by 36 Army outriders on new Kawasaki motorbikes, left Dublin Castle for Áras an Uachtaráin, the President of Ireland sat in the back of her 42-year-old Rolls Royce, gliding past the restored statues of Hibernia, Justice and Liberty standing watch in Dame Street.

The way we are

Chief Feature Writer Justine McCarthy assesses the changes that have seen the Irish people step out of the shadow of the past.

Irish Independent, 1 December 1990

Happy birthday Ireland, you've come of age. After a protracted gestation and decades of severe growing pains, we are, at last, emerging from the time warp of the Celtic mists. The shackles of fear and its twin, prejudice, are being shaken off by a nation heartily sick of insularity and hypocrisy.

The candles are lighting in a new era and a new country. We are witnessing the revolution of evolution. We are an ancient race struggling to stand tall in a young, autonomous state and we have found our voice in a dictatorship of the electorate.

During her election campaign, Mary Robinson challenged us with the notion that, by choosing her as our President, we would be signalling a new maturity. In her victory speech at the RDS she applauded those voters who had "stepped out from the faded flags of the Civil War and voted for a new Ireland".

Now the politicians are scurrying, like bats in the midday sun, to catch up with the people. Those who have been blind now see. The three biggest parties in Dáil Éireann, Fianna Fáil, Fine Gael and Labour, have been forced, at the people's demand, to reassess their trusty philosophes. The ripples of change have reached the shores of power and sands have begun to shift.

Ireland is a different country now. We are a different people. The Glorious Gael is an independent individual who values integrity, recognises realities and draws back the lace curtains to study the world outside the window. Fionn, Oisin and the twinkle-toed maidens are part of what we are: pieces of the giant jigsaw that make up the complex New Ireland.

It is not an overnight phenomenon. Ever since Séan Lemass abolished protectionism and opened up the economy, pubescent Ireland has been straining at the apron strings. Just as the economic reforms propelled us out into the great, big world, the introduction of free education opened our minds to the radical and the untested. Our entry into the EEC, the arrival of mass communications and the urbanisation of our society have changed us utterly.

Seventy years after winning our freedom we have found the confidence to exercise our independence. Ireland has taken her place among the nations of the world, as Dev envisioned, but Mr de Valera would find his emerald in the Atlantic a foreign country now.

The significance of Mary Robinson's election has not been exaggerated. As a woman who proposed a Seanad bill on contraception 16 years ago, who is avowedly in favour of legislation permitting divorce, and who objects to our unconditional constitutional claim on Northern Ireland, as the lawyer who has fought for homosexual rights, access to the law for the poor, and jury duty for women, it is inconceivable that the Ireland of 20 years ago would have offered her the highest seat in the land.

In those days, women were not allowed to continue working in the civil service after marriage (the bar was lifted in 1973) while women performing the same jobs as men were on 20 p.c. lower salaries. In that other Ireland, too, the shadows of the Roman Catholic Church lay over the country. In 1961, for instance, a total of 1.6 p.c. extra-marital births were were recorded, compared to last year's 12.6%.

At the same time, the number of Irish abortions carried out in Britain has risen from 64 in 1968 to an average of 4,000 a year in the '80s. As marital fertility has been declining in recent years, a single woman is now two or three times more likely to have a baby.

In the course of its own research, the Church has found that one of the most distinctive characteristics of Irish practising Catholics is that they are selective about which teachings they accept. This is borne out by figures released this week, which claimed that six out of every 10 couples use contraceptives.

The sexual maturation of the Irish has been dramatic. There is a vague memory of some politician's assertion that sex did not exist in Ireland before the advent of television. The memory grows more remote as subjects like marital infidelity and sexual fantasies are being openly discussed by Gay Byrne and Gerry Ryan on national radio.

The advent of independent radio has further opened up the airwaves and pushed back the barriers. The Bray-based Horizon Radio has been broadcasting a weekly half-hour gay and lesbian programme, Outwaves, since last July, featuring information, advice and "coming-out" stories. There are homosexual literature sections in Waterstones and Books Upstairs, commercially run nightclubs, like 'Shaft' and 'Hooray

Henrys' and several gay pubs and gyms in Dublin. There are active gay communities in Dublin, Cork, Limerick and Galway catering for the 10 p.c. of the population believed to be gay.

The Irish are a predominantly young, educated people. Many of those 50 p.c. who were under 25 in the early '80s, have grown up, travelled, emigrated, lived and learned. Today, the average age is 31.39 years, with 40 p.c. between 25 and 59 years. And our adulthood is being acknowledged.

Though the Censorship of Publications Office persists in banning sexually explicit literature (14 books this year), the film censor has accepted that Irish cinema audiences have grown up enough to handle steam on the screen.

Since Sheamus Smith took over the job four years ago, he has only banned one film and that decision was appealed. It is believed, in fact, that his objection to Personal Services, the autobiographical story of English brothel-keeper Cynthia Payne, was prompted by the scene in which a woman gives her 16-year-old son a present of a prostitute for his birthday.

Meanwhile, as many American cinemas are refusing to play the Hollywood movie, Henry & June, which has been given a restricted over-18 certificate in US, the original, completely uncut version opened in Dublin last night.

The very resurrection of the divorce debate, four years after the country rejected the proposed constitutional amendment, hints at the rapid change that has been occurring in this country. The number of women receiving deserted wives allowance has increased by 50% since the referendum in 1986, when 63.5 p.c. of the population voted against the amendment. Now, for the first time in living memory, an absolute majority of the electorate is believed to be in favour of a divorce law. In the Sunday Independent/IMS opinion poll last July, 51 p.c. of respondents said they would like a change in the law to permit divorce.

It is of more than academic interest that, in the divorce referendum, the electoral constituency of Dún Laoghaire delivered the highest number of 'yes' votes of the 41 constituencies, or the majority of 8,655. Following the same liberal trend, Dún Laoghaire gave Mary Robinson 54.6 p.c. of its vote in the presidential election and, in the abortion referendum seven years ago, the Dublin seaside constituency most resoundingly rejected the amendment, adopted by 67 p.c. of the nation, with a majority no vote of 6,775.

Dún Laoghaire is probably the most affluent constituency in the country. Property prices in places like Killiney, Dalkey, Sandycove and Foxrock have soared as the exclusive cachet has been propagated. The DART line which skims its coastline has added to the area's desirability. Within its boundaries are some of the country's most prestigious schools and expensive restaurants.

Yet Dún Laoghaire constituency also houses large local authority, social welfare estates and, for that reason, it can be seen as a microcosm of modern, urban Ireland. Its liberal leanings can be partly explained by the area's West Brit–Kingstown tradition, as a place where many civil servants in the former British administration chose to live, which boasts a large number of non-Roman Catholic residents and which still records the highest number of votes cast by non-Irish born residents.

The eastern region: embracing Dublin, Meath, Kildare and Wicklow, is the most densely populated region of Ireland and is simultaneously emerging as the most liberal. It also mirrors the urbanisation of Ireland. In 1961, 53.5 p.c. of the people lived in rural areas. By 1986, the majority of the population, 57 p.c. had been scooped into urban life.

As a people our work ethic has also changed. Absenteeism has declined and industrial disputes are less frequent than in the late '70s. In itself, the Programme for National Recovery has shown a greater responsibility in attitudes to the economy. One obvious benefit has been the rise in Irish productivity to 90 p.c. of the highly-industrialised and disciplined German workforce.

The new Ireland is a more tolerant and compassionate society of people weary of nod-and-a-wink politics whose eyes have been forced open by national and personal tragedies. The bitter intransigence searing the North apart, the public humiliation of a young woman in the Kerry Babies Tribunal, the death of a schoolgirl in Granard at the end of her full-term concealed pregnancy, the horror of child abuse and the incest cases pouring into the courts, these have been the painful stages of our journey. Our secrets were spilling out from beneath the carpet and there were no hiding places left.

Late to join this new race, the political institutions have been heaving under the changes. The foundation of the Progressive Democrats, the coalition forged between them and Fianna Fáil last summer and the election of Mary Robinson as President are the accumulated tensions passed on by the people's consensus.

But this is not our final destination. As a pluralist, democratic nation entering an era of cautious liberalism there is much yet to be done. Findings by the Medico Social Research board, when it surveyed under-20-year-old women seeking abortions, that 42 p.c. had never practised contraception, points to the need for more sex education on the school curriculum.

Also in the area of sexual freedoms, the ruling by the European Court of Human Rights two years ago in the Norris Case that the Offences Against the Person Act (1861) and the Criminal Law Amendment Act (1885) were in breach of the Convention of Human Rights, has yet to be adopted.

In coming of age we now have the key and, with it, the confidence to strive for a better future. The ability of individuals to rise above the institutions and the Establishment has given us strength. We can look at the international music scene and boast of U2 and Sinéad O'Connor, the world of cinema and the Pearson-Sheridan duo are up there with the best of them, the world of sport and the Irish football team carries forward our dreams and potential.

Even at home, a woman like the new novelist Patricia Scanlan have shown us what we are capable of achieving and what we are now mature enough to tolerate. Her first novel, City Girl, is a tale of unwanted pregnancies, homosexual love, wife-beating and alcohol and drug dependency. To literary giants like John McGahern and Seán Ó Faoláin, for whom the word 'censorship' has been a middle name, the leap must seem mammoth.

Other women have made quieter strides. Apart from our President-elect, we now have a woman assistant general secretary of the Irish Congress of Trade Unions, Patricia O'Donovan, a woman assistant secretary of a Government Department, Margaret Hayes in Transport, and the first woman legal adviser in the Department of Foreign Affairs, Geraldine Skinner.

The snowball continues to gather momentum, and is even expected to accelerate with the arrival of 1992, when Europe becomes the street where we live. These are exciting times and frightening times for the land of the little people waking from the sleep of mythology. The biggest challenges face the politicians. In the words of Edmund Burke, "a nation is not governed which is perpetually to be conquered." It may not be Éireann go brea, but it will be different, and so will we.

Many happy returns, Ireland.

Eurocrack

A muted gathering of EC Council of Tourism Ministers
in Ashford Castle was transformed by finest Irish
hospitality. Justine McCarthy kept a diary.

Irish Independent, 17 March 1990

Friday 9 March 1990

Dear Diary

This EC presidency lark is the best excuse for a party since
Screaming Lord Sutch founded the Monster Raving Loonies.
Henceforth, whenever I hear the Taoiseach of Ireland and
president of Europe talk solemnly of the dignity and stateliness
of this six-month reign, I shall stifle a private chuckle.

Such revelry and jollity has not been seen since the prodigal
son's father killed the fatted calf.

We're all holed up here in Ashford Castle for the weekend –
the 12 Ministers for Tourism, the Commissioner from Portugal,
the Irish president of the Council, Seamus Brennan, their
spouses, their senior civil servants and what looks like the entire
complement of Interpol. (As I write, there is a detective, with a
parka jacket zipped up to his chin and a Uzi sub-machine gun
slung across his manly chest, scrunching the gravel beneath by
window).

The Government has taken over every nook and blade of
grass in this 19th century castle and demesne on the mystical

shores of Lough Corrib for the pleasure and safety of the 80 delegates. There are uniformed gardaí stationed at all the gates to the estate and on the great cut-stone bridge that spans the gentle Cong River. Garda sub-aqua teams, sheathed in glistening diving gear, glide silently in rippling circles round the lake in a rubber powerboat. Even within the castle portals, detectives sit shadowy in ghostly corners checking the laminated badges on the delegates' lapels. (I suspect that there is actually a garda on overtime and crippled with cramp inside the antique suit of armour in the foyer).

Rory Murphy, a model of the dapper and discreet hotel manager, told me earlier that gardaí insisted the castle be closed 10 hours before the first guests arrived so that they could carry out a thorough security sweep. He said the garda sniffer dogs had done their duty on top of every bed in every room and suite. The thought is a pleasant leveller: I wonder if Commissioner Cardoso e Cunha and the chambermaid have had the same hound's snout stuffed beneath their pillows.

I am writing this at five o'clock in the morning and the castle is resonant with the sound of slumber. It has been a long day. And an education.

The gurus of European tourism didn't exactly look like the jolliest bunch of weekenders when we met this afternoon at the Aer Rianta VIP lounge in Dublin Airport. Even the revelation, courtesy of Council President Brennan's economic adviser Dick Doyle, that three of the ministers are bachelors, hardly ignited our optimism.

For a start, they were all wearing business suits with stuffy shirts and ties. All, that is, except the Danish Minister who wore a frock. (She's a woman). The British Minister, the Rt.

Hon. Lord Strathclyde looked like a pudgy public schoolboy whose only likely form of exercise would be a race through the ranks of the Tory party. The French, the Spanish and the Italian ministers chose to fly directly to the West of Ireland from Paris, Madrid and Rome in their executive jets while the Greek minister was being driven cross-country by his ambassador.

The rest of us were flying to Knock in a specially chartered Aer Lingus 737 and into the eye of the Curse Of Monsignor Horan, as a junior official from our own Department of Transport and Tourism put it. Despite a valiant attempt by the pilot, thick fog shrouding the late Monsignor's miracle made landing impossible and so we were diverted to Shannon. Later, we heard that, as we sipped our champagne on board, there were scenes of panic on the tarmac of Connacht Regional Airport as the motorbike outriders and the drivers of the escort cars and the 13 black limousines – their engines purring in anticipation – watched their passengers being sucked back into the night sky.

You couldn't help feeling a teenshie bit sorry for Séamus Brennan as airport staff at Shannon buzzed around him with pots of hastily-brewed coffee for the unexpected visitors and somebody was despatched to rustle up a couple of buses from Conway Coaches in Limerick. Here he was, prepared to spend between £80,000 and £100,000 on the weekend, and there was still no escaping the potholes of the West.

Lord Strathclyde had other things on this mind when he sought out the nearest telephone to contact his embassy in Dublin and to seek advice on how best to travel to Cong – now that his bullet-proof Jaguar was idling in Mayo.

It fell to the doughty Denis Lyons, Junior Tourism Minister, to rescue our flagging spirits as we bounced along the roads of counties Clare, Galway and Mayo to the dinner, we feared, would be burned to cinders by the time we arrived.

"Here's the hard sell for tourism," the Corkman cajoled his travel-weary visitors staring glumly at the opaque blackness outside the windows of the coach. "You have passed through some beautiful countryside but, unfortunately, you couldn't see it. Have you noticed how freely we've travelled? So little traffic on the roads. So bring your cars when you come back on holidays."

Tired, grubby and stomachs growling with hunger we arrived at Ashford Castle, all warm and welcoming with glowing chandeliers and waitresses in black dresses, with pretty squares of white calico pinned to their hair, stealing a peep from behind the heavy window drapes. Even the gardaí hadn't the heart to make us all walk through the specially-installed security X-ray as the aromas of the kitchen cast their magic spell.

Dinner was a show of silver cutlery, native crystal and white glove service and a banquet of dainty shellfish, steaming soup, tender lamb and a cacophony of strawberry, milk and white chocolate mousse.

Over dinner, a civil servant from Dublin expounded upon the virtuosity of the Irish in the art of hosting the EC presidency. The French, it seems, are bottom of the league at organising informal council meetings like this one. They are, the man explained, inefficient, arrogant and over-the-top. They held a Finance Council meeting in Antibes last year, commandeering three of the most expensive hotels in the swish Riviera town, the cheapest being £500-a-night. For entertainment, they had a ventriloquist, followed by two performing dogs. (My informant delivered the latter in verbal italics).

On the other hand, he said, the Irish were masters of informality. He recalled a meeting in Dublin when the then Cabinet member Ruairi Quinn brought his Euro counterparts to Kitty O'Shea's pub and sang Summertime in deep honeyed tones. The evening culminated in former Northern Ireland Secretary of State Tom King launching into Four Green Fields – probably the most evocative ballad in the Republican repertoire.

Informality, however, is not synonymous with lack of planning. The rest of us mere mortals have no idea of the attention that must be paid to the tiniest of details, he continued. For instance, when you are entertaining the ministers of several vine-growing countries, how do you manage to serve good wine without offending anyone? The answer is that you always chose at least one Spanish, one German and one Italian. That way, you can have as many French chateaux as you like and Portugal will be satisfied with a drop of port.

My confidante – as pleased to be imparting this information as Neville Chamberlain waving the paper of peace – reported that this method has proved most satisfactory. The Greeks are never insulted by their exclusion from the wine list – and everyone else is eternally grateful.

The wine quandary is a cinch, though, compared to the recurring poser of what gifts to bestow upon the visitors. History books and pieces of Irish crystal have, up to now, been the staple diet but, after 17 years in the EC, Europe can add an Irish literature mountain to its various stockpiles. "Jacques Delors (Commission President) must have every book ever written on Ireland at this stage," confided the loquacious civil servant.

We took coffee (Brazilian or Irish), brandy and hand-made petit fours in the drawing room while the ladies and gentlemen of Comhaltas Ceoltóirí did their traditional party pieces. But the real entertainment only came alive later when the hardier souls of the party repaired to the Dungeon bar and let their hair down.

Seamus Brennan got the ball rolling with his rendition of Galway Bay (what else?), followed by his junior minister, Frank Fahy, and It's A Long Way to Tipperary. No more encouragement was required. The three Italians delivered a less than reverential version of Sancta Lucia, the Rt. Hon. Lord Strathclyde ("call me Tom") and his secretary Catherine led us into the Celtic mists with Loch Lomond while the two men from the ministry of Economic Affairs in the Netherlands sang something totally unintelligible. Afterwards, like mischievous schoolboys, they confessed that they had been singing two different songs. Is this what you call Double Dutch?

Goodnight!

Saturday 10 March 1990

Dear Diary

I picked up a most interesting gem of information today. Despite all the squabbles over the CAP, the EMS, the SEA and the MTIW (Margaret Thatcher's Iron Will), there is one common philosophy among these EC Ministers: Madame Stirn, the Frenchman's wife, is the best looking. It was Peter, the Dutch official in the loud sports-jacket, who told me: "We all agree she is *wow*."

It seems Monsieur Stirn agrees more than anyone. During the coffee break at this morning's meeting of the council, he headed straight to the shop in the dungeon and snapped up £800 worth of Irish tweeds, lace and cashmere for his young blonde femme (fatale).

By the way, the meeting was a success. The paper presented by the Commissioner was unanimously adopted and a proposal was passed to have another meeting in Dublin in June. There is a TV crew here from Portugal filming a documentary on the weekend so, naturally, the Commissioner was chuffed with the result.

After a light lunch of chilled vichyssoise, poached salmon and a cheese platter with celery sorbet, the commissioner, the Council president and the Ashford manager departed to the golf course for a leisurely round, while most of us boarded a luxury coach for a tour of Connemara. The guide was somewhat anxious that she would run out of things to say after she had been warned not to mention Northern Ireland, the benefits Ireland had enjoyed since joining the EC or anything potentially political. As we drove through the village of Recess, our visitors remained oblivious to the school teacher who has been sitting in an empty classroom for over two years because she wanted Mass to be said in Irish. (Sure, who would have believed it anyway?)

As you can imagine, all the talk over pre-dinner cocktails was of the session in the Dungeon the night before. Tonight, everyone was determined to get in on the act – literally. Just for a moment I noticed Séamus Brennan's face blanching while we were waiting to go into the dining room. He was talking to a very animated-looking minister from Spain. That, in itself, was something of a shock because I had heard from people who have been to these council meetings before that the Spaniard is normally reserved and a little uptight.

It has emerged that Señor Peña is, in fact, the most heavily-guarded minister in the council and has actually brought his own bodyguards and armour-plated car for the weekend. (He was Spain's Minister for the Interior at the height of the ETA campaign). And what had drawn the blood from Minister Brennan's face? Only his Spanish counterpart's account of his afternoon and how he had travelled into Galway to see the Spanish Arch only to be lured into Naughton's pub, by an Irish newspaper photographer, for a pint of the hardstuff. Nobody can ever remember seeing Señor Peña looking so happy.

After another feast (plateau de poisson fumée, crème de celery, contre-filet de boeuf au sauce poivre and gratin de fruits), the Bunratty Folk singers, dressed in medieval velvet costumes, earned a foot-stomping encore from the VIPs before everyone headed down to the Dungeon bar for a sing-song.

But the sing-song was cancelled. In its place we had a mini-Eurovision Song Contest. And, by now, the Rt. Hon. Lord Strathclyde was being fondly hailed by everyone as Tomás. It was unbelievable. There were delegations of ministers and civil servants gathered in the corridor outside, practising their numbers before taking the stage. Danish Minister Anne Birgitte Lundholdt opted for a solo with a word-perfect Molly Malone.

"This proves the Danes were in Ireland," cheered Séamus Brennan. And then it was his turn as he skipped lightly into the stage with Lord Strathclyde and the Irish and British ministers delivered Living Doll in total harmony. (Could a weekend in Ashford even solve an 800-year-old problem, do you think?)

The night finished with the entire Irish presidency and council delegation (and Lord Strathclyde) on stage, swinging their arms and singing "Que Sera Sera, we're going to Italy ..."

"This is the most informal informal council meeting I've ever seen," declared the president's wife, Ann Brennan, as she reluctantly followed her husband to bed.

At 4.30am, perhaps it was time to sleep.

Sunday March 11, 1990

Dear Diary
The good news is that last night's free bar still came in under budget, despite the fact that it remained open for at least four hours after it had been scheduled to close. The bad news is that the weekend is over.

Before he left, the Italian minister announced that he was going straight back to Rome and packing his children off to Dublin to learn English.

Junior Minister Denis Lyons came down the corridor after lunch, smacking his hands in glee and telling all and sundry that several of the ministers had expressed their intentions to return to the West on holiday. (Not bad for a meeting of the European Tourism Council!)

We left Ashford Castle in a convoy of 13 limousines, 13 garda outriders, a fleet of escort cars and two coaches. On the way to Knock Airport, we bumped along country roads, past deserted thatched cottages and knots of families waving to the procession from their garden gates.

The captain of our Boeing 737 gave us one last glimpse of Ashford as he circled Lough Corrib under streaky whisps of cloud that made the plane shake.

"Your air is as bad as your roods," cried Peter The Flying Dutchman.

And we all laughed. Because we knew that our air is a different thing to our atmosphere. And we knew that, just two days ago, nobody would have dared to utter such blasphemy.

Fear on the Shankill, fear on the Falls

In one of the bloodiest weeks in Belfast's troubled history, when 15 people have died in terrorist atrocities, Justine McCarthy reports from a city where ordinary people on both sides of the sectarian divide are trapped under the same dark shadows.

Irish Independent Weekender, 30 October 1993

The wounded haunt the Shankill and the Falls. Bloodied surgical bandages wrapped around limbs torn and shattered by bombs and bullets. It is like a scene from a Movietone newsreel. There is a man at the prayer vigil on the Shankill Road. He is wearing a black suit with a scuffed collar and a shirt that was once white. His head is completely covered with bandages. Only his eyes are visible.

He is staring at the gulf in the row of shops where John Frizzell and his daughter, Sharon, were serving fish to their customers last Saturday. Behind the man is a phalanx of steel barriers and a policeman in a bullet-proof jacket absentmindedly shuffling the debris of the bomb rubble under his feet.

The hearse carrying 13-year-old Leanne Murray has just passed by the junction connecting her red-brick terraced home in Silvio Street to the Shankill Road. Hundreds of neighbours stand silently on the kerbsides of Paris Street and Brussels Street and Berlin Street and Crimea Street watching a mother take her only daughter to the crematorium. A child screams, splintering the mourners' silence. "Mummy, we're going to get blown up!" The child is three years of age. His mother is lost for words of comfort.

On the back of a truck outside the place that used to be Frizzell's fish shop, Reverend Roy Magee implores his grieving Protestant brethren not to take the law into their own hands. "Leave it to God," he begs, struggling to speak through his own tears. "The voices of the dead are crying from the grave: The violence must end!"

Jim Cameron's workmates from the cleansing depot huddle together on the road outside his widow's terraced house. Only the previous morning they were drinking tea in the yard on Kennedy Way when two men wearing boiler suits and balaclavas ran towards them brandishing machine guns, yelling "*Right, yees bastards*", and sprayed them with 60 bullets. Jim Cameron (54) and Mark Rogers (28) died because they were Catholics. Because they were Catholics and they were there.

One of the men outside Jim Cameron's house in Coner Road has his arm bandaged in hospital gauze, blood dried in the palm of his hand where the bullet went straight through him. He had managed to flee onto the road, a busy feeder route to the motorway, but the gunman came after him and chased him down the road, firing all the time. The man ran for his life.

"There was sparks coming off my shoes. When I looked down I could see my heart beating through my coat."

The men say they will probably never go back to work. They will lock themselves and their families into their homes every evening when the last light fades from the sky. They will not answer a knock on the door. They will be careful about which newspapers they are seen to be reading, what cigarette brands they smoke, the taxis they travel in, the churches they worship in, the pubs they drink in, which side of the street they walk on. In Belfast, your lifestyle can be your death warrant.

Going down Andersonstown Road the driver points to a young man standing outside the Emerald House Chinese takeaway. He is on watch, explains the driver, looking out for strangers who will cruise up the street and shoot civilians because they are easy targets. There are tears running down the driver's face. He rubs them away with his fist.

"I'm sorry," he apologises. "My nerves are gone. I wanted to go to the Shankill Road and sympathise with those people but I don't have the guts to go there."

The man has been a driver for journalists in Belfast since the start of the Troubles. He has seen bombs exploding and street riots and paramilitary show funerals. But, he says, this is the worst it's ever been. He keeps packets of Panadol in the car for his tension headaches and no longer drives his passengers into Protestant areas.

The wire mesh gates are locked at Belfast Council's depot on Kennedy Way. Through the gaps you can see the white chalk circles where the bullets hit the ground and the mechanical roadsweeper the men cowered behind. Bunches of yellow and pink carnations have been stuffed into the wire with gift cards that bear no names. That's fear, says the driver.

On the ground in the corner stands a bunch of flowers, just like the others, a flickering votive candle inside a funnel depicting the Virgin Mary, and a card inscribed with a block lettered message.

"As a Protestant who narrowly missed last Saturday's bomb, I am utterly ashamed of the carnage that happened to innocent workers at this assembly point. This slaughter was not carried out in my name nor in the name of thousands like me. I deeply grieve the tragedy and I extend my sympathy and prayers to the broken hearted. May God guide you through your sorrow and give you strength to endure the awful pain. May He guide all of us to learn how to respect each other."

The Catholics reading the message wonder at the anonymous Protestant's courage. It takes guts for a Prod to cross the Peace Line with a bunch of flowers for a dead Taig.

One hundred yards separate the Falls from the Shankill.

For the love of God, will someone listen! Three-thousand-and-ninety-six people were dead by last Thursday. Fifteen lives gone in five days in Belfast. Almost 70 murders since the start of the year. A city is petrified with fear. There are children who wake screaming in the middle of the night. Hospital blood supplies depleted. Social events cancelled. Status Quo has called off two concert dates.

The annual ball at Queens University has been abandoned because the bands were afraid to travel. The doors of the church were locked during Mass last weekend to protect worshippers while they prayed for peace. But not content with taking their lives, the killers have taken their voices too.

"Our politicians are telling the world we're not speaking, but we are speaking. They just won't listen," says Charlie Butler, uncle of seven-year old Michelle Baird, the youngest person to die in last Saturday's bomb explosion. "Unless the paramilitaries give it up it will go on and on. We feel sorry for the people who were murdered by loyalist paramilitaries because we know what they are going through. We don't have time to feel bitter. We only have time to feel sad, very, very sad."

There was a feeling of an emotional truce on the Shankill after Rev Magee reminded them that Roman Catholic grief was just as terrible and tearing as Protestant grief. Then the news filtered through that Gerry Adams had carried the coffin of the man responsible for nine Protestant deaths and the anger bubbled again.

"It is an absolute sin for a priest to bury him," spat a small woman with permed grey hair and a belted raincoat. "The Catholic Church shouldn't have given him a Christian burial. The worst thing they done was disarm the B Specials. They should bring back hanging. No, hanging's too good for them.

"They should cut off their toes first and work their way up as slow and torturous as possible. A pack of rotten bastards. Gerry Adams had the cheek to carry his coffin. He's the one who caused all this to happen.

"That soldier (who shot a mourner outside Thomas Begley's home on Tuesday night) pulled bodies out of the rubble here on Saturday. Bodies with no heads or limbs. He doesn't need interrogation. He needs a medal. We're signing a petition for him."

Just when it seems that maybe the human leveller of grief could bridge the chasm between Ordinary Catholic and Ordinary Protestant, the polarisation grows more acute. The women of the Shankill remember how their men vomited at the sight of the dead last Saturday, declaring "we are the majority in this country" and "let the Catholics go and live in Dublin." One woman – the mother of the three-year old who had earlier screamed Mummy, we're going to get blown up – told how her seven-year old had picked up the newspaper the day before and, pointing at a man's picture, told her: "That's Thomas Begley, the one that planted the bombs."

Later, leaving the Shankill through the labyrinth of neat working class two-up-two-downs, a local man nods in the direction of a house and says: " That's where Mad Dog lives."

It was the first time the self-declared Fenian killer had been mentioned all day.

A black ribbon hangs on the front door of Mark Rodgers' house in Lenadoon. There is a rubber mat on the doorstep decorated with two frogs sitting on a water Lily and the words "Welcome To Our Pad." Inside, Mark Rodgers' young widow and her two children, Mark (6) and Leanne (3) are being comforted by friends and neighbours.

"The sanctity of human life is gone forever," says Mark Rodgers' father-in-law, former SDLP councillor Liam Hunter. "We're like a pack of animals."

The previous morning, a couple of hours after his son-in-law had been shot to death in Kennedy Way, Liam Hunter had telephoned the RUC and asked them to disperse a gang of thugs sitting on a wall opposite the house, taunting the people coming to pay their respects.

"We need protection. We need help," he says in a voice exhausted by sorrow. "The killing will go on and on as long as we have politicians who revel in the sectarianism. All they do is beat the drum and beat the drum: No Surrender. The politicians in Dublin are too far away from it. They haven't got a clue. They will never help.

"This is a religious war and nobody can underestimate that.

It is nothing about loyalty to the Queen. It is between Catholics and Protestants.

"Mark was working at the depot part-time. He needed the money for Christmas toys. Now there'll be no toys. No Christmas."

Around the corner, in Lenadoon Avenue, somebody has placed fresh flowers on a marble slab marking the death of a six-year-old girl some years ago. She had been killed by a plastic bullet as she waited to cross the road to buy sweets in the corner shop.

"What have we done to them?" asks the man who was shot in the hand on Tuesday morning. "Both sides are sick and tired of it and nobody's listening. The way it is now is, if you're a Catholic you must have be an IRA man, and if you're a Protestant you must be UVF or UFF. I don't want anybody to hurt a Protestant in retaliation for what was done to me. Two wrongs don't make a right. It's us people, innocent working men, who're going to get it."

Everybody is somebody's enemy in Belfast. If your name is Smith you must be a Prod, if it's Murphy you must be a Taig. If you're a Brit journalist you enter Catholic West Belfast with trepidation. A Free Stater takes his life in his hands walking down the Shankill Road. A couple of TV cameramen and photographers were jostled and punched last Saturday by angry Protestants who believed that the media had encouraged the Hume Adams talks, which they blame for the IRA bomb.

In the past year Orange Order newsletters and UDA magazines have been exhorting community groups to improve their relationship with the media so that their side of the story can be told.

If you go to a paramilitary funeral as a friend or relative of the family you are labelled a fellow traveller. If you cross the Peace Line to show solidarity with the other side, you are a traitor. Whatever you are, whatever you do, there is a name for you. Best do nothing.

If you are one of the 30,000 RUC, British Army and Royal Irish Regiment patrolling Northern Ireland you have few friends. On the Shankill policemen stop to talk to civilians. On the Falls at night you can hear youngsters calling to the soldiers: "Who's at home ridin' your wife while you're here?"

Three of the five men who escaped from the Kennedy Way shooting on Tuesday claim that when the police arrived on the scene they "sat in the jeeps and laughed". Yet an RUC officer was quoted in the Belfast Telegraph calling the loyalist killers "debased bastards".

"They have a taste for blood and are actually enjoying it. They just hate Catholics, any Catholics," he said. "It's as bad now as it has ever been. We are fighting a war on two fronts, whereas before it was primarily the Provos."

By six o'clock in the evening Belfast is a ghost city. Work yards have closed early. Taxis have disappeared. Pubs are empty. People who have reinforced their front doors with sheets of steel wait behind them for morning to come.

In the Peace People's office on the Lisburn road, administrator Ann McCann says: "People's nerves are shattered. We take the wives of loyalist and republican prisoners on the bus every day and, this morning, the women from the Shankill were terrified passing by Kennedy Way. We have a cross-community football tournament organised for the weekend, we've had it every year at a neutral venue for the past 15 years. Now we're getting calls from the team managers to cancel it. There is a feeling of despair and fear in the city."

There were four funerals for victims of violence in Belfast last Tuesday. There were seven on Wednesday. Three on Thursday. There is a 13-year-old boy still in hospital after the Shankill Road explosion who may be blind for the rest of his life. There is a 73-year-old pensioner dead after being "interrogated" for an hour before being shot in the head in the house where he lived alone.

Tomorrow is Cemetery Sunday in Belfast, the day when the bereaved traditionally visit the graves of their loved ones. This year, many people are too fearful to make the journey. The terrorist's hold on this city reaches even beyond the graves of the innocent dead.

Annie's Story

Justine McCarthy reports from Connecticut on the love story that has captured the world's headlines

Irish Independent, 9 May 1992

"Would somebody mind telling me what's going on?" pleaded the publisher of the Ridgefield News as the media of the world descended on his newspaper office in Connecticut yesterday morning.

By daybreak, television and print journalists from Europe and the US were converging on the quiet rustic city of Ridgefield, 86 miles north of Manhattan, all with one mission to accomplish: the inside track on the impossible love story that has scandalised a nation and abruptly terminated the career of a Roman Catholic Bishop in the remote West of Ireland.

In sleepy Ridgefield, cherry blossoms and aspens shivered in the damp dawn. Freshly-painted dove-grey shutters were still drawn protectively over the town's candy stores and ice-cream parlours as its 6,000 citizens rose to hear the news that had, overnight, rocketed them into the world headlines.

At 48 Olcott Way, one of a neat line of cinderblock garden apartments in the centre of Ridgefield, Annie Murphy flicked the on-button of the coffee machine in her kitchen for the umpteenth time, for the umpteenth visitor and apologised that there were no doughnuts left.

"I haven't slept for 72 hours," she said.

Somewhere, in a New York hotel, there was a 65-year-old man for whom sleep had not come easily either in the 48 hours since he had announced his resignation from the Bishopric of Galway.

Dr Eamonn Casey had flown into John F. Kennedy Airport in New York on Thursday evening, en route to Chile, dodging the waiting media. A couple of hours later and a two-hour drive away, 43-year-old Annie Murphy was entertaining total strangers in her kitchen as they filled their jotters with details of her doomed romance in the Dingle Peninsula 18 years ago.

One time, when she left the room to answer the incessant ringing of the telephone on the bedroom, two male reporters whispered in surprise about her lively eyes and fine cheekbones. The fact that Annie Murphy had turned out to be something other than an overweight, middle-aged bag lady seemed to have whetted their appetite for the story.

In 1973 she was 25 years old, recovering from the divorce which had just ended her two-and-a-half-year marriage. As a consolation prize, her half-Irish, half-German doctor father, who had never liked the man she had married, had given her a present of a trip to Ireland. On her visit to the old country she would be in the care of her father's friend, the Bishop of Kerry, Dr Eamonn Casey.

"When I stepped off the plane in Shannon it was like *déjà vu*," she remembers. "I know it's corny, but it was like I'd always known him. I hated the expression, but, yes, it was love at first sight for me. I think it was for both of us."

She had only met the Bishop once before – when she was seven and he had taken her to see *On the Waterfront* at a Connecticut Cinema.

From April until August that year Annie Murphy lodged at the Bishop's Georgian house in Inch, overlooking Dingle Bay.

"We used to go for beautiful walks on Inch Strand," she recalled. "Within the first few days, he was holding my hand and kissing me. I was madly in love with him. One night, he came to my room to say goodnight, as he always did, and that was when our relationship became intimate.

"I can't say I found him physically attractive. It was a metaphysical thing. He was great fun. He was like the Bishop out of *The Canterbury Tales*. It was a carefree, fun, magical time. I told him several times that I loved him and he told me several times that he loved me.

"He used to call me The Temptress and joke that I'd been sent from another world to test his Faith.

"I told him I wanted to have his child – we weren't using contraception – and he said: 'We wouldn't like that to happen, would we?'"

But it did happen. According to Annie's calculations, it happened on October 31, 1973, a night of a full moon.

The child, Peter Eamonn Murphy, was born in the Rotunda Hospital, Dublin, on July 31, 1974.

"When I told him I was pregnant things were even better at first. He was more caring. There was a lot of tenderness. At this stage, I was living in Dublin. I had a job in the Burlington Hotel and a flat in the city. Eamonn used to drive up from Kerry during the week and I would go down to Inch at weekends. When I was five and a half months pregnant, I quit the job because the pregnancy had started to show and we didn't want anybody to know.

"I went back down to Inch, but things were different. He

started bringing me prayer books and telling me that I would have to give up the baby. There was a lot of praying and a lot of talk about repentance. He told me I would have to give up the child because it would cleanse me of my sins and I would be able to start over again as a good Catholic girl.

"He wanted me to have the baby in the Coombe Hospital, but I heard that they had a policy of not showing unmarried mothers their babies before they went up for adoption, so I called the Rotunda instead. For the last month and a half of my pregnancy, I lived with a family, the Devlins, in Dublin.

"Eamonn came to the hospital and saw the baby four hours after his birth. He said: 'Annie, that boy has to be adopted. That is not your child.' When he went to touch Peter it was like the baby was liquid fire. He threw his hands up."

After the birth, Annie moved to St. Joseph's Home for Unmarried Mothers outside Dublin.

"I was penniless," she says. "My family didn't know about the baby, only my sister. I needed to raise $500 to get back home. I was trapped and desperately frightened. There was one girl there though. Thelma, she was from the northside of Dublin and she was God-sent. She made me laugh."

Today, Peter Eamonn Murphy drives a Chrysler Lazer the fives miles to Ridgefield High School, where he will graduate next month. He's an all-American kid. He plays baseball, raves about music, dates girls. Just like all the other kids. Except his father is a Bishop.

Says Annie's common-law husband, Edinburgh builder Arthur Pennell: "He looks just like his old man and he behaves just like his old man. He gets dug in.

"I once went to see the Bishop at his palace in Galway. He

offered me tea and sandwiches, but he wouldn't admit that Peter was his son."

The 17-year-old, who first saw photographs of his father at the age of six, plans to study political science at the University of Connecticut and, later, to work for Amnesty International in Moscow.

"I expected newspapers from Ireland and the British Isles to be interested in the story," said the 6 foot 1 inch tall high school student with a shock of black hair and traces of adolescent pimples on his face. "This is more than I expected from the American papers. They're all here.

"None of the kids in school have heard it yet, but two of my friends know who my father is. It didn't make much difference to them. Basically, they're not very religious in the Catholic sense."

Annie first revealed the identity of Peter's father to her son when he was just six.

"I used to tell him funny stories about the people in Ireland and about the fun we had. I remember showing Peter some photos of the Bishop and he wasn't very impressed. He didn't like it that he was bald. He didn't like the shape of his nose either, and he kept saying that he was better-looking.

"Then, when Ronald Regan visited Ireland and the Bishop was interviewed on American television, Arthur sat Peter on his lap and said: 'Do you recognise him?' Peter said: 'Sure, that's the man my Mom says is my Daddy. Maybe I'll get to meet him some day.'"

Peter Murphy met his father for five minutes in 1990.

"His eyes wouldn't meet Peter's," says Annie. "He said he would pray for him twice a day. Then he went into another room and somebody else came out and asked Peter to sign a release form saying he would never bother the Bishop again.

"It was Peter who wanted the story publicised. Five times he had answered the phone to Eamonn here in the apartment and each time Eamonn refused to speak to him. Peter felt that he wouldn't allow him to cast him aside as a nonentity.

"Four months ago, Arthur called Eamonn in Ireland and said to him: 'Your son has requested that I go to the newspapers with the story. We've given you every possible chance. Now we want you to resign.'

Later we got a telephone call saying that Father James Kelly, who represents Eamonn in New York, wanted to speak to us. Arthur called and they offered him money. It came down to payment for Peter's college education. It would have been about $150,000."

Peter was to be the only child Annie Murphy would ever have. After she gave birth to him in the Rotunda Hospital, she developed deep-vein thrombosis in her leg and was warned by doctors that she could never have another baby.

Despite the sadness which she associates with Ireland, she still loves the country where her baby was born. With Arthur and Peter, she moved back to Ireland in September 1990. The family set up home in the hills overlooking the Bandon River in Kinsale, Co. Cork, where Peter attended the local convent school. They only stayed until the following January, however. Peter never quite fostered a love of the country of his birth to match his mother's.

"While we lived there, we used to call Eamonn in Galway and his relatives living in Castleisland, but he never contacted us," says Arthur.

Framed pictures of Peter on his own and Peter and Annie together dot the small apartment, with its basic furniture and venetian blinds. There are no photographs of the child's father and no signs of religious devotion.

The family is not well off. According to Arthur they suffered a foreclosure on a mortgage on a one million dollar house a few years ago, absorbing a loss of half a million dollars. Annie holds down two jobs. By day, she works as a receptionist in a nearby office and, by night, she is a secretary at a local hotel in Ridgefield. Arthur, who is also divorced, continues to work in the construction business.

Yesterday evening, as she patiently answered journalists' repetitive, probing and often intrusive questions about her Irish romance with a Roman Catholic Bishop, Annie Murphy spoke like a woman with few regrets.

"I love my son," she said. "I've told Eamonn that I love Peter more than I loved him. The strange thing is that two years ago I met Eamonn in the Grand Hyatt Hotel in New York and all the feelings I once felt for him came flooding back. A friend of mine made a video of the meeting and you can see him kissing me, hugging me and grabbing me. I don't know if that feeling will ever come back now."

But he never saw me cry

Justine McCarthy talks to 'probably the bravest, strongest person I have ever met' – the Kilkenny incest victim ...

Irish Independent, 6 March 1993

She is sitting on the edge of the single bed in her dingy flat. Her feet do not reach the floor. Her face never smiles. A single shaft of noon sunlight dissembles in the clutter beside the cooker. The irises, daffodils and white carnations brought by a friend slump their heads in the stained enamel sink. She has no vase to put them in.

She is talking about her father: a daughter searching for the right words to describe the first man most little girls love in life.

"He's a small man with big fists," she says. Nothing more.

Of all the reams and reams of words written since he was imprisoned this week for raping, sexually assaulting and battering his own child, these seven simple words uttered by his daughter tell the whole horrible, tragic story.

Last Monday night, after her father had been taken away to Arbour Hill jail to begin his six-and-a-half-year sentence, she kissed her son tenderly and switched off the light in the small bedroom they share. From the darkness his muffled, hurt voice cut in on her own sleepless musings.

"What good has come out of all this?" he asked her.

"I don't know," she said. "Just remember that he was an evil man."

"I will always hate him," he promised her. "I hope he never comes back."

She is cradling a six-week-old puppy, a cross-breed between a miniature terrier and a pom, a gift from another friend. "Young children never forget," she says heavily. Just as she will never forget.

He brought her a cake for her tenth birthday. She scrunched up her eyes, made her little girl's wish and blew out the candles. Two months later he raped her in her own bed.

"When we were in England he seemed nice," she remembers. "He was the sort of father every kid had. He'd give you anything. When we moved to Ireland it all changed. He got harder. He used to keep the curtains drawn in the house because he didn't want people looking in. He thought if he kept it behind closed doors no one would ever know.

"He made you like an animal. He owned you. If he told you to lie down, you lay down. When he bought me the cake for my tenth birthday it was the last time I remember him treating me nicely."

From the age of 10 until she became pregnant with his child five years later, she had sexual intercourse with her father twice a week. She did not know that was what it was called or what its purpose was, other than to punish her for being naughty, and she has never slept with any other man other than her father. The thought of sex as an expression of love makes her whole body shudder with fear. She cannot imagine what it would be like.

When the baby was born she was given some books on the facts of life in the hospital. She read them with horror, slowly realising that what her father had been doing to her was wrong. She decided to confide in the social worker.

"She told me it was a family matter," she says, "but what's more is that she wanted me to sign adoption papers handing the baby over to him. He thought I'd signed them. He actually thought the child was his until I took him out of school last year when I ran away and he accused me of stealing his child. It was only then he found out about the adoption papers."

When she came home from the hospital nothing had changed. He continued beating her and abusing her and demanding: "I want a bit of sex."

He had her mother take her to the GP for the contraceptive pill because, he told her: "If they knew I was the child's father I'd be put away for life."

He called her a whore and told the townspeople that he didn't know who had fathered the child because "that whore would have anything in trousers."

The house felt emptier after the birth. Her only sister, two years younger, had run away – never to return home – when the baby was born. Last Monday she sat with her mother and sister in a Dublin courtroom, prepared to give evidence of her father's brutality, if such evidence was required.

The baby slept in her room until he was five years old. At that stage her father insisted that the child's bed be moved into the room he shared with his wife. The boy called his mother's parents mammy and daddy. Then, when he was seven and she told him that she was really his mother, he grinned up at her and said: "Aren't I lucky to have two mammies?"

"He has had counselling and he'll be having more," she says of her son. "He saw it all, except the sex assaults. He's a happy little boy but he doesn't really trust men. He's very loving and he's great with animals but he can be abrupt with people. He gets bullied in school. He's that soft. The other day he came home from school bawling his eyes out because he saw a small boy hitting a girl and trying to take her sweets. He hates violence.

"No," she says, "he doesn't look like him. He's the spitting image of me." It is the only time during the interview that she smiles.

During the 17 years of her secret hell the woman was beaten by her father with everything from a whip, a hammer and a vodka bottle to a steel bar off the Rayburn cooker, his buckled belt and those fists that she remembers so vividly. She is blind in her right eye; the nerves in some of her fingers have been smashed beyond repair.

One time the sexual abuse was so violent that she bled for three days after it and he prohibited her from seeing a doctor. Another time he sent his wife to the shop to buy an instamatic camera. The photographs taken of the man engaged in sexual acts with his daughter that day were among the evidence collected by the gardaí when they were preparing the prosecution case against him.

"I tried to poison him once," she says, out of the blue. "I got some of that stuff that you get for animals. It says on the outside that it kills humans. I stirred two teaspoonfuls of it into his tea and I sat down and waited to see him die. And nothing. Not even a stomach pain. All he said was that the milk tasted inky that night."

What do you say? Tell her she is probably the strongest, bravest person you ever met?

"On the outside its OK, but deep down it's not." She shakes her head sadly. "The night of the last beating, the night I ran away, I had two pints of blood left in my body when I got to the hospital. I had walked the eight miles to my friend's house with my head cracked open. Her father used to be my little fella's godfather, but he died. I think it was my friend who called the guards when they brought me to the hospital."

It was a dark winter's night in January last year. Her father was drinking poitín in the house. His wife, his daughter and the son conceived from the rape of his daughter were in the kitchen with him when he suddenly exploded. He hit his daughter over the head with the vodka bottle that had contained the poitín.

He picked up a broken salad cream bottle from the floor and flung it at her. Then he undid the belt of his trousers and beat her with it on her arms and back. He hit her on the head again with the bottle. And again. And again. The blood was streaming down her neck, from behind her ear.

He stripped off her sweater and bra and made her son stand before her. "This is the difference between men and women," he told the child.

After he had hunted her out of the house, she lay in the long grass listening to his raving and the sound of splintering delph and her mother's voice saying: "You've hit her enough. Leave her alone."

When they got her to the hospital that night she needed five stitches in her head, three stiches in her arm, she had a fractured finger and bruises on her legs, arms and back.

"That night he had such a look in his eyes that I never saw before," she recalls. "He was intent on killing me. I'm telling you that when he gets out of jail he'll come looking for me and my mother and, after he has done harm to us, I can guarantee he will do harm to some other girl. He is sick in the mind.

"I don't blame mammy in any way, she adds. "Too many people are blaming mammy but she was hurt a lot more by this than I was. Ok. I was being raped, but I was her daughter."

Suddenly she stops speaking. There is the sound of approaching footsteps in the hallway outside. The door opens slowly and a 10-year-old boy with the same eyes as the woman sitting on the bed comes in. His cheeks are bright from the ice in the wind. She tells him to put a spaghetti bolognese in the microwave (borrowed from a friend for the week). He puts one fork on the tiny table and waits for his lunch to heat up.

From the garage down on the street, a man calls up to her that she is wanted on the phone. She excuses herself and goes downstairs. The boy looks over and grins.

"Come here," he says. "I want to show you something," and he takes a tiny silver keyring shaped like a pistol from the pocket of his short pants. "It's the smallest gun in the world," he announces proudly.

When she returns to the room she explains that the phone call was about her counselling session that afternoon at the nearest Rape Crisis Centre, the first since she moved to her present accommodation last spring.

"The worst thing is the way people look at you," she picks up her story, after her soon has gone back to school for the afternoon. "A lot of people recognise my voice from the RTÉ interview. I met a girl I know this morning and she looked at the ceiling and she walked right by me and never even said hello. I wish they'd say what's on their mind and just ask me straight out why I never ran away."

Why didn't you run away?

"It was only when my son was born that I realised that what was going on was wrong," she answers. "I had no money, nothing. I could sleep under a ditch but he couldn't. What sort of a mother would I be if I ran off with my son to sleep under a ditch?"

As it is, they barely get by. While the nation beats its breast with contrition for not rescuing her 17 years ago, she is struggling to rear her child. After the £40 rent for the flat every week, £10.80 for gas and £17.50 to fill the electricity meter, she is left with little more than £20 to feed and clothe herself and her son from the £71 single parent's allowance she receives every week, plus £18 rent supplement and £15-a-month child's allowance. She had to borrow a pair of denim jeans and a jumper from a friend last Monday – good clothes to wear to court.

And yes, she did, in fact, run away twice. Once she fled to her grandmother in England but he came after her and forced her to come back home. On the way to the boat in Fishguard, he beat her so badly she had to go to hospital. Her father told the nurse they had been mugged.

Since the gardaí started compiling the case last year, she has found out that her granny in England – her father's mother – had guessed what her son was doing to his child. Now, says the woman, she never wants to see her son again.

The other time she ran away it was to a hostel in Dublin. Again he followed her. This time he harassed the other women in the hostel so much that the people in charge asked her to leave. He was waiting for her outside the door.

"He never once said sorry," she says. "He would go to bed after a row and wake up at about five o'clock in the morning and shout at me to make his breakfast. Then he'd go back to sleep until around 10 o'clock and when he'd wake up it was as if last night had never happened.

"But I can't blame the drink for it. He has a drink problem, but the beating, that comes from his mind. When he gets out of jail he won't have got help to make him better. He'll come after me and mammy and he'll kill us."

In a way, the praise and the plaudits showered on her by politicians and the media since Monday has put an extra pressure on the woman. Though nobody is supposed to know who she is, Ireland is too small to keep something like that a secret, and even in the place where she lives now her neighbours know that is she is "the Kilkenny incest victim." She is the sort of woman who answers that problem with a brave face.

"I won't cry," she explains. "Not where someone might see me. I went into the toilet in the courthouse the other day and I cried but I will do it on my own. You could hit me or do anything and I would never cry. I never cried in front of him. That was the one thing he couldn't make me do. I wouldn't please him to cry."

How close to tears she must have been the December night – a years before she finally managed to get away – when a garda came to the house and asked her mother and herself if they would care to make a statement about their injuries. No, they said, unable to reach out to the helping hand as her father stood there and watched, full of menace.

A year later, when Garda Agnes Reddy answered the hospital's call about an assault case, the woman was free of her father's ominous presence. It took hours and hours of probing but, eventually, the whole sordid story came out.

"I really trust her," she says of the garda. "She is one person who deserves a lot of credit. There should be more guards like her; women guards made available for rape cases so that you feel you can talk to them.

"Garda Siobhan Connolly in Kilkenny, as well. She's a wonderful person. She did all the paperwork while Agnes went around collecting the evidence."

She has a lot of friends, she says. Friends she can lean on for a while. One of her friends rents the flat next door and allows her to use the heater in the room during the day while she is at work. She is glad of the warmth, not for herself, but for her child.

"He feels safe since we moved here," she says. "He's normally slow to make friends but he's started to open up. No, he never hit him. He used to push him out of the way so as he wouldn't get hurt. But he saw it all."

As for herself, she says she cannot see her future. For now, she is living according to the alcoholics' gospel: one day at a time. Her single cause is to protect her son. Her own family is a thing of the past. Her sister fled, her mother alone in that house filled with terrifying memories, and her father in jail.

"That place in me where he was a father, that is empty," she says. "He died a long, long time ago."

If he had a headstone, she would inscribe it with the epitaph: "He never saw her cry ..."

Up with Billy's boys

Justine McCarthy took the trip north with a group of sensibly dressed Republic supporters to feel the full force of footballing and political hostility.

Irish Independent, 20 November 1993

We can hear the chanting from the Malone Road. A growl of battle muffled by the traffic and the distance. Growing louder as we cross the Lisburn Road to the first police ticket-check. Louder, louder as we walk mutely down one of the black, empty streets in The Village. Four of us from the South, not talking, walking close together, jollying each other along with our eyes. The noise is deafening. We turn left towards the footbridge. We see them coming. Marching jauntily from the east, swathed in the Union Jack and the emerald denied us tonight. Hundreds of them. All singing in one rumbling voice.

"We are the Billy Boys ..."

We had been brave on the 11.20 train from Connolly, where the loudspeakers were playing "We're all part of Jackie's Army, we're all off to Ital-ee" and the young, ginger-haired garda from Store Street wished us luck on the platform. A handful of journalists and a dozen Republic of Ireland supporters, 12 men strong and true off to whisper for Ireland in Windsor Park. We talked about Germany and Italy, Albania, Latvia, Malta, Turkey, Poland ... happy days.

"My wife got me the tickets, T'was cheaper than a divorce,"

laughed Peter Dowling, a bank official in Donnybrook. "You should'a seen her this morning, rooting in all the ould biscuit tins and tea caddies for the insurance policy."

Peter was travelling with five friends – another Peter, Charlie, Dessie 'Metal' Burke, Tom Gately over from London and Donal Kennedy from Long Beach, California.

"You know what they'll all be saying back in Dublin after this?" said Charlie Hurse. "They'll be saying: 'Oh, I was there, in Windsor Park.' An' we'll be saying: 'Were you now? I didn't see youse.' An' they'll be saying: 'Oh, I saw youse alright, but I didn't want to let on. Blow the cover, ya know.'"

We had laughed heartily at that. Too heartily. The two lads from Cork sang "The Boys of Fairhill" and Tom Gately handed out chocolate Lion bars and his last Rolos. One fan got off in Dundalk to drive the rest of the way. We said goodbye to Peter Dowling and the other five in Newry where they were being met by members of the Warrenpoint branch of the Republic of Ireland Soccer Supporters Club. Michael and Tom, who'd got the 7.35 train from Cork, got off in Portadown, to collect their tickets and down a few scoops in The Shambles Bar in Armagh.

As the train pulled into Belfast Central, Dubliner Brian Gaff pulled on a sweater over his tricoloured Opel T-shirt. His mate, David Keogh, was wearing a jacket over his blue Dublin GAA shirt, over his green and white IRELAND T-shirt.

"My girlfriend's from Turf Lodge an' she keeps telling me to watch meself," Brian had explained his layers of clothes.

"God save our gracious Queen
God save our glorious Queen
God save our Queen
No Surrender."

Block N – Row S – Seat 27 on the Upper Deck of the North Strand: eight o'clock and 10,000 Northern Ireland supporters singing their unique, throaty version of the British national anthem. We stand – just two of us now, hoping nobody notices our lips aren't moving.

Knots of RUC men watch from the closed Spion Kop terrace. A British Army helicopter shudders by in the sky. Their Ireland start warming up. They cheer. Our Ireland take off their tracksuit tops. They boo. The "Warning to Spectators" at the turnstiles has been forgotten – that the wearing or shouting of obscene slogans shall result in eviction from the ground.

"If you hate the Paddy bastards clap your hands, clap
your hands,
If you hate the Paddy bastards clap your hands, clap
your hands …"

It was late on Tuesday afternoon when the phone had rung in the office.

"I hear you're looking for a ticket," said a Belfast voice. He said his name was Warren and he'd be in Renshaws Hotel in University Street at 2.30. He'd have the tickets (face value: £12 each). We'd have the money: £160 for two.

The transaction was made over a drink in the bar. A pint of Guinness for Warren, who turned out to be from Hollywood, a posh Belfast suburb. He said there were Northern Ireland followers over from Scotland and Canada and 30 buses taking the local supporters from the Shankill Road the two miles to Windsor Park. He said the players were all fired up to beat "Ireland" tonight, that he'd talked to Alan McDonald after the

Lansdowne Road match and the Northern captain had told him he was physically sick for two days after the southern taunts that "There's only one team in Ireland."

"Did you know there's a Northern Ireland Soccer Supporters Club in Donegal?" asked Warren.

We thanked him for the tickets. He thanked us for the money and the pint of Guinness.

OLE, OLE, OLE, OLE,
F**k the Pope and the IRA …

"Men," smiled the woman beside me – one of about ten in the whole of Windsor Park (thank you, Mother of Divine Jesus and, please, can we win too?). Her man was on his feet roaring their Ireland on. He looked OK. She was nice. Still, best not take any chances. Sit on your hands, plait your legs into immobility under the bucket seat. Don't react. Don't smile. Don't grimace. Find that Mona Lisa look. Stop staring at all those empty FAI seats across the pitch.

"Dick Shpring's here," says a head in a duffle coat in the row behind.

"Who?"

"Dick Sphring, the Irish foreign minister. See the blue board an' two mon with orange on thum. He's the one in white beside 'um."

Dick Spring's in America – where we're going. We have to tell them. We can't tell them. Oh. Lord don't let there be trouble!

English ree-jects. English ree-jects. OOOH-AAAH.

We'd started out for the match in the Wellington Park Hotel on the Malone Road. Declan McPartlin, Larry Goodman's former press officer, was in the bar with a few friends, waiting for their tickets to arrive in the pocket of a Northern business colleague.

Five members of the RDS Gang (Rovers Destruction Squad) sat under the TV, waiting for the England–San Marino match to start on the telly – Roger the butcher, Paul the printer, Paul the book binder, John with the sports shop and Noel, the undertaker (honest). All from Dublin.

"We'd go anywhere to support Ireland," said John with the sports shop, "because we consider ourselves real football fans. The Northern Ireland fans think we're frightened of them. They call us Jack's Yellow Army but the only reason there aren't more of us here is because we couldn't get the tickets."

"Ya, I think it's a disgrace that the FAI f****d out those 400 tickets that were distributed," agreed Paul, the book binder. "Please put that in the paper. They should be looking after the real supporters and not the corporate businessmen."

Declan Cummins, a Chapelizod publican, and a Dub called Jack were over at the other side of the bar with a gang of pals from the First Shankill Northern Ireland Soccer Supporters Club who had come up trumps with the tickets for the Dubliners. The two Dubs were wearing 'civvies'. The Northerners were wearing lovely green, navy and white IFA tracksuit jackets and green scarves.

"We met Declan on an RTÉ programme called 'Over to You' at the last match in Lansdowne Road," said a man called Winston. "He got us a hundred tickets for the match and had a party for us afterwards in his pub. We love Dublin. It's a nice city. Very friendly. We'd rather see the southern Ireland team going to the World Cup than to see England going. Nobody ever wants England to win."

Football, he said, was their religion.

"We want to rub Jack Charlton's nose in it because of his arrogant English attitude to Northern Ireland," chipped in a man called Ronnie. "The closest some of them boys (in the Republic squad) have got to being Irish is a pint of Guinness. If you want to play for Jack Charlton all you have to do is own an Irish wolfhound. We're disappointed that Alan Kernaghan, such a talented young man, would play for a foreign country."

As we left the Wellington Park, Jack from Dublin had his arm around Winston from the Shankill Road. They'd met in Genoa during the World Cup three years ago. Tonight, Jack was going to sleep on the floor in Winston's House – "50 yards from where the bomb went off in the fish shop."

"There's only one team in Ireland. There's only one team in Ireland. One team in Ireland ..."

The middle-aged man in the grey raincoat must be one of us. He's been sitting in front of us, rigid, since the game began. He hasn't spoke to anyone. Hasn't smiled. Hasn't groaned. The giveaway is the way he's been chewing his fingernails to the quick. Our suspicions are confirmed when their Ireland score and the man in the grey raincoat stays in his seat. Like us. This is hell. They're winning and we're sitting here like Lot's wife. They must be able to hear the jeers in Inisvickalaun.

You're not going to the USA. You're not going to the USA.

It looks like all 10,000 of them are on their feet, stabbing the bitter gale with a synchronised two-finger salute. Then Alan

McLoughlin puts the ball in the net. Silence. Stunned, gut-churning silence. Slowly, the gentle hand-clapping reaches us from the FAI stand across the pitch.

"Shut the f***ing Fenian bastards up," screams a fellow in the row behind us.

"That's not nice," says another fellow, who's been quiet until now. "They have the right to support their team too."

It's over. The whistle's gone. A draw, Jack Charlton's kissing Ray Houghton. Christ! We've qualified!!! The nice man behind us taps us on the shoulder and shakes our hands, smiling. He's sussed us all along. Now we can sing together.

There's only one team in Ireland. Only one team in Ireland. There's only one team in Ireland ...

It's Thursday morning now. The first of the heroes are heading for home on the nine o'clock train from Belfast Central. We feel brave again. We did it. We were there. Ronnie, a truck driver. Dugo, an unemployed electrician and Tony, a bus driver, are refining their stories for the lads in the 'Dragon Inn' in Tallaght tonight. They'd gone back to a Republican club on the Falls Road after the match and a stranger had given them the use of his maisonette in Twinbrook for the night – complete with six bolts on the front door.

"We were like the Pope in the club," says Dugo. "They were all coming up, shaking our hands, saying: 'Thanks for coming'. Nobody there would go to Windsor Park. It's too dangerous. But they were all in the club wearing their Irish T-shirts. Everybody's been really nice. Even the guys at the station in their Northern Ireland Railway uniforms, and the taxi drivers who wouldn't charge us, and the pubs that wouldn't take a penny from us for the drink. It would've cost us more to stay in Dublin."

Ronnie admits he was scared. "It's a pity we couldn't wear our colours last night. Remember Cardiff Arms Park in the snow storm? The temperature sub-bleedin'-something and we took off our coats and stood there in our T-shirts. We were like the Ready Brek Kids standing there in the snow with a glow in our T-shirts."

Were they going to America? Were they wha?

"The problem is this," says Tony. "We got to Italy on our own and when we came back our wives told us: 'Never again. Next time, we're coming too.' It's amazing the number of women we saw at the matches in Italy."

"Jaysus, don't say that," says a distraught Ronnie. "My wife reads *The Indo*—"

Dugo is clutching a plastic carrier bag as he gets off the train at Connolly. A bag stuffed with copies of yesterday's *Belfast Telegraph*, with a colour picture of Dugo and Tony and Ronnie, arriving in Belfast on the front page: Jack's Army.

"Shit, I feel brave," grins Tony, rubbing his hands with unapologetic, unashamed, macho feel-good smugness. "I was there."

As we said goodbye, we were already singing ...

OLE, OLE, OLE, OLE, WE'RE OFF – TO THE USA!

The last goodbye

For now, there are no words to say. Only goodbye.
Goodbye wife, mother, daughter, sister, friend, colleague,
brave lovely lady. While she makes her final parting,
let the words of anger and vitriol, the political points-
scoring, the incoherence of frustration, make dumb leave
to honour her passing.

Irish Independent, 29 June 1996

In life, Veronica was a woman who transcended society's
most sinister barriers. In death, she is a leveller of the great,
the good and the plain ordinary. The scene outside Staffords
Funeral Home on the Malahide Road in Dublin last night
was a poignant epitaph. Against a sorrowful backdrop of her
neighbours, her readers – the friends she never knew she had –
the three most powerful politicians in the land stood helplessly
bent with sadness. The Taoiseach held his head in whitened
hands. The Tánaiste, seemingly shrunken, stared unblinking at
the ground. The Minister for Justice was crying.

The funeral director, former Fianna Fáil TD and Veronica's
friend, John Stafford, was encouraging everyone who knew her
to go and say a last goodbye. She looked beautiful, he said. She
was wearing her television suit, the beige jacket we had seen
her wear on *Questions & Answers*, with a cream polo-neck. A
single red rose lay across her waist. She was a vision too much
to bear. A woman with eyes shut to the world she had tried to
make a better place.

"There was no malice in her," said an elderly woman who had never met Veronica but who felt she had a relationship with her through reading *The Sunday Independent*. "Her fine mind has been whipped away from us just like that."

Her crime was that she had loved her country, and she believed it could be a better place. At her wedding reception in the Gresham hotel, another white-haired neighbour remembered, she had wooden plaques with the Irish flag on each table. "She wore a hat that day. Ronnie wasn't one for dressing up and, as soon as she got into the car she threw the hat out the window. Of course, the rest of the cars in O'Connell St drove over it."

Her concern for her country was evident in Veronica's journalism, and is well documented. But what few people knew was that her love of people, her fellow country people, squandered any spare time she had. At night she used to run discos for the Artane Summer Project. On carefree, sunny days, she accompanied up to 150 city children on outings to Butlins. That was Veronica Guerin, the woman viciously murdered in the city she loved.

"I never remember any death that has had this effect on people," the Taoiseach said, recalling that the last time he had met Veronica Guerin was at the funeral in Limerick of Detective Garda Jerry McCabe. He had been having a light-hearted conversation with the Tánaiste at Leinster House on Wednesday when the Dail's newest TD, Brian Lenihan, came to tell him the awful news. "You could see the loss in his face," said John Bruton, a man who, like so many others, has shed tears for Veronica.

If the man who ordered the assassination of Veronica thought that, by killing her, he could shut her up, he can think again. The outpouring of sadness across the country is ample evidence of the public's want for someone to defend their lives.

It was fitting tribute that people like the Taoiseach, the DPP, the Garda Commissioner, and the leader of the Opposition should fill the modest airport church last night. Fitting too were the forests of floral wreaths from Amnesty International, the NUJ, Irish Actors Equity, the Garda Representative Association, the Irish Bank Officials Association, the Oireachtas Press Gallery, the School of Journalism at the Dublin Institute of Technology …

But most fitting was the sobbing presence of people who had never met Veronica Guerin and yet believed she had made a difference to their lives. Among them, at the Church of Our Lady Queen of Heaven last night, a son of Garda Jerry McCabe. When the woman soloist sang *Be Not Afraid*, the entire congregation spontaneously joined her sweet voice in the chorus. It could have been Veronica's own anthem.

Of all the gestures made to her memory in the last three days, the contents of a decorative gift bag left among the floral tributes in the front office of Independent House are the most eloquent. A newly-bought blue and white soft toy in the shape of a bunny rabbit has this message attached: "For your little boy, Veronica. I will remember you because you cared."

Last night, her little boy, Cathal, did her proud. Immaculate, in navy shorts, laced-up canvas shoes and a white polo shirt, he held his daddy with one hand and his Robocop in the other. Outside the church, Veronica's husband, Graham, brought yet more tears to her colleagues' eyes when, in honour of his wife's profession and her readers' affection, he gently took the Robocop from Cathal, slipped it into his jacket pocket, and held his child in his arms by his wife's coffin long enough to allow the media cameras take their pictures. It was a moment of intense emotion, made unbearable when Cathal raised his little hand to the cameras, and waved. Tears ran down the face of John Bowman, so often Veronica's host on *Questions & Answers*.

The memory of white-faced reporters writing the story of Veronica's murder in the newsroom last Wednesday, their hands shaking over the keyboards, is one which will be impossible to eradicate. Her killing was a collective punch in the stomach for all of us, even those who did not know her. If only we could tell her how her brutal end has not only galvanised public opinion but has elevated the profession which she proudly represented. The media, often a hate word these days, finds itself supported, encouraged and wanted. Thanks to Veronica.

The priest was right last night when he said: "There is no church in Ireland that could adequately accommodate all the people who wish to be here." If only Veronica had not been there. She was a woman who loved her husband and child, their cottage home that Graham had taken a year off to make it like they dreamed, her zippy red car, life itself. A woman who had been beaten up, shot, threatened and intimidated in the most horrible way. One time, when her car was stolen two years ago, she got it back with a chilling message: "This time it's the car. Next time it will be you."

And yet, last Christmas, she sent a card to her colleague in *The Sunday World*, Paul Williams, saying: Happy Christmas to you, Anne and the children. Please be careful."

Now another card already grows yellowed and crinkled on the railing of Leinster House. "Veronica," it says, "thank you for all you have done."

The day Haughey gave old Ben Dunne the boot

It is the best-kept secret in the country. A mystery of Lord Lucan proportions which has been exercising inquisitive minds everywhere. Never more so than in the past two months. Most of those who were privy to the story at the time it happened are now dead. The survivors have long since taken the vow of omerta, swearing to take the secret to the grave with them.

Irish Independent, 19 July 1997

Their silence is a mark of respect for a man who, when he died 14 years ago, was interred in the firmament of legends. He had been one of the most successful, one of the richest and possibly *the* most enigmatic businessman to emerge from the Lemass cub economy. But the feud that erupted two decades before his death would come back to haunt his children and rock the political establishment.

On a warm sunny day last April Margaret Heffernan took the witness stand at Dublin Castle to give evidence to the Dunnes Payments Tribunal. It was to be one of the most sensational days in Irish politics. The suburban doctor's wife who heads up a £1 billion-plus retail empire told her gasping audience about a day in July 1993 when she drove to Abbeville in Kinsealy to ask former Taoiseach Charles Haughey if her younger brother, Ben, had given him £1m of Dunnes money. Her memory of that day was of her host repeatedly dodging the question and, instead, raising doubts about Ben's mental stability.

But it was what Margaret Heffernan declined to say during her testimony last April which proved to be most tantalising. Asked by Tribunal counsel Denis McCullough if she had approved of her brother's friendship with the former Taoiseach, which she described as "extremely close", she replied that she "certainly would not have agreed with him being friendly with Mr Haughey". Then she added enigmatically: "It goes back a long way and I wouldn't want to go into it. It was something between my father and Mr Haughey."

That cryptic allusion to the famous rift between two men who have touched the lives of all of us all sowed the seeds of wild speculation in Dublin Castle. Most people of a certain age had always known that bad blood existed between Charlie Haughey and Ben Dunne Senior but few knew the cause of it. Some mistakenly assumed that it had been a tiff, possibly about the horse-racing which was a passion of both men. In his second appearance at the Tribunal, just last Monday, Ben Junior said he was unaware at the time of his father's death that there had been a falling out between the two men. And with Margaret Heffernan privately refusing to ever divulge the details, the mystery took on the magnitude of Fatima's Third Secret.

Now that secret can be told.

What happened was this. It was the late 1960s. Jack Lynch was Taoiseach. Charles J Haughey was the youngish, bullish Minister for Finance. The Minister was nearly 20 years younger than a Rostrevor-born, self-made millionaire, rapidly building a hugely successful retail empire. His name was Ben Dunne.

He had a reputation for anticipating new business trends long before his competitors, regularly travelling to America where, for instance, he discovered the concept of a supermarket. He was also known to be a hard taskmaster and a ruthless negotiator with his suppliers. He once famously said: "I don't get ulcers, I give them."

This was the age of economic growth put in train by the Lemass era and T.K. Whitaker's Economic Development programme. Irish business had discovered the vast market to be tapped in America where the dollar-rich diaspora formed a ready-made customer base. The government here, under the auspices of old Córas Tráchtála, was investing heavily in the promotion of Irish merchandise Stateside. Irish fashion became something of a travelling roadshow, showcasing native crochet, knitwear and tweeds in major cities across America.

It was in this thrusting economic culture that the mysterious feud erupted between the young Finance Minister, who would soon be exiled to Purdah in the Arms Trial, and the earthy draper whose St Bernard label would feed and dress endless generations of Irish men and women.

The occasion was an Irish Trade Fair in a swanky New York hotel. It was designed to promote the finest products from home in the land of plenty, with the backing of generous State funding. Amont the exhibitors were Waterford Glass and Foxford Rugs, showing the range of quality crafts that went down a bomb in the States.

The Minister for Finance flew into Manhattan to officially open the exhibition. It was the sort of engagement that appealed to the burgeoning swashbuckling pretensions of a man destined to become the most controversial figure in Irish politics. It was a good-news gig: glamour piled upon glamour. Nothing could go wrong.

At least, that was how it looked – until the Government Minister's beaming gaze, proudly sweeping the panorama of all that was best from home, came to rest on an incongruous exhibitor's stand. It bore the trademark of St Bernard and there, in front of the stand, was one Ben Dunne busily answering visitor's queries about the new clothing phenomenon he was promoting: the drip-dry bri-nylon wonder shirt.

Charlie Haughey blew a fuse. He stormed across the exhibition hall, coming face-to-face with the father of his future benefactor. "What do you think this is?" he demanded, his face purple with fury. "The f***ing Iveagh Market?" Then he gave orders for the Dunnes stand to be dismantled, sending Ben back home with his tail between his legs. It was a humiliating episode for the wealthy trader and one he never forgot. Ben's rage was still palpable when he returned to Dublin. Charlie Haughey had become his sworn life-long enemy.

All these years later, the story of how Charlie Haughey fatally crossed swords with Old Ben Dunne is a veritable parable of what-goes-around-comes-around. No Hollywood scriptwriter could better a plot which culminates in the total disgrace of a near-mythical figure by the munificence of the son of a man he had so publicly disgraced 30 years previously.

The story of the falling out between Ben Senior and Charlie Haughey also puts into perspective Margaret Heffernan's anger over her younger brother's charity to the politician her father detested. In her Dublin Castle evidence, she made her lack of regard for the former Taoiseach crystal clear. Replying to counsel's questions, she said she couldn't remember if she had ever been in Abbeville before that July '93 meeting and her recollection of her chance encounters with him, at a fund-raising event and at a race meeting, screamed with the vagueness of a woman deeply unimpressed.

They say of Old Ben Dunne that when he passed on his business empire to his children, he bequeathed them not just a chain of shops but an entire way of life. Their father had handed them the Dunne Stores flag and it was their duty by birth to fly the standard high. For some of them, Ben Junior especially, it proved too onerous a task to honour.

But Margaret Heffernan fits her father's mantle like a glove. She is a religious woman, like her father, whose remarkable lifestyle (living in a £60-a night Shelbourne Hotel room; dinner every night in the Berkeley Court) involved making the Stations of the Cross every morning before going to the office and reciting the Rosary every night with his wife Nora. Like Old Ben, Margaret cuts an imposing figure in the boardroom and on the shopfloor. She is a formidable, forthright woman whose loyalty to her father has gagged her all these years from talking about that defining incident in New York when Charlie Haughey became a persona non grata in her family.

She told the Tribunal in April how the former Taoiseach had interceded with her to patch up her differences with Ben in the litigation over the family trust. Though we now know that his motivation at the time was the instinct for survival and a desperate attempt to keep the recorded €1.3m payments out of the public arena, the idea of Charlie Haughey meddling in the affairs of Old Ben Dunne's family must have galled Margaret Heffernan to the core. And when, last Tuesday morning, he tried in vain to brazen it out at Dublin Castle after admitting that he had consistently lied in 70 separate pieces of correspondence to the inquiry, it must have made Margaret Heffernan's blood boil to hear him contradict her own earlier evidence.

"She talked about his (Ben Junior's) difficult and unpredictable behaviour," he countered. "I may have said: 'From what you describe, Margaret, it may appear that your brother is acting in an unstable way, giving an indication of instability.'"

The friendliness implied by the use of her first name, slowly and deliberately given in his testimony, gave a false impression of warmth in the relationship between Charles Haughey and Margaret Heffernan.

The real irony of the enmity between Ben Senior and Charlie Haughey is that, in other circumstances, they could have been the best of friends. They had much in common. Both came from relatively humble origins, nurturing grandiose ambitions. Both liked to hobnob with the privileged classes while relying on their street-wisdom to further their own careers. They were straight-talkers who believed in themselves. They had in common a fascination with horse-racing, both having led their own charges into the winner's enclosures. Had they not met, so briefly and tempestuously, in New York three decades ago, they could have been lifelong friends, rather than sworn enemies.

But it was the pride of both men which caused one of the most talked-about rifts in the country and which was still subtly at play in the Tribunal at Dublin Castle. Ben Dunne's pride was seriously wounded in New York that day the young Government Minister sent him packing with his drip-dry shirts. He was a man justifiably proud of his achievements in business.

And, though his youngest son may have been blissfully

unaware of the history that existed between Old Ben and Charlie Haughey, when he stood in Glasnevin Cemetery to deliver his father's graveside eulogy, Ben Junior unknowingly fired a shot on his behalf. His father, he recalled, had once been distinguished by a prestigious American organisation which voted him 'The Most Outstanding Retailer in the World.' The same retailer who had been sent packing from a deluxe trade affair in America by the former Minister for Finance, one Charlie Haughey.

And the same retailer who built a multi-million pound empire, some of the proceeds of which went towards maintaining the lavish lifestyle of the same Charlie Haughey.

The lion in the winter

It is as if his life has been frozen. Everything awaits
the day of judgement. And what is at stake is Charles J.
Haughey's place in history.

Irish Independent, 28 March 1998

Séamus Brennan's State Mercedes straddles the double-yellow lines outside the Four Courts, two of its wheels planted resolutely on the footpath. Poised for flight and impervious to the bellow of juggernaut traffic thundering up the city quays in its path.

Inside the austere monolith of justice, the diminutive Government Chief Whip is being ushered along a pastel institutional corridor towards Court Six and the High Court action being taken by Charlie Haughey against Ireland, among others.

The Minister of State at the Department of the Taoiseach, Government Chief Whip and Fianna Fáil party whip has been subpoenaed by the Haughey side to testify to advice he gave the parliamentary party on how the TDs, Senators and MEPs should respond to a letter sent to them by the Moriarty Tribunal. The Minister is being interposed as the first witness in the hearing to facilitate his imminent departure to the US for a promotion of the 1798 commemorations.

As he is about to enter the courtroom, however, the doors swing open to squeeze a stream of spectators and lawyers into the hallway. The Minister looks bemused. He wasn't expecting Judge Hugh Geoghegan's court to rise for lunch before hearing his evidence. He is still standing at the doorway, unsure what to do next, watching the hangers-on milling in the hall. There is a hush, partly reverential and utterly expectant. All eyes are trained on the courtroom door.

The dawn of realisation breaks across Séamus Brennan's face in a storm. Of course, they are waiting for Haughey to come out. Panic springs to his eyes. He spins around, away from the door, searching out the solicitor who has brought him here. "Ivor," he calls urgently. The solicitor nods. And the two men stride purposefully down the corridor, disappearing around the corner just before the former Taoiseach hobbles into view with his standard hospital-issue crutch.

During the lunch break that follows, one of the court's busier barristers inadvertently barges into a consultation room near the Law Library, looking for his own party of litigants. When he finds the room is occupied by Charles Haughey and his family, the barrister apologises and withdraws. To his surprise, when he opens the door of the next consultation room, there is Séamus Brennan – the Minister awarded his first portfolio by Haughey – dining separately.

You could feel the isolation of Charles J Haughey in court this week. He arrived alone, but for his garda driver. He sat with his wife, Maureen, his daughter, Eimear, and sons Conor and Seán. Sometimes, Maureen would whisper something to him. Only occasionally. He never looked around at the rows of reporters sitting behind and the spectators standing four-deep. He looked old, tense and thin. When the court clerk swore him in on the witness stand and asked him to state his name for the record, his reply was so low that only the judge and his own lawyers could hear it.

An English journalist who had never before seen him in the flesh but knew him to be a legend of imperialist magnitude, professed amazement that this was the man who had held his country in a grip of fascination for three decades. At the adjournments, when the few bravehearts came to shake his hand and slap his back in the old how's-she-cuttin' style, the gestures made him seem more inescapably marooned than ever. "You're a real Irishman," a giant of a man bent low to tell him. "You stood up to Thatcher."

But that was a lifetime ago. A time when standing up to Thatcher got them cheering in the terraces. A time when Charlie Haughey could imbue a silver teapot with all the symbolism of a nation squaring its shoulders. A time when he had the entire machinery of the State at his command and citizens boastfully regaled one another with bloated stories of his machismo. They loved him then. They hated him too. But they could ignore him like they ignored breathing.

Now they ignore him for their very survival. So acute is his sense of having been abandoned that, according to a friend who has remained loyal, he was inordinately chuffed when the Finance Minister, Charlie McCreevy, recently credited him on the *Late Late Show* with the economic boom. It is poignantly illustrative to think of Charlie Haughey, a man always destined for immortality in the history books, sitting in watching the *Late Late* on a Friday night, finding comfort in the praise doled out by someone who used to be a thorn in his side.

It is as if his life has been frozen. Now is the time he should be enjoying retirement – the chrysanthemum-growing and bucolic pursuits he sign-posted when he quit the Dáil. Instead, everything is on hold, awaiting the day of judgement. The staff has been let go at Kinsealy. The house and the island may or may not have to be sold. Acquaintances have scattered. And the bills are mounting.

Now, instead of the courtesans and the sycophants, he has only the company of his family, a few stalwart friends and phalanx of professionals engaged to rescue him from obliteration in his declining years. In his oral evidence on Wednesday, and again on Thursday, he revealed that he has retained accountants and lawyers to reconstruct more than half a lifetime of work. The court heard there is no guarantee that he will be recompensed for the expenditure necessitated by the Tribunal's inquiries.

His potential liabilities are already estimated at double the £1.3m which the McCracken Tribunal established he received from Ben Dunne. The Revenue Commissioners have levied a tax bill of £1.7m and he did not seek his legal costs of roughly £100,000 from the McCracken Tribunal. Added to that is the cost of the current High Court challenge, which is expected to finish on Tuesday, probably with judgement reserved. Should he lose and have costs awarded against him, they could run to £500,000 for the six senior counsel, six juniors and four solicitors attending the hearing, if the ordinary rates apply. The perceived wisdom among lawyers is that, whatever the outcome, the case is likely to end up in the Supreme Court, where costs usually work out at between 25% and 33% of the lower court's costs.

The legal team representing the five Haughey plaintiffs includes former Attorney General Colm Condon who, ironically, led the State's case in the Arms Trial and whose reputation and 54 years' experience at the bar allow him to command generous fees. He is accompanied by Eamonn Leahy and Eoin McGonigle, the senior counsel who famously made £1m from the Beef Tribunal. The instructing solicitors are Ivor Fitzpatrick, a frequent table host at the annual Cáirde Fáil fundraising dinner, and Deirdre Courtney, a partner in Fitzpatrick's firm.

Another partner in the practice is Michael O'Connor, the son of Haughey's former solicitor, Pat O'Connor, who is currently ill in hospital. The firm has also acted for Dermot Desmond in the past, the businessman who issued a media statement after Christmas detailing his financial relationships with members of the Haughey family.

On the accountancy front Haughey has engaged three financial advisers. The highest-profile of these is believed to be fellow northsider and Mensa-member Des Peelo, who stoutly defended Haughey on television in the run-up to the McCracken Tribunal. Haughey has also engaged tax specialist Terry Cooney, a former president of the Institute of Taxation and a partner of property developer Paschal Taggart.

The third adviser is thought to be Paul Moore, who has a practice on the southside of the city. Some of the top financial advisers in the country can charge £300 for an hour's work, but it is expected that, in this case with its vast brief, an all-inclusive fee would have been agreed. A further expense is that, as a non-trader, Charlie Haughey does not qualify for exemption from the 21% VAT imposed on professional fees.

Off the record, nobody denies that Haughey is broke. The sums simply will not add up. But friends of his insist that nothing is for sale yet. With 200 acres of the Abbeville estate, valued at £10m, as well as Inishvickaullaun held by his four children in Larchfield Securities, Charlie and Maureen Haughey have 20-acres and the Gandon mansion itself to call home. It is here that his former Government Press Officer, PJ Mara, comes to see him once a week. And it is from here that he sets out each day for his morning ride-out on Portmarnock strand with his neighbour, the builder Standish Collen.

Every Saturday night, Charlie and Maureen Haughey go out to dinner in Malahide or Howth with Standish Collen and another neighbour, Brian Dennis of HB Dennis. The architect Arthur Gibney, who developed an amateur sideline as the designer of Haughey's Christmas cards when he was Taoiseach, has also remained close.

Maybe it's sheer bloody-mindedness – or maybe it's not – but a friend of Charlie's claims that the real reason for the frailty of his appearance these days has less to do with the Moriarty Tribunal and more to do with his riding accident in January when he broke his thigh bone. It seriously dented his self-image, says the friend, and his pride in being fit and active at 72. This is despite another hospital stay last year when he underwent a procedure to clear a blocked coronary artery.

In fact, there is a story about the fall from the horse which suggests that the old Haughey spirit remains unquenched. According to sources near Kinsealy, the horse that threw him that morning was not his usual mount but a younger, far livelier horse with a reputation for chomping at the bit.

He will need that spirit to sustain him. Apart from a peaceful retirement and a modicum of financial stability, he is fighting for a noble place in history. The odds appear to be stacked against him. After being publicly outed as a liar at the McCracken Tribunal, open season was declared on Charlie Haughey.

The general legal advice to journalists – who for so many years tiptoed around him in trepidation – is that it is virtually impossible to defame the man because his reputation is in shreds. To other politicians he is radioactive, a contaminant to be avoided at all costs. Now it is known that he took £1.3m from Ben Dunne and led a lifestyle in the 80s that cost £300,000 a year, questions about his career have openly multiplied.

There is a demand for those questions to be answered but there is a danger too that because of the man's very personality, it could degenerate into a vindictive exercise of self-gratification. He and his wife of 46 years have already had to endure one British newspaper's sensationalist and highly inaccurate report that their marriage was over. At least one journalist who covered this week's hearing confessed that he took great delight in watching Charles J Haughey's discomfort.

At one juncture, when Judge Geoghegan queried the Haughey lawyers' emphasis on cabinet confidentiality, he drew a spontaneous laugh from his courtroom for his own unintended sarcasm. "His own money arrangements were not made at cabinet," said the judge, perplexed about the relevancy of the issue.

In the High Court reporters' office during one of the breaks, a veteran of the courts listened to his younger colleagues' animated swapping of Haughey stories. "I remember the days when you'd be afraid to say his name," he said, shaking his head in wonder.

As the DPP considers whether or not to prosecute him for his conduct at the McCracken Tribunal and the team of professionals he has engaged labours over his tangled financial history, Charlie Haughey is living in a time capsule. As he entered the courthouse on Thursday morning, he defiantly told media photographers that he never looks back. Nor can he look ahead, at least no further ahead than the Moriarty Tribunal.

The last time he so dramatically appeared in a courtroom was nearly 30 years ago for the Arms Trial. Significantly, last Wednesday his son Seán, the TD, sat beside him in Court Six even as Bertie Ahern was placating the Fianna Fáil parliamentary party over Articles 2 and 3 of the Constitution, a matter which goes to the heart of the organisation's republicanism.

For now, Charles Haughey, the man who stood up to Thatcher, has his own territorial claim to defend. His place in history.

The 2000s

The 2000s

To school through the shields

This week, the eyes of the world became focused on a short stretch of road in north Belfast. For a community of mothers and their children, the walk along the Ardoyne Road to Holy Cross primary school with her two children became a journey down a tunnel of hate. Justine McCarthy reports.

Irish Independent, 8 September 2001

Anne talks despite herself. She protests that she's worn out from giving interviews to the media. She doesn't want to see herself on the television again. She draws her daughter's blonde head into the pleated waistband of her skirt and shoos away the circling newspaper photographers. "No more pictures," she forbids them fiercely, waving them away with the child's honey-brown teddybear. "For God's sake, she's only little. She's six. I don't want her to be a target. No more pictures."

Most of the parents are nervous about setting their children and themselves up as targets since the RUC informed three mothers that the Red Hand Defenders had threatened to kill them, but Anne talks anyway. "I can't walk the walk," she confessed. "I'm too frightened."

Anne had taken her two daughters, the six-year-old and the 10-year-old, up to Ardoyne Road for the first day of the school year at Holy Cross Primary on Monday morning. Like most of the Catholic mothers, she was expecting a protest. But what she encountered was something she never imagined.

In the narrow cracks of the grotesque security tunnel formed by armoured cars and plastic riot shields, she saw faces screwed up with hatred. The faces were straining to show themselves to her and her children. Their mouths were screaming curses at them. "Whores! Fenian bastards!" one voice yelled. She could feel her neighbours' fear too. They huddled tighter, instinctively, squeezed between the tensed line of armed police and soldiers. Her six-year-old stumbled and fell in front of a man with a placard. Anne saw his face and reckoned he was at least 50. The man looked down at the child on the ground and screamed: "Fenian scumbag, your mother was out with her legs open last night. You're the bastard of a slut."

Anne was panicking. She tried to pick up her six-year-old, vaguely aware that her older child was tugging her forward, desperate to reach the safety of the school. She felt a hand on her shoulder. She turned in dread. It was a British soldier. "Walk on, love," he urged her, in a soft Scottish burr. "If anyone's scum, it's him."

The soldier stayed with them until they got to the gates of the school. Anne thanked him and hurried inside. Everyone was congregating in the assembly hall. The mothers were shaking. The principal, Anne Tanney, was trying to comfort the children. Then they heard a series of loud bangs. The parents and the children threw themselves onto the floor.

"Jesus," Anne thought. "They're throwing bombs at the school." There were children lying on the floor, screaming. Some were only four years of age, on their first day in school. "Babies, really",' Anne said. When she realised that the noise outside was coming from fireworks, she looked around for her 10-year-old and found her in a corner of the hall, vomiting.

That was it. She caught her two girls by the hand and led them back to the safety of their home, past the goldfish tank in the corridor and the childish paintings hanging off the staircase.

They have not been back up the road since. "If I wasn't afraid, I'd be going up there every morning with the rest of them," Anne says. "I lowered myself on Monday because, for the first time in my life, I actually called someone an Orange bastard. It sickened me because I have Protestant friends living up there on that road. I've been bridesmaid to two of them up there and one of them was my bridesmaid.

On Tuesday, Wednesday and Thursday, Anne woke the children an hour earlier to take them to school by the "alternative route". She says it takes them 40 minutes longer to get there. "Uphill and downhill and across a boys' football pitch." And past an entry-way to Hesketh Road, a main Protestant artery.

She does not feel safe going that way, but her eldest daughter will sit her 11 Plus exams in six weeks' time in the hope of qualifying for Fortwilliam Grammar School over in leafy Cavehill. She wants to be a teacher. The girl has refused to stay in school unless her mother stays as well and so, each day, Anne has waited with other parents for six hours until classes ended.

She believes there is still hope for her daughters. As for herself, she vows: "I'll never again have anything to do with cross-community things. I'll stick with my own people from now on."

She is the embodiment of how the hatred keeps perpetuating itself. The more the majority wants change, the more some people are determined to keep things as they are. The powerful pictures of little girls being shouted and spat at in their pretty red-and-navy uniforms had not been to everyone's disadvantage.

Further up the road, where the UDA and UVF flags flutter from the lampposts and the parking meters are painted red, white and blue, a Protestant man tells a joke. "Ardoyne," he says, "is like the Aborigine who bought a new boomerang and then spent the rest of his life trying to throw the old one away."

The joke-teller is from Upper Ardoyne. This is Protestant Ardoyne to outsiders. Some residents call it Alliance, but that is not entirely accurate because, while Alliance Road might be Protestant, the neighbouring Alliance Avenue, visible across the cul-de-sac wall, is Roman Catholic. When the wind blows from a certain direction, the competing union and tricolour flags that mark out the territories appear to be dancing a gentle minuet wrapped in each other's folds. One third of all killings in the Troubles have occurred here in north Belfast.

Roughly, there are 7,000 Roman Catholics and 1,000 Protestants in Ardoyne. A short section of Ardoyne Road itself and four streets running off it – Glenbryn Drive, Gardens, Parade and Park – make up the Protestant patch. All the roads seem to finish in dead-ends here. They run along nicely for a while, neat red-brick rows with faux shutters and the bric-a-brac of family lives strewn in their front gardens. Then you reach the inevitable wall. It's the same in Springfield and the Markets and the other enclaves. All the better, someone explains, for the security forces to corner their prey.

According to the joke-teller, a square-built man dressed in a funeral suit for the burial of 16-year-old Thomas McDonald, the Protestant schoolboy killed by a Catholic woman's car on Tuesday, Ardoyne is a boomerang. No matter what the politicians do with the Peace Process, he argues, you can count on Ardoyne to bring the past bouncing back every time.

In some ways, Ardoyne – Catholic and Protestant – is like the Republic used to be about two decades ago. It remains untouched. It would be a lovely place to live if it wasn't for the terror. Nobody is in a hurry. People stroll, they chat, they smoke, they go to church, they still believe in communal sharing and respect as if, having had to consciously safeguard their dignity, they treasure it all the more. They hold the teacher and the doctor in high regard and the priest remains undisturbed at the top of the social pyramid.

It was the priest they gathered to hear yesterday morning outside the little parade of shops at the bottom of Catholic Ardoyne. He borrowed a step ladder and climbed to the top. Against the drone of a watching security helicopter, he thanked them for the respect they had shown Thomas McDonald by their silent walk and shared prayer with the Presbyterian minister outside the school. Then they said an Our Father together and the priest blessed them, invoking the Mother of Good Counsel. He cut an heroic figure, his black robe moving in the wind above the heads of the people.

Before the first riotous school run last Monday, hardly anyone in Ardoyne had even heard of Fr Aidan Troy. By Monday night, his name and face were seen right around the world. Like Fr Edward Daly, waving his white hanky in Derry on Bloody Sunday, and Fr Alex Reid administering the kiss of life to a soldier in Andersontown, the image of Fr Troy leading a procession of little girls to school through an avalanche of sectarian abuse has joined the iconography of Northern

Ireland. It was hardly what he was expecting when he arrived in Ardoyne just five weeks ago as the new superior at Holy Cross Monastery.

Originally from Bray, he lived in Mount Argus in Dublin for several years. He returned to this island last month after completing a degree in Rome. For the six years before that he had travelled around the world as a liaison with the international Passionist Order, using Rome as his base. He lived in South Africa for a while, where he saw what apartheid did to people. When he was invited to transfer to Belfast, he thought he could make the transition easily, as he had lived in Downpatrick after his ordination.

Three nights after his arrival five weeks ago, an attempt was made to burn down his monastery on Crumlin Road. Fortunately, the people who poured fuel in through one of the windows were seen running away and the nearby fire engine responded quickly. No physical harm came to the eight priests in the community, including a deaf 89-year-old and a blind 83-year-old. The fist person to phone Holy Cross the next morning was President McAleese, who was baptised in the church and whose family was machine-gunned out of its home at 657 Upper Crumlin Road 30 years ago.

Fr Troy readily admits that he has been scared walking up Ardoyne Road each morning this week. "I was very frightened and very, very distressed. I think shock set in with me a few hours after the blast bomb on Wednesday morning. When it went off, some of the children started running back down the road and some ran towards the houses where the protesters were. I was trying to pull them back and get them to the school. I'm not used to this."

It was 6.20 yesterday morning that Fr Aidan Troy lay in bed watching the BBC news on television. The reporter was talking about a planned silent protest by the Protestant residents of Ardoyne as a mark of respect to Thomas McDonald. The scene had been set for a highly incendiary encounter when the Protestant residents asked the Catholic residents not to bring their children up the road to school.

That was when Fr Troy had a flash of divine inspiration. He phoned his opposite number, Rev Norman Hamilton, the Presbyterian minister of Ballysillan Church, and suggested they meet outside Holy Cross School to say The Lord's Prayer together. It was a brilliantly simple plan to defuse a dangerous situation and turn it into something positive.

"I suppose we say it all differently," said Rev Hamilton, uncertainly, as he led the Catholic parents in the Our Father.

"That doesn't matter," replied Fr Troy. "We know your ending."

What this week's events in Ardoyne have done is to cause everyone to reassess the peace process. Like Fr Troy says, there is no point in changing the structures if the hearts and minds remain unchanged. In that latter cause, he has already carved out a role for himself. Perhaps, as someone from the outside, he is better equipped to see how much the two communities have in common.

Both suffer from casual violence and persistent intimidation. Whether it is the initials of the IRA painted outside a house or the name of the UVF C Company, the nearest houses will have wire mesh on their windows to safe-guard against missile-throwers. Brendan Bradley, a spokesman for Survivors of Trauma, confirms that the violence visited on the two communities is "in equal measures, but bombs are not the same as stones". Loyalist pipe bombs have prevailed in Belfast in the past year.

Yet, the Protestant population is declining in Ardoyne, down to nearly a quarter of what it was a decade ago. There are claims that Protestant women have been ordered by their community to desist from shopping on the Catholic part of the road, there are counter-claims that Catholic traders have told them to "starve".

The present violence erupted after a Protestant man was knocked from his ladder on June 19 last as he hung a Union flag from a lamp-post. But some Catholic residents believe that it has been exacerbated by the internecine loyalist feud and the relocation of people from the Shankill, creating further tensions between the UDA and the UVF.

"We don't blame the kids. We feel complete compassion for them," said a 21-year-old mother in Upper Ardoyne on Thursday, after participating in the whistling protest. "But my granny couldn't walk down the street to collect her pension in the post office. I couldn't bring my two-year-old son to the library." Seemingly unaware of the contradiction, she added that she would not expose her son to the protest if the roles were reversed. While she was speaking, four middle-aged men standing a short distance away repeatedly shouted "Today and every day." The woman said the men were her father and three of her uncles.

After a week that began with such horrific images and talk that the paramilitary ceasefires were over and the peace process was collapsing, it ended more hopefully, but, while Fr Troy and

Rev Hamilton prayed together in an attempt to change hearts and minds, there was no sign of Anne.

She had been watching from the school on Wednesday and had seen the blast bomb explode. "I saw a reporter pick up a wee child and run to safety," she recalled. "And I saw the mummies standing at the side of the road. They were cheering and clapping and saying 'You Fenian bastards'. Those people aren't Protestants. They're sick psychotic monsters. I will never again let my children become involved in cross-community projects," she pledged.

Wheatfield Protestant Primary School stands directly across the road from Holy Cross Primary. The children of both schools regularly work together – often assisted by their parents – as part of the non-segregation policy built into the education curriculum. Yesterday morning, as the Catholic children walked silently up the road, young girls from Wheatfield stood at the side of the road with their parents, their backs turned to the procession. Some held black scarfs over their heads.

As the procession was turning into the school, a pretty Protestant girl turned to look over her shoulder at it. The expression of contempt on her face was chilling, as much as for its intensity as for its familiarity down through the generations.

Keeper of the flame

Brendan Kennelly will turn 65 this month, though you would not think it by his youthful mischievous face. Yet, Brendan Kennelly's life has been dogged by alcoholism, by a failed marriage and heart surgery. He has been dry now for 15 years and still he can say 'I like drunkards. I like drink. I don't like myself.' Ireland's best-loved poet talks to Justine McCarthy

Irish Independent, 7 April 2001

He is leaning backwards against the black iron railing. His arms and his feet are crossed. His eyes are watching. Not watching for anything. Simply watching. His demeanour looks ready to be amused. Students and tourists lurch past him into the cobbled otherworld of the university. If the sightseers knew he was a famous Kerry poet, they might decide to forgo the Book of Kells and queue instead to capture his soul with their instamatic cameras. But they do not know him and so they go on, leaving him still and watching at Trinity's entry way, washed in sunlight between the shadowless statues that stand guard with him. Goldsmith. Kennelly. Burke. Keepers of the village gate.

I see him at the out-turn of Grafton Street's last curve and feel a sickener of anxiety. We have never met, but we did speak – once – on the telephone. It must have been seven or eight years ago. I had written a throwaway line about him in the paper. He rang me up.

"Do you really think I have a *pained voice*?" he asked, echoes of befuddlement and hurt lingering on the line.

I am walking towards him now and hoping he has forgotten; hoping that his rich mellifluous Irish voice will greet me as someone with whom he has no past. He stretches out his right hand. "Hello," he smiles, and two dimples as deep as wells spring forth in his cheeks.

He leads the way across the cobbles. It is the first day of the year's final term; the Trinity term, when the madness of the annual ball and the perennial exams will produce the next generation of educated rat racers. They flow past with their bicycles and their books. "Hello professor," a young man mutters shyly.

These leafy groves have been the professor's home for most of his adult life; bar his early flirtations with the ESB and punching out tickets on the London buses; bar the 10 years of his marriage when he lived in Sandymount; and bar the accumulated lost years at the bottom of a whisky glass in O'Neill's pub. He was a scholarship student in Trinity and joined the staff as a junior lecturer in the 1960s so that he has been teaching here now for 40 years. It was in his college rooms this morning that he rose at seven o'clock. He washed and shaved and when he looked in the mirror over his sink he saw "a face with a fair amount of tiredness. As the Dubs say, a face only a mother could love."

Having completed his ablutions, he picked up a book by a writer called Heine and read with immense pleasure. Heine wrote that, while his mother was pregnant with him, she had seen a lovely apple in her neighbour's garden. She resisted the temptation to steal the apple so as to ensure that the child in her womb would not grow up to be a thief. Instead, the child grew up to love apples and to seek to respect his neighbour's property. Brendan's blue eyes dance as he relates this story.

His own book, *Glimpses*, his sixth published volume of poems, is fresh from the printers, bearing the image of Jan Vermeer's *Girl with a Pearl Earring* on the cover. The verses are vivid jabs of observation, full of wisdom and wish and ruthless truth.

He spent time killing time
until time killed him.
What's his name?

He says a fella once declared to him that "poetry is bad enough without being long into the bargain." Hence *Glimpses?* His laugh is delighted. Such are the joys for someone whose writings have been translated into Greek, Italian, French, German and Arabic, who has reworked the tragedies of Euripides and Sophocles and who gets invitations to read his poetry on the continent. He knows the critics are waiting and he quotes Conor Cruise O'Brien's dictum that the first thing an Irish writer needs is sensitivity. The second is a thick neck. "We love kicking the shit out of each other," says the professor of modern literature. "I think I've got some unfair criticism. I think in Ireland what we do is label each other. The label of the Kerryman, the Trinity college professor, the jovial person, the 'good old Brendan Kennelly' figure, and then they bring these to bear on what you write. I don't expect warm criticism. George Moore said a good literary movement is a number of people in a city with a cordial hatred for each other."

We're seated now in an odd little bar room fitted with low-lit tables and beer taps, upstairs in the Dining Hall. We have arrived here by way of a stone staircase, watched over by a portrait gallery of daunting academics and sweeping past the open double doors of the common room where teachers are boning up on the day's news before lectures. It was he who poured out two cups of coffee at the help-yourself table in the corridor. His pouring hand is steady as his gaze.

"You have a steady hand," I say.

"I had to beat the drink," he says.

"Are you lonely?" I ask.

"I shouldn't be," he answers. "I don't like saying it's because I have good friends."

"Is there a woman in your life now?"

"There is someone, yes," he says.

"Do you remember we spoke once before?" I ask.

"No," he answers, "when was that?"

He will turn 65 this month, though you would not think it by his sturdiness or his mischievous face. Nor would you think to look at him that his ivoried life had been chipped by alcoholism, by the failure of his marriage to Dr Peggy O'Brien, an American academic, and by the necessity for a quadruple by-pass of his heart. "In the summer of 1986, I spent two months trying to think about alcoholism. I walked from St Patrick's Hospital to Ballsbridge one Sunday and when I was walking, my mind told me to stop drinking. I wondered: "Is being a lapsed alcoholic a form of betrayal?" I had to think about that.

He has been dry for 15 years and still he can say "I like drunkards. I like drink. I don't like myself. I don't like being afraid of life. I am timid. I'm not shy any more. I love the pub for an hour or an hour and a half. The great thing is they are centres of transformation. People change after a few drinks. They drink articulately to another planet and you are left alone on yours."

He calls himself "an olic", as in alcoh-olic (two bottles a day in his pre-sober years), workah-olic (four plays, two novels and more than 20 books of poems), a walkah-olic (he has a Joycean intimacy with his city), a bookah-olic (he reads two or three a day). He says his brother died from chocolate. He craves intensity. "I love football. I love drinking and rogues and fellas that will not answer you. Abuse, curses, insults, blessings, all these things that have the mark of intensity." The thing he dreads is the benign. His language explodes with words like 'love', 'devotion', 'compulsion', 'tragedy' and 'adventure'.

It is this appetite for the extreme that has him living in the capital between holidays in the Kingdom. "I love being in the heart of Dublin and on the edge of Ireland." In the summer, he will once again rent his cottage from Mary Collins, 20 yards from the sea in Ballybunion. Each morning, her husband, Seamus, will go down to the strand at daybreak to gather the weeds off the rocks. Then the university professor will sink into Mary Collins' famous seaweed bath for a languorous soak. Afterwards, he will go running down into the sea. "I leap around and pretend I can swim."

His home village is busy organising the inaugural Brendan Kennelly Summer School for next August. The fact that he mentions this betrays his pleasure until the possibility is raised that it could be jinxed by the foot-and-mouth crisis. Then his face accordions into ruffles of wicked laughter.

His landmarks for his Ballylongford childhood are mostly female. There were the women living on either side of his house and his school teacher, Jane Agnes McKenna, who taught him languages. Such a love did she inculcate in her pupil that he hungrily read Latin, Greek, French and Irish. When he took Irish mythology for his PhD, he read the European myths too, Homer and Dante.

And then, there was his mother. Her name was Bridie. She came from north Kerry and worked above in Cork as a nurse. At a dance in Ballybunion in 1931, she met a man from Scrolm Hill in the parish of Ballydonoghue who returned from America. They wed and set up home in Ballylongford on the earnings of Timmy's Old Tin Shed, the garage where Mr Kennelly repaired cars and clocks.

One day, Bridie was standing in front of the range when the third of her eight children asked her: "What is the secret of life?" She paused and thought before replying: "Give as much love as you can." He preserved that moment in a collection called *Begin*, the same poem that the monks of Glenstal Abbey recite every Christmas morning.

Ah, Brendan Kennelly and the women! He loves them. They love him. They expand themselves in his company, straining to live up to his grand idea of them. "I have never met an evil woman," he announces. "I remember the women's faces when I was growing up. It was devotion and humour. The way the women in my village worked and how they reared their children and got them ready to go to America. You would never see them out for a walk. You know that whiteness a woman gets in her face if she does not go out walking? They had that, a dedicated pallor." He's spellbound by us women. It makes him likeable. And vulnerable too.

The old Irish word for kiss
  is drink.
When a man drinks a woman
he knows how stupid it is to think.

Dublin is something else entirely. He has made it his city by walking its streets, carpeting its pavements with his footprints, and by striving to live meditatively and "sensorially" at its epicentre. "In a frantic world in a frantic city, to get the smell of cars, to see the faces behind the wheels, to close your eyes and hear the voices in a café, to touch the books in the shop." His waking hours are spent in lecture halls and book shops and, on Sundays, he goes to mass in John's Lane, the Augustinians' byzantine church over on Thomas Street.

It cheers him now and then to declare his active Catholicism in the humanist environs of intellectualism. "It is a religion for poets and drunks and people who sense the inadequacies of reason and logic." Yet, he is not judgmental, believing that materialism and spirituality can co-exist and refusing to decry the economic culture.

His daughter and only child, Doodle, is part of the lucky generation. So too are her children, his three granddaughters, Meg, Hannah and little Grace Mary, whom he loves taking to the shops "to buy things".

But even Brendan Kennelly's Ireland has its flaws. He recoils at what has been done to two of his friends, fellow Kerry man Hugh O'Flaherty and honorary Kerry man Charlie Haughey.

He suspects that the odium heaped on them was mined from a communal thirst for revenge.

Our Irish style is changing, she said.
We have a new mode of attack.
It seems we prefer steel kicks in the head to stabs in the back.

"I think people have taken out on Charlie what they might have looked at in themselves," he says. "Here is an *ard rí*. I think he sees himself like an emperor. He likes land and big houses and money. He does. But I'm talking about something essential in him. He can recite Latin poetry. I think he's a kind man."

He recalls an encounter on the street with the former Taoiseach sometime in the 1980s.

"Where are you off to?" Charlie asked the poet.

"Up to Mountjoy to teach the women."

"Here," Charlie said, handing him £50. "Buy them something."

"What'll I buy," asked the poet.

"What every woman loves: soap, ya eejit. Go into the Body Shop and buy them some soap."

He does not hesitate in the telling of this story though he knows "what people will say".

It is easy to be cynical about Brendan Kennelly. He seems almost too bright and jolly and Irish-y to be true; always an anecdote or witticism or a dimpled grin to electrify his audience. It is easy to be cynical, that is, until you meet him. Then the overwhelming impression is of a man trying his damnedest to be as good as he can; reading his books, saying his prayers, teaching his students, walking, listening, flattering, watching.

In the stiff dining room, he absently swallows forkfuls of pasta as the parade of well wishers drops by. The junior dean stops to tell him that a very rich property developer paid £7,500 for a collection of Brendan's works at a charity auction in aid of a girl's orphanage in Moldova. Next the professor of theology wants to thank him for giving a talk to a footballing audience at the weekend. The college GP, who first detected his cardiac condition, jokes that "we always knew there was no heart in there".

The first sleeveless students of springtime are draped on the granite steps as he walks me back to the front gate. These are the young people who will benefit intellectually from their sojourn here, if they're lucky. If they are not lucky, they will leave with "a posh accent" at least, but only after the professor has concluded his "Socratic dialogue" with them. He shakes hands at the main entrance and says goodbye in a voice of cream and the salty sea and – yes – of pain too.

Return to gender is a big minus for ad' industry

After Charlie McCreevy was forced by sectional indignation to dilute his budget measures for tax individualisation a couple of years ago, a journalist asked one of his staff why the Finance Minister had proposed something so politically naive. The minister was bewildered, the official revealed. "He thought women's liberation had been achieved."

Irish Independent, 8 June 2002

Maybe the alarm bells should have started ringing then, but, of course, we were all too cosy in our smug rug. We were the denizens of Hip Hibernia, after all, land of the right-on, with a woman in the Áras and the bearded masculists away in the corner group-hugging their inconsolable grief.

But then there appeared a photograph in the newspaper of a lovely young woman with shiny hair and pointy hips, heralding a McCreevy Moment of enlightenment. The woman was wearing a bikini featuring a football on each of its three strategic triangles and she was lying all seductively curvy on her side. A sushi assortment was laid out on her uppermost thigh, over which three 'lads' in green shirts drooled, chopsticks aloft. The photograph was contrived to publicise a World Cup song called 'Oki Doki Karioki' and the woman was serving the purpose of a table, which, I suppose, is a step up from a doormat.

Now this could have been entirely innocent and no more than a crude attempt at supposed post-feminist irony. According to those who study these things, the genders have had so many role reversals since the 1960s we're in danger of turning into a Lada with a Lexus complex.

Satire was the excuse offered to the Advertising Standards Authority (ASA) by the makers of a billboard campaign for the Rover 75 showing the quintessential figure of authority – a man in a suit. Behind him and the gleaming car, three lovelies pranced about on a yacht. The people responsible argued that it was intended as a spoof of the 1970s genre of advertising but the ASA ruled that such demeaning stereotyping was no longer acceptable. And, you would think, that would have been that.

But no. Next thing, the pages of the property supplements are being blitzed by purveyors of the marketing theory that sex sells. Instead of chimneys and pebbledash gable walls and period tiled fireplaces, we get shapely slaves and toothy smiles. Well, well, there have been reports of a housing shortage, but nobody warned us we were going to have to shack up in a des-res well-turned ankle on an elevated site over a vertiginous stiletto. One of the silliest of this breed of advertisement has a long-legged woman striding down a catwalk without benefit of apparel or a house in sight. "Super Models at Super Prices", boasts the slogan and, naturally, the thoughts of all hot-blooded males turn instantly to septic tanks and double-glazing.

You could convince yourself that all this is coincidence,

or Art, or Good Old Harmless Fun. Or you could convince yourself that you have been kidnapped by little green men, tossed into a buckety time machine and whooshed back 30 years to a place called the Dark Ages. These images of female sexuality and submissiveness are the stuff of long ago when Crystal Carrington sported plunging lamé across the breakfast table from her cardiganed husband.

When did the slide start? Perhaps it was all that filthy Celtic lucre and the artificial value it put on appearances. Maybe it got so that lobotomies assumed the same quick-'n'-easy appeal as botox or colonic irrigation to achieving the divine state of skinny, wide-eyed unwrinkledness. Or maybe - just maybe - the models who collude in the creation of these images are having the last laugh.

If so, let it be that - the last laugh. There was nothing at all funny about the recent picture promoting a certain race meeting that shall remain nameless, on principle. Vivienne and Gail, two beautiful-looking women who cannot claim to be witless teenagers, strapped a riding saddle each around their otherwise bare bosoms and frolicked for the cameras. I suspect that the people who paid for this photo-op thought the whole thing a hoot. But the women who lent their bodies for the exercise should remember the single greatest truism of the bloodstock business. They shoot horses.

Give me Cruz and a couple of Mumbas

It promises to be the ultimate shopping experience. Leave home in the morning; return in the evening a new woman, literally. The neighbours won't know you. Nor will the postman, the kids' school principal or the desk sergeant in the wanted posters archive. Come to think of it, neither will next-door's Doberman, your own family, the pet iguana, or the bathroom mirror. Crikey, you won't even know you. How sublime is that?

Irish Independent, 9 November 2002

For, folks, the day is coming when we'll be able to buy new faces for ourselves. It's going to knock Prada into the tuppenny ha'penny place and humankind into a frenzy of indecision. I'll take Michelle Pfeiffer and two Britneys for the girls. No, no, make that one Penelope Cruz and a couple of Sam Mumbas. On second thoughts, gimme three Shirley Temples with matching ringlets and raspberry-flavoured lollipops ...

The boffins say the medical advancement that allows surgeons to transplant faces will be exclusively used for cases of debilitating disfigurement and is not intended for the mass market. Now where have we heard that before? Didn't they say the same about slimming pills, stomach stapling, Viagra, rhinoplasty, skin grafting, leg stretching and botulism injections? I bet the inventor of the wheel only ever intended it to be used by crippled nonagenarian mountainy men with no social life as opposed to your average time-impoverished urbanite with zero tolerance for physical endeavour. Little could the world's first Big Wheel have imagined that what he had really conceived was the origin of the expression, a spare tyre.

Besides, who is to judge the extent of another's ugliness? For all we know, Quasimodo might have been drop-dead gorgeous if only he had spent a little less time hanging in the bell tower and a little more time at the barber's.

Perhaps the Elephant Man was so dazzled by his own pulchritude he was saving civilisation's blushes by donning his paper bag. And, come on now, do you honestly think it was, his sparkling wit and debonair disposition that made Jessica Lange fall for King Kong?

Somebody has, it would appear, seen the future – and it's worth billions.

Every town that once boasted a Greasy Spoon will henceforth host a New Face Emporium, festooned with catalogues and the kind of receptionists who make Julia Roberts look ugly. Here, amid the plush upholstery and the sound of flutes imitating babbling brooks, we will be able to find perfection, at a price.

I quite fancy looking like Nigella Lawson. Her colouring lends itself to the wearing of black, the staple of easy dressing, and her skin is that smooth Dublin City Council could lease it as an ice-skating rink for Christmas. With her face, you could nearly wear a granny print apron and they'll still call you a goddess.

Poor Nigella.

Hold on, what do you mean poor Nigella? You are talking

the queen of the great English tragedy who can spear a man as readily as a marinated monkfish kebab with one of Cupid's little arrows?

The very one. Poor Nigella is likely to become an endangered species, rather like the elephant or the crocodile, once the inveterate shopaholic recognises her potential. You've heard the expression that, say, a Lainey jumper is "to die for"? Well, watch out Nigella.

One thing bothers me, though. Is there any guarantee that the consumer will actually acquire the face of perfection chosen from the catalogue? Suppose (and this is a deliberately ludicrous supposition to defray any possible defamation damage) someone chose Cher's face. Six months after the operation, there she is schmoozing the bank manager to extend the overdraft when the Botox finally runs out and everything collapses – the forehead, the eyelids the cheekbones, the lips, the chin. And the bank manager finds herself discussing the finer points of economy with the Bride of Frankenstein's mother.

Unless you're one of the super rich, you're more likely to be reaching for the yellow pack shelves than scouring the fresher plots in the cemeteries of Beverly Hills. Such generic distribution could make for some very interesting encounters.

Think on this. Just when you thought you'd got rid of the taciturn, sour curmudgeon of a husband you were stuck with for 40 years, there he is beside you on the 46A bus. The fact that he refuses to talk to you, or even to acknowledge your existence, is only confirmation of your worst nightmare.

Maybe we'd be better off sticking with the arrangement of facial features we already have. Let's face facts.

A wake-up call where the Shannon flows

Billy rang this afternoon. He has a bugbear he keeps haranguing me about. Suffice to say it is an esoteric constitutional hypothesis probably best suited to a scholarly thesis. Anyway, he rehearsed his case this morning for the umpteenth time.

Irish Independent, 6 July 2002

"How are things down there?" I asked him when he was finished.

"The usual," he said matter-of-factly. "We all have thrush in the back of our throats. To tell you the truth, I don't remember it ever as bad. My three neighbours have all been in hospital at the same time and I've a year-old calf that has its two front legs deformed."

The first time I met Billy it was around this time of year, a perfect sunny day with a sheen on the grass. He brought me up to the field at the back of his handsome stone farmhouse to see the cattle. There were red burn marks the size of splayed hands on the animals' backs, submerged into the flesh where strips of hide had peeled off.

Afterwards, Billy drove me to meet one of his neighbours about a mile away. Two other farmers joined us at the rambling house on a wooded hillside. A couple of sheepdogs snoozed in the yard and a family of ducks quacked in an ornamental pond. The four farmers sat at a circular table on the veranda discussing the mystery deaths and illnesses on their lands, passing a two-litre bottle of aloe vera among themselves, rubbing the substance into their arms and faces and the backs of their necks. They swear by it as an emollient for the constant itch.

Billy and his neighbours live in the environs of Askeaton, close to where the River Shannon flows into the Atlantic Sea in west Limerick. On a sunny day it has the allure of paradise. But this is no paradise. It is Purdah. See no evil, hear no evil.

Something perturbing has been happening here for the best part of two decades. Freakish animals with five legs and no heads have been born at an uncommonly high rate. Mature beasts have been dying like flies. Leaves have been scorched off trees in early summer, denuding chestnuts and silver birch and browning the hedgerows when spring is at its zenith. A cat gave birth to a three-eyed litter. Men, women and children have sore eyes and skin, wheezy breathing and burnt noses. Some of them, inspired by Pat and Nuala who are scared stiff for their two little girls, conducted a survey amongst themselves. It indicated that the incidence of cancer in the community far exceeded the national average.

Yet the Republic to which they pay their implicit allegiance has failed to help them. The Environmental Protection Agency, primarily a licensing body for potentially polluting industry, oversaw a two-year study from which a number of the farmers dissociated themselves when it was insinuated that their own farm practises, passed down through generations, were suddenly causing their nightmare. After several years of procrastination and the expenditure of €5.3 million, the EPA finally published a weighty report which, in summary, shrugged its shoulders and said: We're stumped.

That was a year ago. Since then, Ireland has gone about its business, dealing in exemplary fashion with a foot-and-mouth crisis and rightly prosecuting farmers who endanger the wider population by using prohibited substances. We have had a general election and reselected the government. Meanwhile, the homes of Askeaton continue to be eerily distinguished by the sound of incessant dry coughing, both animal and human.

Doris, a Howth woman who married Andy, a substantial landowner, many years ago and went to live on his stud farm in west Limerick, believes that "if we would all just disappear down the Shannon they would be very happy."

There is, however, still a chance for the rest of us to redeem ourselves in the matter of Askeaton. We can insist on the appointment of an environmental ombudsman, as the EU Commissioner, Margot Wallstrom, has proposed. Such an office would hold out the hope of justice for citizens who have been isolated by a State locked in the handcuffs of conflicting interests. Even if we are too ungenerous to do it for our neighbours, we might at least do it for our children.

As Billy observed before he hung up this afternoon to go and tend his cattle: "These things are the warning nature gives us. If whatever is doing it does that to the animal kingdom what's awaiting us in the years ahead?"

The $33bn reason why we'll back the war

As the world divides itself into pro- and anti-war camps, the Irish government will soon find that it cannot keep sitting on the fence. Which way will we jump? A politically respected senior Fianna Fáiler is privately unequivocal about the commercial realities. "What is our national interest? It's not to upset the Americans."

Irish Independent, 15 February 2003

Millions of earth's citizens will assemble today in its greatest cities. They will march for peace in New York, London, Sydney, Hong Kong, Berlin, Bangkok, Paris, even Tel Aviv, in what could turn out to the be the greatest peace time mobilisation of humankind in a single cause. Tonight, television stations across the world will broadcast pictures of the protests in the most strategic capitals. The march in Dublin is not likely to be among them. Ireland is small, peripheral, a bit player in the United Nations, and a nonentity in NATO. It does not matter in the global scheme. Or does it?

"In a military and diplomatic sense, Ireland isn't hugely important but, in a sentimental sense, yes it is and that sentimental sense has a political consequence," says The *National Review* columnist John O'Sullivan, who is also editor in chief of United Press International in Washington. "Americans have a sense of connection with Ireland."

Irish politicians would rather their opinions on an Iraq war were extraneous to the greater good. That way they could retreat into the background, unnoticed until the whole horrifying business was concluded. But the world has changed, and so has this obscure green patch on the edge of it.

Next Monday, when the European Council meets for an emergency summit in Brussels, Ireland will have to stand up and be counted as a participant in world affairs. With Europe riven over the prospect of an unprovoked onslaught on Iraq, the time for dissembling is over. In Bush-speak, we're either with 'em or against 'em. In making that decision, Bertie Ahern's government will be clearly choosing between the economic, political and kindred ties with the US on the one hand, and, on the other, the burgeoning monolithic Europe where lie future power and fortune. Both sides of the chasm claim the moral impetus.

Roger Cole, a Labour Party supporter and the chief steward of today's march in Dublin, claims there is a disunity both within government and within the Department of Foreign Affairs. He characterises the military presence at Shannon Airport as "the President, as Commander-in-Chief of the Irish Army, who are now known as Bush's bodyguards". Others, however, believe that Ireland can no longer make a virtue of its shilly-shallying.

"Everybody has to take his responsibilities in the matter. We are adults," opines a French observer who wishes not to be identified. "Sometimes you Irish criticise us because France is a big state and we do what, supposedly, we want. Other times, you say 'we are only a small country, we want you to protect us'.

"It is difficult for Ireland to jump off the fence because you have two loves: the love of Europe and the love of the US. Ireland has the same problem within the EU. There is not complete agreement with the EU because of this divide. A materialistic vision of your self-interest is dominated by the US. Despite this, there is an idea that you belong to the EU."

The choreography of this weekend means that, following Dr Hans Blix's report to the UN yesterday and the international peace marches today, the leaders of the European Union will be under pressure to present a united front.

It appears, at this stage, to be an impossible task, with Britain, Italy and Spain on one side confronting Germany, France and Belgium on the other. Of the remaining nine members, Ireland, Finland, Sweden and Austria are the four militarily unaligned nations.

One of the many ironies is that Ireland was credited with facilitating the EU's expansion by passing last year's referendum on the Nice Treaty, the government having shut off an avenue of anti-treaty attack by vowing that neutrality would not be compromised. For this country, with its exceptional emotional and trade connections with the US, the "political neutrality" coined by Foreign Minister Brian Cowen does not contain an opt-out clause. Or so many in the ruling Fianna Fáil party believe.

"What is our national interest? It's not to upset the Americans," is how one politically respected Fianna Fáiler sees it. "Most people in the party feel the Iraq crisis should be sorted out through the UN but, if push came to shove and the Americans went off on their own, you're not going to see us condemning them.

"If Iraq is invaded, the Iraqi army will desert in droves and it'll be over in a jiffy. Everybody has grave reservations about the Anglo-American alliance going it alone but, if it comes down to it, we will not turn on America. It has been our ally."

To most people marching for peace today, the choice is stark: either bomb millions of innocent Iraqis in an act of unprovoked aggression or allow the UN inspectors to continue working with Saddam Hussein's regime to dispose of its illegal weaponry.

"We expect millions throughout the world on the streets today," says Wisconsin native and Dublin resident Mary van Lieshout, founder of the peace movement, US Citizens in Ireland for Alternatives to War. "I hope it sends a very clear signal to politicians that people have not been convinced of the need for war, and that this is not a show of support for Saddam Hussein but a show of support for a non-military solution.

"We invited Ambassador Richard Egan and Minister Brian Cowen to a debate on this issue, promising it would be respectful, and we did not even get an acknowledgement. I think Ireland should be pursuing a more mature relationship with other governments. There is a sense that if the Irish government doesn't go with the US they will lose trade. Somebody has to take the first step to that mature relationship.

"What Ireland does now is absolutely critical. This war is not inevitable and it's critical that Irish people stand up and say that. Ireland should use its rich and warm relationship with the US to act as an independent agent to resolve this."

Exports from US operations exceed €26bn. In the past week, the Irish Government will have noticed the anti-France vitriol in Washington where Congress is preparing to pass motions of condemnations. The French cheese exporter fromage.com has announced that its sales to the US have fallen by 15% in recent weeks.

"We've received emails from American customers saying they've thoroughly enjoyed eating our fine French cheeses and will miss them, but that, as long as France refuses to align itself with the US on Iraq, the orders will stop," says the company's chief executive, Marc Refahart.

With a cooling in the emotional relationship between Ireland and the US since Bill Clinton's departure from the White House and against a backdrop of the trial in Columbia of three Irish republicans, the peace process is especially dependent on goodwill. The Anglo-American alliance, built on solidarity between Bush and Blair, also changes the complexion of Dublin's relationship with London.

"The sentimental attachment with the US has become detached from the political attitude in Ireland," says John O'Sullivan. "Even the younger people who have travelled here to live and work no longer have the commitment to a close American relationship that would once have been the case. They look more towards Europe, probably as some kind of rebel gesture because of Britain's latent anti-Europeanism.

"I think it (Ireland going with the Franco-German alliance) would have a bad effect on the Irish reputation here," he suggests, "because the US are looking at divisions in Europe as between friends and enemies at the moment. People are already looking beyond the crisis to how relationships that have gone sour can be repaired and, secondly, what European arrangement could be reached to dilute the influence of France and Germany and increase the influence of countries like Britain or the surprising supporters like Poland."

A more surprising aspect of the crisis is the sympathy for Ireland's dilemma expressed by some of the people closest to the looming conflict. Palestine's delegate general to Ireland, Ali Halimeh, says he understands the quandary for the Irish government in having to choose between an historical friend like the US and some of its European neighbours.

"Coming from the region, it is a matter of grave concern for us," says the Egyptian Ambassador Ashraf Rashed. "Ireland's role is of great importance because we need the European contribution to be united and to reflect a position that supports what the UN is doing. Ireland, in the last two years on the Security Council, has played a very important role. Sometimes Ireland voted with resolutions that the US vetoed. We understand quite clearly that Ireland has a special relationship with the US, but it does not mean that they follow blindly. We do not think war is inevitable."

In Dublin, like most other administrative capital cities, the jaw-jaw of diplomacy has increased its tempo. Bertie Ahern and Tony Blair met in Belfast; Brian Cowen and Joschka Fischer in Berlin. One thing is sure: they did not spend their time discussing the weather.

Over the heads of those trying to talk terms, megaphone diplomacy blared away with the US and France swapping accusations of selfish interests in oil and arms. (Before the US started moving its army to the Persian Gulf, it had 247,000 personnel in 752 military installations in more than 130 countries.)

In Italy, a country, like Ireland, with a strong emigrant link to the US and a traditional influence by the Catholic Church, the centre-right coalition has toed the US line. Again, like Ireland –

and many other countries – its government's position seems to directly contradict the feelings of the people.

"What we have seen happen in Europe is the first move by France towards a super power but the others have decided not to follow," says Roberto Menoti, research fellow in Rome at the Aspen Institute, the American-founded think-tank which hosted George Bush Senior and Margaret Thatcher in 1990 to plan military strategy during Iraq's invasion of Kuwait. "The rift that is evident in NATO particularly affects the prospects of any common EU foreign policy. There is also a secondary concern that the Baghdad regime may try over the coming weeks to play one country off against the other.

"Irish neutrality is something we in the European Union have to respect as a legitimate choice and, since there is no more Cold War, it is something less of an obstacle and an anomaly.

"My biggest fear is that the positions in Europe are so entrenched it will be extremely difficult for all of them to shift quickly. What they need to do on Monday is reach some kind of fluffy compromise that they can agree on. A holding position."

Women pay for wrong constitution

Willie O'Dea wants to know why woman workers are paid less money than men. So keen is he for answers he is prepared to contract researchers to come up with an explanation. As if opening his eyes would not suffice.

Irish Independent, 13 September 2003

The reason why women earn less than men is that the boss is a man in 97.5 cases out of a hundred. Men make the rules. Conscious discrimination is only a minuscule part of the phenomenon that leaves third level women graduates with 18 per cent less money than their male counterparts. The culprit is the culture of the workplace where the rules and the code of behaviour have been handed down from one generation of men to the next. Dig deep into the corporate psyche and you will find a suspicion still persists about women's commitment to the job.

Even in the third millennium, the men in the office are regarded as family breadwinners; the women are seen as hobbyists earning their pin-money. Young women joining the workforce, especially at the professional level where economic necessity is less obviously a motivating factor than, say, in the contract cleaning industry, are the employment equivalent of It girls. No matter how well-educated or highly qualified (most of their academic achievements having out-shone the boys'), there remains a deeply embedded unacknowledged resistance to taking women workers as seriously as their male counterparts. They are not expected to be there for the long haul.

This attitude has been compounded by a history of women exiting the labour force for such reasons as home making, child rearing, parent care and the civil service bar on married women. Even though society has all but eliminated that pattern of premature retirement, there still exists a male instinct that the women seek and stay in the job for less urgent reasons than themselves, money being the least of their needs.

Male employers cannot be altogether blamed for this, whereas Minister O'Dea and his political cohorts can. When the founder of Willie's party composed Bunreacht na hEireann, he painstakingly unstitched the ethos of equality that had distinguished the birth of the nation.

The Constitution became the gospel of a patriarchal state. To this day it promises to protect women from "avocations unsuited to their sex," because of the "inadequacies of their strength". Further, it enshrines woman's "life within the home" as being for the common good.

It ill-behoves any politician who fails to campaign to have this antiquated stereotype excised from the Constitution to then condemn employers for not rewarding women in the workforce. The golden rulebook of our society tells them that is precisely how they should treat the "fairer sex".

There are those who argue that the Constitution is an aspirational document and that, apart from the odd Supreme Court skirmish or Council of State conflab, it has little relevance to daily life. Think again. The tentacles of Dev's framework for society reach into every corner of life. It is as philosophical it is functional, setting out the values by which the State comports itself. It is no surprise, therefore, that Dev's successors in Fianna Fáil decided against buying Lissadel, the homeplace of the State's most loved female champion.

Constance Markievicz was one of those women who never needed to work, for money or status. She was, by birth, a turn-of-the-century It girl: aristocratic, well-to-do and accomplished. The very prototype of the female employee seen as temporarily amused by her job today. Even history cannot suppress a giggle whenever it is moved to describe her Cumann na mBan uniform at the College of Surgeons in 1916.

Yet, when she died, the streets of Dublin bore witness to an unprecedented display of mass grief at the passing of a true hero. Half a century on, the inheritors of her republican legacy see fit to spend €29 million on the architecturally dubious home of a brewing family, but not €3 million on hers.

It is that subliminal diminution of women's contribution outside the home which causes employers to pay their female staff less than their male staff. Such is the traditional masculinity of the work environment, where the boys pile into the pub after hours and jockey for favour with the boss, that promotions are often decided across the counter rather than across the desk. The National Women's Council has found that women workers lose out on approximately €300,000 in pay compared to men in the course of their lifetime. Were Minister O'Dea a woman, methinks the facts would have concentrated his mind long before now.

Prison? You gotta be joking. I'm getting ready to rebuild Baghdad ...

Justine McCarthy – on four extraordinary days at the Mahon tribunal

Irish Independent Review, 12 July 2003

Were his name anything other than Liam Lawlor one would have to conclude that the man was quite, quite mad. His attitude to reality is that of affable indifference.

The earth is flat, but we won't fall out over it.

Black is white, and sure what of it?

It never happened, Your Honour.

His inability to acknowledge the facts puts one in mind of those people who are rescued by their loved ones from the abyss of sweet-singing suicidal cults. There is nothing gung-ho or belligerent or obsequious or histrionic in their accounts. It's just this brick wall of denial. That implacability of the brainwashed.

Didn't do it, Your Honour. Shrug.

How long does Liam Lawlor stare into his own eyes in the mirror before he leaves the house in the morning? Actually, does he *have* a house? Does he have a *mirror*? Poor man can no longer afford a habit-of-a-lifetime chauffeur to zip him over to the Castle in his BMW. Gets a pal, a dead ringer for the old driver, mind you, to do the biz for him now, or so he told the tribunal.

No readies, you see. Liam's as good as broke. Can't afford a lawyer. Reckons he's on a shoestring budget of €1,000-a-year for travel expenses. Said on Thursday he'd spent the all-in sum of €15,000 on himself and his business activities since last January. So up yours, Mister €2,500-a-day Big Shot Senior Counsel.

The tribunal insists there are "millions" unaccounted for.

What? Naaah.

Come Friday, the tribunal suggests he's spending four or five times more than he said the day before. Closer to €200,000-a-year, perhaps?

You could be right there.

Hi there, Liam. Nice tan. Didn't get that colour in the Joy, eh? Been anywhere interesting? Sicily, wasn't it? Sixty guests at the daughter's June wedding among the serpentine grape vines of omerta. A real glam 10-day gig with lots of gorgeous models, according to the gossip columns. They say it cost the guts of €50,000. Ain't life a bitch.

Any other trips during the year? Washington, no less? DC? Hobnobbing with the Bush brigade before it headed off after the invasion to reconstruct Iraq.

Ah, Iraq and fond memories of another tribunal. Our Liam sure gets around. It was the Beef Tribunal that discovered he'd joined a delegation to Baghdad in January 1989 to make representations on behalf of the Aer Lingus hospital subsidiary, Parc. Saddam's regime was under the impression that the Irish politician was there as a go-between for his government but Liam, who happened to be a director of Larry Goodman's Food Industries, was – by an extraordinary coincidence – accompanied on the trip by the company's sales director.

Quelle surprise – it was Goodman's beef that fed the Iraqi army in the '80s. And everyone knows the one about armies and their stomachs. Must have been a bit of a shock for the Lucan globetrotter, all the same, to hear that his friend, the minister for health, got taken out and executed for criticising the boss.

(Publisher's Note. The following is not fiction but a verbatim report of what Liam Lawlor told this newspaper during the lunchtime break at the Planning Tribunal on Thursday, immediately after two witnesses testified that he was a cheat).

"I've been doing a lot of correspondence about business in Iraq. I've had correspondence with the Kabaretti brothers. K-A-B ... I don't know how to spell it. Kabaretti. They're Jordanian but very prominent in Baghdad. I'll be making introductions and acting as agent for international business."

A few months ago when first he signalled his intentions for the region, he explained: "I want to make things happen for Iraq. I want to bring the same pioneering and entrepreneurial vision to Iraq that I brought to Dublin County."

On Thursday, he expounded. "I'll probably go there (Iraq) in September. I've been to Washington, before they left for Iraq and met the people who are rebuilding it.

"I have contact with a senior legal person in Prague, someone who was a principal in a firm in Prague and is now part of the American government team in Baghdad. There are lots of Irish companies that could get work there and they need somebody to go out and get tender documents and bid for business for them while they get on with the work. So, yeah, I'll be going in September."

After lunch, Judge Alan Mahon asks him if he might be able to cobble 10 grand together to pay his lawyers.

Sorry, no can do, Your Honour.

Next day, he's reminded that he has a Dáil pension now, not to mention a self-proclaimed overseas account with 40 or 50 grand in it.

Right so, he'll be off to see the lawyers in London about complying with the tribunal's discovery order – probably Ryanair to Stansted and thumb a lift into town on the back of a coal lorry.

He looks the richest man in the room. Smooth tan, hand-made suit, compact chrome mobile, gold-tipped pen, gold-rimmed glasses, a gold ring on each hand. He sits with his arms folded high on his chest, legs stretched out and crossed at silken ankles. Mr. Big, compliments of Central Casting. The lawyers and journalists (who qualify for a lifetime's free supply of Mogadon and/or danger money for the hypertension brought on by his evasions) are wondering how soon and for how long he will be going back to the slammer. Fourth time lucky, maybe. What they don't know is that he's planning to be schmoozing in downtown Baghdad round about then.

Prison! You gotta be joking, Your Honour.

It will be three years in October since the High Court ruled that the then Dublin West TD had to comply with the tribunal's discovery order. Mr Justice Tom Smyth declared that his court recognised no such thing as an untouchable.

"Mr. Rogers (Lawlor's senior counsel at the time) stated of Mr Lawlor that: 'He is a person in public life and has to cope with that. I think it reasonable to assume that in over 30 years in public life he appreciates the sentiments, if not exactly familiar, with the words of Edmund Burke that "People who would carry on great public schemes must be proof against the most fatiguing delays, the most mortifying disappointments, the most shocking insults, and worst of all, the most presumptuous judgment of the ignorant upon their designs."

Fatiguing delays? Now we're talking Liam's lingo. He was due to give evidence for a day this week. It ran every day, and has not yet got around to the substantive matter of planning corruption. In the four years since the tribunal has been painstakingly investigating him, it has lost its inaugural chairman, Liam has lost his Dáil seat, the economic boom has ended, the World Trade Centre in New York has collapsed, and there is a new millennium. In the Lower Castle Yard, it's *plus ça change, plus c'est la même chose*.

The Revenue Inspectors sit at the back of the room, taking notes of the tax dodging. The Criminal Assets Bureau keeps a beady eye on the money trail. The DPP watches for perjury. The High Court may have to revisit the question of non-cooperation with the tribunal. And still, all these matters are peripheral to the nub of planning corruption, the tribunal's *raison d'être*.

(Publisher's Note Two: the following is a truncated but accurate account of an exchange between Liam Lawlor, witnesses, Des O'Neill SC, and the chairman, Judge Mahon, at the Planning Tribunal on Thursday, honest!).

Des O'Neill: "Is it a false invoice, Mr Lawlor?"

Liam Lawlor: "I don't think it is, no."

Des O'Neill: "Tell me what there is about it that is true?"

Liam Lawlor: "I don't agree they're false in their totality."

Des O'Neill: "Did they type up the invoice or did you type it up?"

Liam Lawlor: "I can't be certain about that."

Chairman: "Mr Lawlor, you've been asked a simple question. Did you type it up or did they?"

Liam Lawlor: "As far as I know, Seddon's office typed it up."

Chairman: "Did you type it up?"

Liam Lawlor: "I don't type, chairman."

Des O'Neill: "So it's a false invoice?"

Liam Lawlor: "It's an invoice, yes."

Des O'Neill: "Will you agree it's a false invoice?"

Liam Lawlor: "I don't believe it to be false, no."

Chairman: "We'll adjourn for lunch."

The invoice related to the sale by Lawlor of one acre of land running alongside the avenue to his big house, Somerton. He had sold off much of the estate in July 1995 for £410,000 and, when it was rezoned three years later, the value had shot up to £7 million. So you can see why a paltry acre would warrant a price tag of £820,000 in 2001, £1,000 of which was the subject of the iffy receipt he supplied to the purchaser, Maplewood developments. Liam said the cheque was a finder's fee earned as a property scout for Maplewood but Michael Whelan, the company's managing director, said he never employed him or asked him to look at any property.

What was most hair-raising about the revelation was the timing of the transaction: a year after various trips to the High Court culminated in Liam Lawlor's three stretches in jail.

The morning of this damning evidence, as he was being driven by his friend to the tribunal, his wife, Hazel Lawlor, had phoned him on his mobile with the tragic news that their daughter's father-in-law had died suddenly. "This is nothing compared to that," he says, casting a glance across the hearing room in Dublin Castle during a break in proceedings.

As he speaks, Michael Whelan, the witness deemed to have blown his cover, passes by on his way to lunch with his legal team.

"How'ya Mike," says Liam, all friendly-like.

"Liam," replies the other man, never breaking his stride.

Straight after, the politician is telling a journalist he will not be contesting the local elections next year, to return, so to speak, to the scene of the crime at Dublin County Council. But, hold on now, he wouldn't be ruling out the next general election just yet.

Mister Lawlor, the consensus is that this has been a very bad day for you?

"No, I don't see it that way," he smiles. "I don't see it that way at all, Your Honour."

Can Mick the mouth really conquer the world?

A few years ago, Ryanair was on a flight to nowhere. Now it has zoomed to the threshold of superpowerdom and its lippy boss Michael O'Leary brags it'll be the world's biggest airline. Not bad for a guy who was an anonymous trainee accountant.

Irish Independent, 7 June 2003

Look out world, here comes Mick with his flying machine. It's got no tickets, no frills, no apologies and, sometimes, no charge. Lampooners in snooty English aviation have christened it 'Eireflot'.

The pernickety eurocrats in Brussels are pulling on their bifocals to investigate it. The Belgians are still bristling after their famous statue of a child urinating, the Mannekin Pis, appeared in a Ryanair ad under the banner question, 'Pissed off with Sabena's high fares?'

And the dour Germans, bless them, haven't stopped gawping at the sky over Frankfurt since Mick dropped out of it last year with his usual aplomb. Along the full length of both sides of his 747s, he'd painted a message to break the ice between strangers: 'Auf Wiedersehen Lufthansa', it saluted.

Next stop: world domination. That's after Palermo, and another jab at nicety-going-native with a jet livery screaming 'Arrivederci Alitalia'.

Ryanair, the brat-in-the-pack alternatively known in comedy halls as Leery Air or Yuck Airlines, has a billion quid in the bank, and the same again in chutzpah. It has zoomed, on a wing and two fingers, from the brink of bankruptcy 12 years ago to the threshold of superpowerdom. In less than three years time, brags Mick, it'll be the biggest international scheduled airline in the world. Not bad for a bog-trotting, spud-thick Paddy farmer?

Mick is the only one who calls himself Mick. On the verdant boarding school playing fields of Clongowes Wood where he played third-team rugby, they used to call him Ducksie.

In the Ryanair HQ, its walls festooned with snapshots of exuberant staff parties, they call him Mollie, a play on his initials.

Trinity College's transport economist, Seán Barrett, was queuing with the boss, a former undergraduate and long-time friend of his, in Ryanair's cafeteria, when one of the staff hailed him with an airy, 'How'ya Michael?'

"I suppose," chuckled the university don as he related the incident to a friend later, "if the poor fellow had said 'hello Mister O'Leary' he would have been fired."

Last Tuesday night, after announcing the company's phenomenal end-of-year results in London (59pc increase in profits, reaching €239.4 million after tax), Michael O'Leary hopped on a plane to America for an "investor roadshow" – briefings with financial analysts and brokers.

The tour began in New York, where Ryanair is one of only 12 European companies listed on the by-invitation-only NASDAQ, and went across to Chicago, over to California and up to Canada.

When asked which airline his lippy boss traversed the Atlantic with, head of communications, Paul Fitzsimmons, replied: "The first one that came along." Therein lies the key to Ryanair's 46A-bus philosophy: fill 'em up and dump 'em as quick as you can at the other end, with all regulatory decency and haste. If the company had an anthem, the chorus would go, 'Well, what did you expect for the price?'

The ingredients of the supersonic miracle are simple: short-haul routes (only one of the current 125 routes exceeds two hours' flying time); fast aircraft turnaround (20 minutes between arrival and departure); uniform air fleet (it uses only Boeing 737–800s); no paperwork or airbridges; no in-flight meals, hot towels or any of "that nonsense"; a small workforce (Air France, with 42,000 employees, carries the same number of passengers as the 19,000-strong Ryanair).

These are the reasons enumerated by the fast-talking company managers known as Zs (last letter in the alphabet – bottom of the pile) for the transmogrification of a company haemorrhaging £5 million in 1991 into the third biggest in Europe with "enough cash to buy British Airways with change".

"We're a one-trick pony," boasts Paul Fitzsimmons. Ah, but which is the pony and which is the trick? Michael O'Leary and Ryanair are inseparable; both saucy, tireless, fascinating, ruthless, bolshie, unconventional, ungallant, running on high octane and very, very rich.

If an airline can have a personality, then Ryanair is the first recipient from a donor-boss. His personal wealth is about €500 million. He shares his 250-acre estate home with a herd of prize-winning Aberdeen Angus cattle, a stable of race horses, a couple of Irish wolfhounds, some Burt Bacharach CDs and a game of Who Wants To Be A Millionaire, espied in the sitting room by a nosy visitor.

For someone who protests that he dislikes personal publicity, his appetite for the most attention-seeking stunts is insatiable, making him quite the blossoming corpo-celeb in downtown Europe.

Last Saint Patrick's Day, he kitted himself out in green robes and a mitre to host a media conference in London in the guise of Ireland's patron saint.

When his airline opened a route to Reims in France, he disported himself as a sommelier cracking open the champagne.

In London, he togged out in military fatigues and shimmied into the turret of a World War II tank to lead his foot soldiers to Easyjet's HQ where he yelled provocative slogans through a loud-hailer to the musical theme of *The A-Team*. For run-of-the-mill photo-ops, he has perfected the Mad Max-rolling-eyeballs acrobatics patented by Mel Gibson.

The Guardian newspaper described him last Tuesday as one of Ireland's four living icons, after Bono, DJ Carey and Orla Guerin. The following evening, in a BBC Money Programme half-hour special on him and his flying machines, he threw a verbal wink at the camera and pronounced: "This is the most fun you can have with your clothes on."

"He's very brash when you're doing business with him but he's a really nice guy. I know he's very helpful to people in a whole range of areas," says Peter Bellew, spokesman for Kerry Airport where Ryanair operates two flights a day to London and one to Frankfurt. "They work at hyper speed. They'll screw the best possible deal out of you but once everything's agreed, they'll stick with it."

It is already part of the legend that, in the week following September 11, as flabby flag carriers were being grounded by the most adverse commercial aviation conditions ever encountered, Ryanair was in Boeing's head office ordering 125 new 737s.

The Irish company placed a second order for the same number last year, sparking renewed speculation that the formidable manufacturer had conceded to a discount of 50pc-plus on the $60 million-a-piece planes. Whatever the deal was, Boeing has been reported as saying it will never sell its aircraft as cheaply again.

As global terrorism, the Sars threat and an international economic downturn colluded to take more planes out of the sky, Ryanair, the second-biggest airline operating in Britain, upped and bought the KLM-owned Buzz, the number three, for €20 million. From the 700,000 passengers it was ferrying between Dublin and London in 1991, it now carries 15.8 million and plans to add three million seats in the coming months.

It has no intention of moving into the US market, what with 370 million travel-hungry Europeans on its doorstep and 10 more states about to join the EU.

So, when Michael O'Leary says Ryanair will be the biggest international scheduled airline in the world in 2006, the word "international" is the operative one.

Unlike US operators, it can still describe itself as such while restricting its operations to one continent.

The Irish company opened 50 new routes in the past 12 months – 22 of them last month alone – and is ready to roll with another 40 airports. Meanwhile, it's waiting to see if Séamus Brennan gives it the go-ahead to build the controversial second terminal at Dublin Airport.

Its proposal, costed at €114 million, envisages two or three hotels with the same number of multi-storey carparks and 10 million passengers a year; the construction to be 100pc funded by Ryanair but the resulting complex not owned by it.

So far, Séamus Brennan seems keener on the Ryanair option than did his predecessor, Mary O'Rourke, but the silence from the cabinet is lengthening like the notes of the *Dead March*.

Somebody who has observed the protracted animosity between Ryanair and Aer Rianta over Terminal 2 believes that Michael O'Leary's failure to secure the contract is symptomatic of an Achilles heel in his character. "He was so arrogant in his rows with Noel Hanlon (Aer Rianta chairman) that it was the worst possible tactic he could have chosen," this man argues.

"He got it horribly wrong. I suspect he could have his terminal by now if he hadn't been so aggressive. Also, during the baggage handlers' strike, when the Taoiseach tried to act as an intermediary, Michael O'Leary refused to take a phone call from Bertie and Bertie won't forget that."

To what extent realpolitik matters is moot. Ryanair's greatest strength is its cartel-busting messianic reputation. Beneath that tieless informality there may beat the acquisitive heart of a post-modern capitalist but what counts with the punter is the price of a plane ticket.

Thanks to Ryanair, it has plunged from the equivalent of a week-and-a-half's wages in 1985 to a day's pay.

In Michael O'Leary's vision, the time is approaching when airports will pay the public to fly in order to maximise the retail potential of their shopping malls. Seems unbelievable, doesn't it? But then, the entire Ryanair story rings with the implausibility of overblown fiction. Twelve years ago, Aer Lingus could have bought it as a going concern for £20 million. Today, the state airline is saving its own skin by copying Ryanair's formula, which itself is a copy. When Tony Ryan asked the 29-year-old whippersnapper who succeeded Denis O'Brien as the multi-millionaire's PA if he would rescue his dream of an airline, O'Leary said it could not be done. Then he hiked off to Texas to study the original of the species, Southwest Airlines.

The pioneer of no-frills, Southwest was founded by an Irishman called Herb Kelleher, reputed to hail from Kanturk in County Cork, the native town of O'Leary's father.

Kelleher is a zany, plain-speaking, chain-smoking, Wild Turkey whiskey-drinking entrepreneur who believes in "having fun while earning a profit". He once arm-wrestled a competitor for the right to use the trademarked slogan, 'Plane Smart'.

Aspiring pilots being interviewed by Southwest are required to climb into a pair of the company's bermuda shorts and lark about. Those who baulk don't get the job.

Michael O'Leary returned a changed man from his introduction to Herb Kelleher.

The middle-class scion of a partner in a Midlands textile factory had never drawn widespread attention before now. After graduating from Trinity with a good business degree in 1981, he had joined the old accountancy firm of Stokes Kennedy Crowley in Dublin's Hatch Street to serve his articles on a salary of £4,000.

One of his contemporaries in the office remembers that O'Leary wore a suit and tie like everyone else and probably kept his sandwiches in his briefcase. But he remembers nothing else about him from that time. "He was quite average."

Whether he reinvented himself to reflect the ethos of the company he was deputed to rescue is unclear.

Two things are certain, however: within a decade, he was a household name; and he had £17 million in the bank from a three-year bonus scheme he worked out with Tony Ryan. Despite his Clongowes-Trinity-Gigginstown-affianced-to-a-banker bourgeois pedigree, he made a virtue of getting up the nose of the establishment.

David McWilliams once asked him on TV3's *Agenda* what single catastrophic event he could imagine would destroy Ryanair. "I suppose we could join IBEC," he shot back, in a vein of startling truth.

The iconoclasm has become an art form. His irreverent and often personalised press advertising has ridiculed everyone from Mary O'Rourke – whose Department of Public Enterprise he dubbed 'DOPE' – to the Pope. Mostly the creations of the chief executive, only about one per cent of his brain factory ever gets published.

One that didn't was inspired by a stand-off between Aer Lingus and Ryanair over the use of the mortuary at Dublin Airport at a time when the independent airline was specialising in bringing the remains of deceased people home. 'Ryanair, for those who wouldn't be seen dead on Aer Lingus,' it gloated.

When David Bonderman, the chairman of Southwest Airlines attended a Ryanair AGM in Dublin a few years ago, an Irish journalist asked him: "How good exactly are Michael O'Leary and Ryanair?"

"Son," the American answered, "Michael is as good as it gets. He eats the model."

Sometimes, the manic energy gets him into trouble. His

audience was less than enchanted when he told an Oireachtas committee, having been chastised for using unparliamentary language, that 'bugger' was a term of endearment in Mullingar.

But his purchase of a taxi plate to allow him use bus lanes and his conviction for dangerous driving have dented the maverick image.

An earlier high court case, in which Jane O'Keeffe, Ryanair's lucky one-millionth passenger, sued the company for reneging on a promise of free flights for life, was more damaging.

In his 7,000-word judgment, Mr Justice Peter Kelly found that the airline boss had been bullying, aggressive and hostile.

Now an even graver matter looms as the EU transport director is investigating rumours that Charleroi Airport in Belgium gave Ryanair a 50pc discount in landing charges and makes sweetheart payments for every new route the airline opens.

"I think Ryanair will win the Charleroi case," says Seán Barrett, the country's most enduring and vocal champion of transport deregulation. "The EEC has sat on its very well rounded posterior and done nothing about the control of small airports. There are about 400 airports in Europe that are unused."

Michael O'Leary returns to Trinity College every spring to speak to the final year students in the economics faculty. It is he who renews the annual arrangement.

He turns up with his prepared script, slides and even a power point. Two years ago, as he waited to enter the lecture hall, his mobile phone rang.

"Tell then to f*** off," he said, before switching it off. The call had been to inform him that Rimini Airport was demanding increased landing fees.

Within weeks, Ryanair was flying to Ancona instead.

When he eventually took his place in front of the starry-eyed students, he told them the same thing he always tells them: don't let the new order slip back into the habits of the 1980s.

Then, in one of the most telling statements he has ever made – and one he is unlikely to utter in public – he declared what many might interpret as his business motto.

"It's economics. It's not society," he explained. "I don't do bonding."

Iarnród has ideas beyond its station

Heard the one about the train with no toilets? Cork-to-Dublin and not a *leithreas* in working order. So the train company allows an unscheduled comfort stop in Charleville. An hour out of Cork. 300 discombobulated passengers pour onto the platform to find the two conveniences in the small country station locked and bolted. Back on board and onward to Limerick Junction: teeth gritted, legs crossed.

Irish Independent, 8 March 2003

The train company promised to refund half the price of the tickets, which is mighty generous. Sure, all the passengers wanted was to spend a penny.

Heard the one about the Kerry train station with no left-luggage facility? It's in Killarney, home of the highest-per-capita concentration of hotels in the country. The railway station was recently given an expensive sprucing up. Even the porters were decked out in eye-catching blue livery. Only problem is, visitors to the tourism mecca who have to vacate their hotels by midday have nowhere to leave a suitcase until the 2.30 pulls into the station. A jaunting car ride through Muckross National Park does not have quite the same appeal when your travelling companion is a bulging 3" x 2" Samsonite.

Then there's the one about the new commuter train earmarked for the Gorey-to-Dublin line. This was designed to alleviate the road traffic jams caused by daily commuters to the capital who cannot afford to live there anymore. The train company made an announcement last month. *Attention please, the train scheduled to arrive in Gorey next September will not now arrive until the year 2004.*

Had enough? No? How about the Cork-to-Dublin train (again). When the theoretically three-hour trip stretches into seven hours, an ambulance is called to rush a heavily pregnant woman to the Coombe Hospital. Rumours have not been confirmed that the enceinte lady was only three years old and clutching a Barbie doll when seen boarding at Kent Station.

At the rate the trains run, she might possibly be the same woman who travelled with her husband and three children on a €94 family ticket from Mallow-to-Dublin. So crammed was the train the mother sat on a toilet with her four-year-old on her lap for the duration.

Iarnród Eireann has to be the biggest joke in the country. The trains are over-crowded. There is no guarantee of a seat. The fares are astronomical. (A colleague paid €4.25 for a return train between Desenzano and Brescia in Italy last year. A comparable Irish journey between Dublin and Wicklow costs €12.70.) Many of the carriages could double as props in a period drama. The heating doesn't always work. Most trains have this eccentric compulsion to stop for half-an-hour and for no apparent reason in the middle of nowhere. And, of course, no explanation ever given. When announcements *are* made, they are as comprehensible as Shane McGowan speaking Mandarin through a hosepipe. Altogether, it's not a very funny joke.

Take the 6pm from Limerick on an icy night last month. I

did, to my regret. Our train disgorged us at Limerick Junction half an hour later and chugged away into the night, whereupon an announcement boomed across the platform that the connecting train from Cork was delayed 40 minutes. The 40 minutes turned to 50 minutes, then 60 minutes. We squeezed into a small waiting room with sufficient seating for about half of our contingent. An hour and 40 minutes after the first announcement, the Cork train arrived. We piled on, frozen, hungry and cross. The snack trolley, however, had already completed its trundle-through and the dining car was taking last orders.

When we reached Heuston Station, we were told there would be no charge for the bus into the city centre and that any passengers using the car park would go free. But the exit from the car park was so narrow we sat in a queue for another 20 minutes, glaring at each other through iced windscreens. I got home just in time to hear that song, *Rome wasn't built in a day*, blaring from the telly and a voice-over, rich as malted whiskey, declaring: *We're not there yet, but we're getting there.* Definitely not funny.

Iarnród Éireann is paying a ballpark figure of €350,000 for its feel-good television ad campaign on RTÉ. Whoever commissioned it cannot possibly have taken the train lately and lives by the maxim that ignorance is bliss. What sort of management considers it best practise to throw scarce money at inane PR when the people it is targeting are shivering on some platform witing for a train to limp along?

The tiger's back – but can we tame it this time?

Yipee-dee-yay! The good times are back. Loadsa-money coming through. More upgrades, more trade-ups, more fit-outs, more workouts, more soft-tops, more Prada tops, more over-the-top and more – multitudes more – stunted spherical-sculpted trees for outside the front door. Our dear, departed Celtic Tiger has got the kiss of life and is arisen. The store windows are glittering with "all the scenes of alimentary and vestimentary festivity". Opportunity knocks twice. Last one to answer is a ninny goat.

Irish Independent, 10 July 2004

Happy? Us? We're goddam pinch-ourselves-silly delirious. What we thought was dead and buried has come back to slinky, prowling life. And not just any life either, oooh no. It's the High Life – Mark II. This time, we are going to get richer than Finland, na, na, na, na, na. Two plasma screens for the downstairs jacks, anyone? Can't you just feel the good times roll?

Er, not wanting to be a party pooper or anything, but ... have you been on the Tralee train lately? No heating, no trolley service, no chance in hell of reaching Dublin before Starbucks. No "sorry". That's the legacy for you of the High Life – Mark I. A lousy train service, banks ripping off customers, the sick competing for attention in the A&Es , nobody trusting anyone else, prisoners still slopping out in Mountjoy, traffic snarls, glowering shop assistants, exorbitant prices, the courts chock-a-block with too many litigants and not enough judges, toxic waste dumped in gentle green valleys, the dearest child care in Europe, factory-line houses sprouting like Martian weeds, roads that were built for a 10-family-per-car nation. We don't even have a sports stadium, for pity's sake.

And don't get me started on the ramifications for the human spirit.

Jeez, this country. Why must we always beat ourselves up? We've got a lucky break.

OK, two – right? Let's enjoy it. Success is good. Prosperity is good. Lose yer oul' Catholic guilt and smell the bread. Be proud. Boast, why don't you, to your English pals about that two-bed-no-parking garden-in-the-window-box semi that was guided at a million and sold for half that again. Some French philosopher type said that "the conspicuousness of surplus" was "the final and magical negation of scarcity". Beat that. We put up the Spike. We're tearing down the Ballymun towers. Metaphor heaven. Way to go.

There's no denying we're in the money. A fabric designer flew to the Riviera for two days last month to deliver and hang a curtain – a curtain – in the cinema of an Irishman's villa. A midlands businessman paid €10 million for a five-bedroom house in Dartry last month to be his family's home – €9.1 million more than the vendor paid for it in 1995. There is a queue from here to Arcadia for Louise Kennedy's €15,000 crystal chandelier.

A dozen Irish names joined the waiting list for the Merc

Maybach (basic model €585,000 with sterling silver champagne goblets, two TVs, cordless phone, fridge, DVD and four-climate control). Ten others own a Bentley, 14 have Aston Martins , 46 Daimlers and 337 Porsches. That's before you start counting the private jets and ocean-going yachts.

Some 50% more of us holidayed in the Virgin Islands and Oceania in the first three months of this year than in the same time last year. We spent €800 million on travel in those 91 days. Craziest thing of all is that these excesses no longer electrify us.

Been there, done that, bought the T-shirt – at an extortionate price.

"I've always liked it [the Celtic Tiger]. More chrome bars and flower arrangements that could eat you. Lovely," says novelist Anne Enright, whose motherhood memoir *Making Babies* will be published next month.

You're being sarcastic, right?

"Only slightly. We've built a two-tier society now and the descendants of people who are not on the property ladder will be looking at the descendants of people who are on it and asking: "Where did it all go wrong?" I actually think it's worse that we're creating a new poor rather than a new rich. I don't go along with this thing that it's vulgar. That seems anti-democratic to me.

"It's sort of a lie that, if you make rich people richer, the rest do better. For some people, it's really hard to stay above the line. The good that a boom does is it lets people get a job and freedom from the moral restrictions that poverty used to bring. That people wouldn't be terrified any more not to live a meat-and-two-veg life – married with two kids."

"The Celtic Tiger economy has made people more greedy and selfish and, yet, more disenchanted. Young people thought if they had more money they'd have more happiness," says Fr Tony Byrne, a suicidologist and community educator. "People are smelling wealth. Everyone wants to get to the top. The tendency is to feel you have to get out of the gutter, punch your way through because top is best.

"I am totally against liberal capitalism that says money is more important than people. This sort of economy causes bullying. In the workplace, the kick-ass type of person tends to get promoted because it's believed they get the job done. Then the bully surrounds himself with other incompetents, like himself. One-in-10 people is bullied in the workplace.

"I don't think it's a coincidence that in 1998, the year the Celtic Tiger arrived, there were 504 suicides, the biggest number in any year. In two years, there were 899. Last year, 11,000 people attempted suicide. This is the reality.

"The great threat with the recurrence of the Celtic Tiger economy is to the dignity of the human person. That's what the hard-sell targets."

This week's *Time* magazine contains a two-page paean to Bloomsday in Dublin. The writer of the piece has joined the annual pilgrimage to the holy grail and finds himself in the cleaners on Westland Row, which was the post office a hundred years ago when Leopold collected his mail. An actor is re-enacting the *Ulysses* scene, gamely abetted by the man behind the counter, when a scuffle erupts at the door among impatient customers.

But a tall, white-haired commuter intervenes. "It's Bloomsday," he booms. "Show a little respect for James Joyce!" We all erupt in a round of applause. Even the dry cleaner is amused.

Ha, what other capital city would have such rush-hour reverence for a book? Don't tell me that when prosperity comes in the door, the soul flies out the window.

"If you want to be an artist, you have to be one of the poor," says Anne Enright.

Why?

"Because you can't afford the rents. Not if you're starting out in your garret. That's why the cultural centre will not be Dublin."

Is there less inspiration in a boom?

"As Yeats said: 'All things can tempt me from this craft of verse.'"

("One time it was a woman's face or worse,

the seeming needs of my fool-driven land.")

"It's how we use the wealth that's created by the Celtic Tiger that matters," says the director of Combat Poverty, Helen Johnston. "There were people who did not benefit from it at all the last time. I would argue for a redistribution for people on lower income. The feedback from the European and the local elections would suggest that the public wants to see it done differently this time.

"The boom is good, of course, because it gives people jobs and opportunities. But you have to realise that not everybody is in a position to take up a job. What we want is a virtuous circle rather than a vicious circle."

All the deluxe destination spas on the Ring of Kerry cannot make a silk purse out of a sow's ear. Bling-bling rules. The gaudier, the more to die-for. Taste is for timid, bottom-of-the-heap wimps. If you've got it, flaunt it. Mow through the over-crowded streets showing off your luxuriant abundance. Tell the gossip writers and let them worship at your kid-clad feet. Give them details, details, details. Love ostentation and the way it ricochets off the poor.

Former US vice-president Hubert Humphrey said nearly 40 years ago that "slumism" was the pent-up anger of people living outside of affluence. It was what decayed the human spirit and bred demagoguery and hate. In plain words: Them and Us.

A profit-driven society is exclusive by its nature. Most older people, people with disability, those who care for them, people with other priorities, are automatically outside the loop if Mammon is all that is celebrated. Non-producers.

The reports published on Wednesday by the Enterprise Group, entitled Ahead of the Curve: Ireland's Place in the Global Economy, preambled with the audacious claim that this society depends on the enterprise sector for its quality of life. Nobody said boo. This is the gospel now. Ponder it in your top-dollar flotation tank or wrapped in cellulite-busting bandages of seaweed in the Land of Miss World.

One of the Enterprise Group's most startling forecasts was that we will need skilled immigrants to fill nearly 400,000 jobs in the next five years. Startling because it comes a month after a huge majority voted out a Constitutional right to citizenship for everyone born in the State. Hired help preferred. No Irish need apply.

Some economic Einstein has tracked the demise of the Celtic Tiger Mark I back to a nanosecond circa 9.53am on Wednesday, March 15, 2001. That morning, Ireland woke up to the news that the Nasdaq was poorly and a giant US multinational had decided to park its lavish investment plans for Ireland. You could feel the dream start to drain away like water down a plughole. What it left behind were some fabulously rich people, a bigger number of slightly better-off people, and many others who felt cheated and sore. The ones who never made it to the lifeboats. Or were thrown overboard by sharks.

In the 40 months since then, there has been great upheaval. Organised crime regrouped. A murder trial collapsed because witnesses refused to give evidence. Alcohol-soused street killings never let up. *Prime Time* found traces of cocaine in most of the club and bar toilets it tested in Dublin. Banks filched money from their customers. Conrad Gallagher and the Commons Restaurant became casualties of the new economies. The Government suggested we shop around for value-for-money while the café in the National Museum charged the equivalent of Imelda Marcos's shoe bill for a small bottle of 7 Up.

At the same time, more laws were passed to govern the way we live our lives. The plastic bag tax. The smoking ban. Penalty points. The ban on children in pubs after nine o'clock at night. A possible ban on the use of mobile phones in public venues is being debated. So too a legal prohibition on slapping children. The cumulative impression is that we cannot be trusted to act responsibly of our own accord.

Yet alcohol consumption has fallen significantly. It was said, after the first boom from 1998 to 2001, that champagne sales tumbled because stockbrokers' bonuses had stopped and there was nothing more to celebrate. Now the bubble's back in the bubbly. Brand Ireland has even bought the Dorchester and the Savoy. It's as you were, no?

"All I'd ask is that we learn from the last time," wishes Fr Tony Byrne, "but I fear the notion is coming in that money and profit are more important than anything."

Prosperity versus egalitarianism. There's the eternal conflict. Always one or the other. In an ideal world, they would coexist. Maybe that's what money would say – if it could talk.

Tragedy of the mother State forgot

June Morris should have had a wonderful life. She had intelligence, good looks, a talent for art, a kind heart and a strong will. On St Stephen's Day, she told her husband she was going to visit a friend. Soon after, she left the house and fulfilled the final act of that once so promising life by walking into the sea.

Irish Independent, 24 January 2004

In a way, it was a formality. June's life had stopped six years ago when her beautiful 17-year-old son, Steven, was murdered on the front doorstep of the family home.

Months earlier, Vincent Flynn's girlfriend had recited the names of local boys she fancied, including Steven Morris. On the night she tried to break up with Flynn by telling him she regarded him as a friend, her boyfriend grabbed an eight-inch hunting knife from a collection of 15 in his house. He called first to the home of another of the boys whom the girlfriend had identified as attractive but he was out. Next he turned in the direction of the Morris' house.

Steven was home, sharing a pizza with his girlfriend as they crammed for the Leaving. He was 6"3'. 'Player of the Year' with Guinness Rugby Club and had only recently laughed off the cajoling of a talent scout on a city street to enlist with a modelling agency. His dream was to be a full-time cartoonist.

He would have heard the doorbell ring, would have looked up casually from his books at the kitchen table when a family member told him he was wanted at the door. He might still have been pondering a maths problem when he went to the door and felt the knife pierce his chest and mortally slice his aorta.

June got through the funeral with the help of family, friends, ritual, and the natural expectation that her child's murder would be abominated by his homeland. The trial began in the Four Courts. One day, a psychotherapist who had been attending Vincent Flynn said in evidence that while awaiting trial on bail in the care of his aunt, a school principal in Limerick, Flynn had gone from school to school in the city giving talks to children about his life. The words hit June like a train. She slumped in her seat and had to be carried from the courtroom.

That week, family members and friends had written a dozen letters to individual politicians and the departments of Education and Justice requesting information about Flynn's lecture tour in Limerick. They got nothing in reply but platitudinous buck-passing. Many responses expressed the aspiration that its like would not happen again, but there was no attempt to honour the memory of Steven Morris or to ease the anguish of his family or to show any remorse.

Meanwhile, Vincent Flynn was convicted on November 12, 1999 of murdering Stephen Morris and everyone packed their briefcases and moved onto the next case. It was about a year later that June first telephoned. Even before she told her story, the listlessness in her voice betokened a tragedy. She said she could not get over the need to know what Flynn had said about her son in those classrooms. Had he uttered Steven's name.

Had he tried to justify his crime by attributing some blame to her child for his own death? Had her son's good character been hijacked for some sort of freakish educational experiment?

Why would nobody tell her anything?

She was instinctively private. She disliked public attention and arranged to avoid it.

She suggested the *Irish Independent* investigate what had happened and how the authorities had dealt with it. There was no need to quote tear-jerking comments from the grieving parents, she argued. She was a woman to whom it was hard to say no.

The Department of Education said the matter was the responsibility of the relevant school's board of management. The Catholic Church declined to comment on the role of a diocesan priest in organising the tour. More of the same no-answers. Joe Duffy read the story in the paper and invited June to go on *Liveline*. She baulked, protesting that the programme did not need her input, but when the "Talk to Joe" interval breaker faded out the next afternoon, there was June's voice. She would do anything to acquire the information she craved.

"We've lost the plot," she was saying. "What is the value of a human life?"

There is no doubt that the State is partly culpable for her death. When she most needed its help, it shrugged her off with flim flam and walked away. It could not even utter the word "sorry". In the end, June gave up. I imagine she chose the day to do it with careful deliberation. For it was the day that shared its name with her stolen child.

A fitting welcome for George W Bush

The appropriate way to receive George Bush when he steps onto Irish soil next Friday is by clapping a pair of handcuffs on his wrists and marching him onto the next plane to the International War Crimes Tribunal. Alternatively, keep the handcuffs on and wedge him between a pair of Special Branch men in the back seat of a Mondeo, then give him an eyeful of the lush Irish midlands en route to Mountjoy for trial in the Special Criminal Court.

Irish Independent, 19 June 2004

Let the world's most powerful man sample our famous Irish hospitality in an eight-foot by eight-foot cell. He can work out in the exercise yard, watch telly with the other inmates, read about himself in the daily newspapers and eat supper on his bed before lights out. In the Joy's library, he will find a well-thumbed copy of Michael Moore's *Stupid White Men*.

He will not be required to wear a hood over his face, be stripped naked, suffer sexual humiliation, forego his right to a lawyer and a fair trial, be deprived of sleep, be raped or murdered and buried without a post mortem. Unlike the jails in his home state of Texas, he will be nowhere near an execution chamber and, unlike Camp Delta in Guantanamo Bay, he will be entitled to the full panoply of democratic rights that goes hand-in-hand with the presumption of innocence.

But, as Chris Tarrant might say, we don't want to do that, do we? We'll be doing our Paddy the Irishman céad míle fáilte, tugging the forelock to the leader of the world's only superpower. He will enter this country without an obligatory computer decodable passport containing a wealth of personal details. He will not be ordered by some surly guard to take off his boots and put them on the x-ray machine or be selected for a random second or third frisk because he looks shifty.

No, we'll mobilise the Garda and the Army to keep him safe. feed him scrumptious delicacies and tuck him in to sleep in a pillowy bed within the battlements of a luxury castle. His bag-carrier with the nuclear red button will want for nothing either from the moment of touchdown at the same airport that thousands upon thousands of US troops have passed through on their way to invade and occupy Iraq.

We will excuse our craven obsequiousness by pretending that we are only fulfilling our duty as incumbent President of the European Union. But that is not the reason. No such protocol inhibited Washington last year when it insisted on hosting the annual EU–US summit even though it was Europe's turn. We will do it because we haven't the backbone not to.

When Bertie Ahem reaches out to shake Bush's hand next week, however, the Taoiseach could be flouting both international law and the law of the country he leads. The Criminal Justice Act 2000 legislates for Ireland's fidelity to the Geneva conventions on war crimes. As a signatory to Geneva, Ireland is expected to hand over suspects, not give them shelter. The Criminal Justice Act allows for the DPP to determine if there is sufficient evidence to mount a prosecution in this jurisdiction. Otherwise the UN court will pursue it, on foot of the suspect's extradition.

These are no fanciful reveries. They are considered legal opinion. Last month, members of a Department of Foreign Affairs standing committee on human rights wrote to the Taoiseach, the Minister for Justice, the Garda Commissioner and the DPP urging them to consider either extraditing or charging George Walker Bush of 1600 Pennsylvania Avenue, Washington DC, according to national and international law.

The correspondents were not your typical radicals. They included charity worker, lawyers – one of whom has worked at the International War Crime Tribunal in The Hague – a rich, Irish businessman and members of Amnesty International and the Red Cross, both of which produced reports on torture in Iraq long before the world woke up to it.

The Irish government's defence of its planned hospitality is that Bush will get a chiding from Bertie over the outrages perpetrated by his regime, but those tactics have already been tried. After enduring a morality lecture from the world's numero uno religious leader, Pope John Paul, the US president – who likes to invoke God as an alibi – is unlikely to lose sleep over a scolding by the shamrock-bearing leader of a small European state.

What both Washington and Merrion Street have yet to understand is that the legions who object to George Bush's visit here are, in the main, sane, responsible, reasonable, law-abiding and unthreatening to civil harmony. They are not the ones who ought to be locked up.

Polls apart

In this week's Assembly elections in the North voters moved to the extremes as Ian Paisley's DUP and Sinn Féin emerged as the strongest parties. However, there was also a significant drop in the percentage of people who turned up to vote. A greater divide has emerged between nationalists and unionists but also, it seems, between ordinary people and their bickering politicians. We assess the mood on the street in Belfast.

Irish Independent, 29 November 2003

"It'll be the same old shit on TV. Nothing changes," he sighs, exhaling a cloud of cigarette smoke. His accent is strangulated Belfast, that variant that impels the BBC to provide subtitles for "mainlanders".

"What would make things easier?"

"A nuclear bomb."

He has the Christian name of an American cowboy but, he says, "call me Martin in the paper".

It is polling day for the second Assembly elections since the Good Friday Agreement. Martin is in his mini-mogul's office in the city centre. Outside, City Hall's wedding confectioner's facade has been affixed with millions of Christmas spangles and shoppers are poring over toy catalogues inside the steamed-up windows of aromatic cafes. It's 5:20 pm – three hours and 40 minutes till the polling stations shut. In the old days, Belfast would have been a ghost-town by this time on a winter's evening; abandoned and futilely shuttered against the terrorists.

"Och, it must be one of the most beautiful cities in the world," croons Jane, Martin's mother, gazing down on the street, besotted. Yet, she would leave it in the morning if she had to. And she would have to, she believes, if she woke up to a united Ireland.

"McGuinness is probably right. It's going to happen. The Catholics are growing. I'd go to England. I wouldn't stay. Everything would change. It wouldn't be the British way of doing things. It'd be alien to me."

Jane (not her real name either) and her savvy son-cum-boss, Martin, have not voted because they are unregistered after moving house. Jane describes herself as "a British socialist" but sees no contradiction in her admission that had she been enfranchised, she would have voted for Trimble's party. "I'd honestly say that 75 pc of Catholics want to stay in the Union," she argues. "This poor old down-trodden-Catholic card has been played to death. Sinn Féin will get £50,000 a year now they're elected. Tell me this, would your Dáil allow the UVF in if they were elected?"

Martin, who has been off in a side office making the photocopier whirr, strolls back to his desk to light another cigarette. "We've much more in common with the south of Ireland than the English," he butts in. "Look, people here go to the extremities when they feel vulnerable and weak and that's why you get Paisley and Adams getting in. I don't think anybody should go back to war or nothing but nothing ever happens. It'll be the same old shit on TV."

The contest is billed as the Patricians versus the Boot Boys, on both sides of the divide. UUP farmers, professionals and Trimbleesque academics prowl the pig pen of the King's Hall, scowling at the jumped-up pulpit thumpers of the DUP here to snatch their crown. The hot bloods are trouncing the blue-bloods. The floor in the count centre slopes to drain away pig urine during the annual agricultural show but the human bile has no outlet. Ulster Unionist intellectual and West Belfast candidate Chris McGimpsey watches the numbers go up on the results board from the vantage point of his plastic chair by the cappuccino dispensing van. The word "forlorn" was coined for this man, in his mossy tweed suit and bespectacled bereavement.

Three hours since the first box was opened, he is accepting defeat in Belfast West where just 18 pc of the population is unionist/loyalist. "I did the best I could," he says, as much to himself as to anyone who might listen. "I'm satisfied there wasn't another thing I could have done. We don't have the organisation. I spent my time every evening with two other people out canvassing. In some estates Sinn Féin would have 50 people working the doorsteps. We don't have any members. They have a paramilitary wing."

The novelty has worn off Semtex chic. In 1998, when 68.8 pc voted in the first Assembly election, the sight of Armani-ed terrorists rubbing softly-padded shoulders with the enemy sent thrilled shivers through the count. Now two uniformed policemen watch from inside the door as yesterday's gunmen twitter around the ballot box, and only the idlest mind conjectures how a net thrown over this place a decade ago might have landed half the city's fugitives.

The PUP's Billy Hutchinson is bemoaning a "dead campaign" in Belfast North, a recent rendezvous for internecine loyalist warfare and spitting assaults on Catholic school girls. "The people who came out to vote are the most dedicated," he deduces. "I don't think we'll get an Assembly up and running. I don't think the stalemate is breakable while we have the system we have. We either need a miracle or to change the formula we have. I think it would be easier to change the formula."

Outside the front gate, a loyalist prisoners' group is protesting about jailhouse segregation as Gerry Adams's Merc briefly halts for a security check before purring on down Londonderry Road to his victory declaration.

The funny thing about downtown Belfast is that nobody talks about arms decommissioning or renegotiating the agreement. It is a city in the process of industrial shutdown. Shorts' workers have had their pay frozen. The once titanic Harland and Wolff has shrunk so much it qualifies for membership of the Small Businesses Federation. Yet another factory on the city's outskirts switched off its lights one last time the other week.

From the taxi's back seat, it looks grand. The Christmas tree is alight. Cash tills trill in Debenhams and M&S and Littlewoods and Easons and Dunnes and Xtravision. Dirty Den is playing in the panto at the Grand Opera House.

Did you vote? "No," says the taximan, uncontrite. "In this

town you're voting for a flag or what flower goes outside parliament at Easter. Until they have a box saying 'none of the above', I won't be voting."

The car is crawling past Belfast Central train station, beneficiary of a £6 million refurbishment and host to eight trains a day from Dublin. More than £900m has been invested in retail, office and residential developments, and it shows. Over at the Odyssey, the biggest indoor arena in Ireland and home to the Belfast Giants, there is an international horse show going on. Listed redbricks house, glittering telecentres and the Cathedral Quarter of town is being transmogrified into a demi-Temple Bar.

The ubiquity of cocaine and ecstasy stays invisible to the tourist eye. Likewise, the car thieves executing handbrake turns and wheel spins in the estates, competing to amputate wing mirrors from parked vehicles as they hurtle through back streets. So too, the increasingly frequent attacks on old people. A senior citizen wrote a letter to the *Andersontown News* deriding the IRA's new-age passivity while hoodlums kept her neighbourhood awake at night. As Sinn Fein is ready to step into the SDLP's Stormont loafers, she hinted darkly, there would be others waiting in the shadows to climb into the Provos' boots.

The taxi stops at traffic lights. A newspaper gets squelched under foot but, in a momentary lull, an SDLP election ad grows legible on its upturned page. "We have no private armies," it boasts. "We are not wreckers of the institutions."

On the lamp-post illuminating the discarded newspaper, a Sinn Féin poster urges, "Let's Make History". The juxtaposition is a lesson in the power of positive marketing.

So what would make you vote?

"I want politicians to talk about why my rates are going to pay for councillors' junkets to Rio de Janeiro," wishes the taxi man, unperturbed by the rush-hour traffic. "Maybe the next generation will have time to talk about things that matter."

Officially, there is an acceptable low level of violence in peacetime Northern Ireland. This is the dividend.

On Wednesday, voting day, more than 50 petrol bombs were hurled at police stations in Derry city. That night, an 18-year-old male was shot in the knee in East Belfast, emulating a paramilitary punishment attack. In Dungannon two nights earlier, a 60-lb homemade bomb partly detonated outside an army base while shots were fired from a car at a PSNI station in Armagh city around the same time. The night before that, a man lost an eye and suffered multiple fractures when he was set upon by a gang armed with hammers and hatchets, shouting, "Kill him, kill him".

The Loyalist Action Force, a cover name for the UDA, later claimed the attack. Last week, a 21-year-old man was beaten to death in Lisburn. The crime is being viewed as sectarian.

In the toney Malone area, leaves bud and wither on the trees with the seasons and period-terraced houses sell for £300,000. The Troubles have retreated.

Not so in the estates east, west and north of the city centre where the stranglehold of history is slower to loosen. These are the people who cannot afford the luxury of electoral apathy because here everything is so much more personal, down to the colours of the paving stones.

Outsiders might look at a place like West Belfast (voter

turnout: 65.9 pc) and wonder who were those 6,199 devil-worshippers who gave the Republicans' leader their first preference votes only weeks after Jean McConville was finally buried in a proper grave. But people who vote Sinn Féin, like people who vote DUP, do not have tails and horns. What they do have are good reasons for voting as they do. Unemployment (pockets of 60 pc in a region where the average rate is 6 pc or 7 pc), crime, money, isolation, poor access to benefits are the real issues in their lives. And Jean McConville, murdered for helping a wounded soldier, then dumped?

"It was a bad time," says one man. "Shit happens."

Asked if a realignment of party politics could come about with the inescapable message that UUP and the SDLP have more in common with one another than with their respective unionist and nationalist brethren in the DUP and Sinn Féin, Chris McGimpsey thinks not. "There will always be a little matter called the border," he answers. "The border will always be an issue."

Perhaps, in that reply, lie the ashes of his election campaign.

Back at the count centre, Sinn Féin's Malone candidate, Alex Maskey, endorses Martin McGuinness's view that there could be a united Ireland by 2016 to commemorate the Easter Rising. (It tallies with a passage in the newly published autobiography of former Secretary of State, Douglas Hurd, in which he states that the common view in London's Foreign Office was that Irish unity would be in Britain's best interests).

"I don't accept that people south of the border don't care about what happens north of it," Maskey argues. "The Agreement provides for a border poll every seven years and the first one doesn't have to be called until there's a belief it would be successful."

As he speaks, the DUP's deputy leader, Peter Robinson, glides past on his way to the victory podium where he reiterates his party's insistence that the Agreement must be renegotiated. Gerry Adams has already left with his wired-up security men, fondly known as the "sandbags" but other Shinners mingle in the audience.

"They'll never talk to each other," an English journalist predicts, confident of the accuracy of his story.

"Don't you believe it," warns a local reporter. "Paisley's on the way out and Robinson's a pragmatist. They'll talk alright."

At the bus stop, under a sky of frosted velvet, Ross Hanley (21) wonders, with the enthusiasm of a chess master forced to watch a snakes-n'-ladders marathon, how the count is going.

"My only experience of politics in this country is that they bicker and squabble like kids," he says. "A lot of people I know see it as morons fighting on a hill. They don't discuss things that affect the running of the country, like the NHS or water rates. My folks are Protestant. I don't go to church. If anyone asked me I'd say I'm Irish rather than British. I like being Irish. Look at the reception you get wherever you go. To be honest, I don't give a damn what flag flies over my head."

The arrival of the bus heralds a quick goodbye.

"I hear the music scene's good in Dublin," he says in valediction, turning to leave.

"So I hear. Hey, did you vote?"

"No," he calls back, as the night starts to swallow him up. "I mean, what's the point?"

On the way back into town, Queen's University glows ethereally magnificent. The city's seat of learning; cradle of the civil rights movement. Sinn Fein laid on a bus at the Students Union office at 3pm on Wednesday to ferry young voters to Armagh. The eight o'clock return journey was free of charge.

Like the man from the newsletter said over a latte at the count: "Brace yourself for a lot more sharp suits and a little less ideology."

He was a psychological cocktail of rampant egotism and professional ineptitude but, amazingly, there are still those who swear by him

Things started to go wrong soon after Sheila Hodgers discovered she was pregnant with her third child. Neither she nor her baby would survive to tell the harrowing story.

Irish Independent, 4 March 2006

All these years later her husband contextualises his account of what happened by saying: "I've been listening to the horrendous stories of these other women who were his victims and I have mixed feelings about Dr Neary because he was the one bloke I put my trust in. I can only say that, for me at the time, he was my champion."

Brendan and Sheila Hodgers were "very strong as a couple". Their dearest wish was to have another child to join their two daughters, then aged seven and six. Sheila had undergone a mastectomy for breast cancer but she was feeling fit and well when the pregnancy was confirmed. That was when the Hodgers were sucked into what Brendan describes as "our own Mother & Child situation".

At Our Lady of Lourdes Hospital in Drogheda, Sheila was denied all investigations, pain relief and treatment for cancer when symptoms appeared early in her pregnancy that the disease had returned. Though she was experiencing severe pain from a suspected tumour in her back, the hospital would not X-ray her on the grounds that it could endanger the foetus.

"A junior doctor said to me that if she'd been knocked down outside the gate and broken all her bones they would have no choice but to x-ray her," recalls Brendan, a senior trade union official. "But they did have a choice and they chose not to do it. She was in agony. One time, when I was getting out of the car in the car park, I could hear Sheila inside the hospital screaming in agony.

"We were never actually told the treatment was being denied. They just withheld it. I felt so helpless getting the run-around. I could see she was being neglected. I was a brash young man and I asked the hard questions but these were educated guys and I wasn't getting anywhere with them.

"Dr Neary came to me and said 'If you leave her in my care, I'll commit to you that she will not have any pain. I will look after her.' And he did that. He made her pain-free as best he could."

Sheila and Brendan Hodgers's third daughter, Gemma, was born at full term on Saint Patrick's Day 1980. It was not necessary to inform her mother that the child was dead. Sheila knew.

"I asked her did she want to hold Gemma and she said no," Brendan recounts. "I asked her why and she said: 'you have a funeral to arrange. Go and bury Gemma'.

"She said she didn't want a dog and pony show with a mother and child being buried together.

"That was the second last time she spoke to me. The last

time, she told me she'd been talking to Elvis Presley. I said, 'what did he want?' She said, 'a kiss' and I said 'wasn't it a kiss that got us into this trouble'."

Sheila Hodgers died, age 26, two days after her baby's stillbirth.

Judge Maureen Harding Clark notes in her report of the Lourdes Hospital Inquiry that the Catholic ethos imposed by the Medical Missionaries of Mary order of nuns, who ran the hospital until the State bought it for IR£5.5 million in April 1997, prohibited the use of all forms of contraception.

The Sacred Congregation of the Propaganda in the Vatican, set up by Pope Gregory XV in the 17th century, was one of the chief funders of the Drogheda hospital and still remains a dedicated opponent of what it labels "sexual sterilisation".

"Sterilisation for contraceptive purposes was not permitted," Judge Harding Clark writes about Our Lady of Lourdes Hospital. "The ethos allowed for 'indirect sterilisation' where the primary purpose was for medical reasons, although the end result was that the woman could no longer become pregnant."

The judge says there is abundant evidence that the unwritten ethical code was rigidly applied and that Dr Michael Neary and his fellow gynaecologist/obstetrician at the hospital, Dr Finian Lynch, repeatedly sought clarification of their position from the Department of Health, the Medical Defence Union and the North Eastern Health Board. The report states that the doctors were "obliged to operate in a grey area of indirect sterilisation."

No tubal ligation, whereby a woman's fallopian tubes are tied to prevent conception, was ever performed while the nuns ran the hospital. Yet speculation that Dr Neary was motivated by compassion to provide covert sterilisation for his patients does not fit with the facts of the appalling tragedy he inflicted on so many of them.

Some of the women were on their first pregnancies. Some of the babies born at the time of the hysterectomies died either at birth or shortly afterwards so that some women were doomed to childlessness. In the case of Kathy Quilty, who settled her action against Neary and the North Eastern Health Board for €425,000 in May 2004, the hysterectomy following the birth of her brain-damaged son led to depression, bladder surgery, attempted suicide and homelessness.

But Dr Neary boasted as he did in many cases, that he had saved her life. "I lost her twice on the operating table," he told Kathy's mother, Valerie. "I've had to take out her womb. In my 30 years as a surgeon, I've only seen this twice and I lost both of those women."

There is no unanimity of opinion about Michael Neary. Those who suffered at his surgeon's hands would be saints to ever forgive him but there is sympathy for him among his more fortunate patients. Some women still swear by him.

"I suppose somebody can be the two things. He was real no-nonsense," says Angela McCormack, a locally-based journalist who had four children under Dr Neary's care, without negative consequences. "He was very witty. People who didn't like him called him Sneery Neary. You had to know how to handle him. If you told him, for instance, that you weren't sleeping, he'd say, 'ah, sure you'll have that'. You learned there was no point in moaning to him. You didn't argue with him. You did it his way or no way."

Alarm bells were ringing about Michael Neary as early as

the 1970s when a hospital matron voiced concern about the number of hysterectomies he was performing in Drogheda. Later, an anaesthetist who had come from the Coombe Hospital in Dublin, became alarmed. This week, a GP in the hospital's hinterland confirmed that his family doctors' practice made a decision in the 1980s not to refer pregnant patients to Drogheda for fear Dr Neary would be assigned to them.

Conscious of the divisions of loyalty caused by the Neary scandal, this GP declines to be named. He says he was alerted to Dr Neary's psychological cocktail of rampant egotism and professional ineptitude when they clashed over a patient's treatment and he realised that the gynaecologist fabricated a medical diagnosis to support an idiotic argument.

"I know one or two colleagues over the years who would have had run-ins with him," says the GP. "There was an initiative in the mid-1980s to have a closer relationship between the GPs and the consultants in the hospital and he resisted that. Another time, when trainee GPs wanted to do a clinical issue audit for a research project, he wouldn't cooperate. He was somebody who couldn't tolerate his authority being challenged."

Michael Neary, the son of a non-medical Ballina, Co Mayo couple, trained and worked as a doctor at hospitals in Hammersmith, west London, Portsmouth and Manchester before his appointment to a consultancy at Our Lady of Lourdes at the exceptionally young age of 31. He moved to Drogheda with his wife Gabrielle, a native of east Galway whom he met in St Mary's Hospital, Manchester, where she worked in the laboratory. The couple married the day after her 21st birthday and subsequently had three children, one of whom is a doctor.

These days, Dr Neary lives alone outside Drogheda town,

though he is frequently visited by his grown-up children. Gabrielle died on August 23, 1996, two months before her 50th birthday. She had suffered from a chronic gynaecological condition called endometriosis, which can cause bowel problems and infertility. Her mother had died of breast cancer and Gabrielle, in the last year of her life, was treated for uterine cancer in the Mater Hospital, Dublin. Though he shared a love of sport with his wife – they used to go wind surfing in Cork together – Michael Neary only plays the occasional round of golf now. He shops in Drogheda and is often seen engaged in friendly conversations in the town.

A non-smoker and a non-drinker, he goes to daily mass but the exact nature of his religious belief is debatable. There is anecdotal evidence that he toes an orthodox line and has disapproved, for example, of his patients seeking fertility treatment.

"I don't believe he wanted to liberalise the code of ethics in Lourdes," says the GP who decided not to refer his patients to Neary. "That's a load of baloney. He would have had a very Catholic ethos."

In the Lourdes Report, Judge Harding Clark retells Michael Neary's account of a meeting he was summoned to by the late Cardinal Tomás O'Fiach, Archbishop or Armagh and, therefore, patron of the hospital in Drogheda. Neary told the Lourdes Inquiry that the Cardinal threatened at the meeting that if he attempted to flout the hospital's ethics code, the Cardinal would ensure his brother would lose his teaching job in Cork.

Sheila Martin, an accountant, a local health campaigner and Neary's most vocal friend, claims that meeting was triggered when one of the gynaecologist's patients vowed to go to the court to assert her right to have a tubal ligation performed at the hospital. Sheila Martin says that Neary told her Cardinal O'Fiach had phoned his own bank during the meeting to ascertain the balance in his account. After the phone call, she says, he told the doctor he had that much money available to pursue Neary through the High Court if he did not drop the case. Martin says that Neary also told her that he was checked for a concealed tape recorder at a meeting with the nuns on the same issue.

She says he has often mentioned the case of Sheila Hodgers and she claims he boycotted the 1990 formal opening of the new maternity unit because of his conflict with the Church authorities. He was particularly perturbed, she says, in 1996 when the hospital's ethics committee met to discuss a patient of another consultant who was pregnant after purportedly undergoing tubal ligation at a different hospital. She says Neary thought it repugnant that a dozen strangers would discuss the intimate details of this woman's life, and he stayed away from the meeting. The minutes of that meeting show that Dr Neary was one of two absentees.

Sheila Martin has provided this newspaper with a photocopy of a letter to the Secretary of the Department of Health in December 1993 in which Michael Neary wrote: "... I have been informed by various Medical Missionaries of Mary that failure to implement their policies in this matter (the ethics code) could result in my dismissal from the unit ..." But he states too: "... we have been quite prepared to abide by the Rules as laid down by the Medical Missionaries of Mary."

Neary phoned Sheila Martin from Spain this week after the

report was published and "swore he had nothing to do" with files that have gone missing from the hospital. (Both Neary's and Martin's homes were raided by the National Bureau of Criminal Investigation over a year ago in the search for the files and Martin says she has given the name to the gardaí of the person she believes was responsible).

Meanwhile, Brendan Hodgers has to concede defeat in seeking legal vindication for this stillborn child and his young wife. After their deaths, he initiated proceedings against the hospital with the help of a public fund-raising campaign. "Even the discovery process was so slow," he remembers. "Papers were coming one page at a time with lines blanked out all over the place. In the end, I ran out of money. I had to let the case lapse."

This week, Senator Mary Henry, herself a doctor, requested a special Seanad debate on the impact of ethics codes in all hospitals on women's health. Such implications are the fall-out from the heart-breaking suffering caused by Michael Neary.

"There's no point in saying this culture has gone away," she warns.

I will die within the next couple of months

She told the nation on radio that her name was Rosie,
and she had been given a death sentence because of
hospital waiting lists. Now, this 41-year-old mother
can only hope her campaigning will save others – and
make her children proud.

Sunday Tribune, 9 September 2007

The tiredness was gnawing inside her. She ached for sleep.
Her mind was swamped with the vision of her bed at
home, waiting for her. It was always like this after the chemo.
It left her "wrecked" for three whole days.

It was dark by the time she got home that night last January.
She went to her bedroom and kicked off her shoes. She flicked
on the television and prepared to sink under the duvet, already
surrendering to the balm of slumber. That was when she saw
the public health advertisement filling the television screen.
Indignation spread to every extremity of her exhausted body.

"The earlier the diagnosis, the better your chances of
survival," an authoritative voice was warning, urging viewers
not to delay, to go and get tested for bowel cancer.

She could not let it rest; would not allow herself to rest.
What appalling, cruel hypocrisy. She reached for her mobile
phone and tapped out a text message about the advertisement
to RTÉ's *Liveline*. "If Bertie Ahern or Mary Harney or Michael

McDowell were within reach (when I saw it) I would have killed them. Literally. I'm not joking," she wrote. She said her name was Rosie; the name the midwife had mistakenly called her throughout the delivery of her two children, to her and her husband's giggling delight.

"Hello Rosie," said Joe Duffy on the radio the next day. From her empty, silent home in Callan, Co Kilkenny, her children oblivious in the midst of their school labours, her husband teaching a computer class, and her own body begging for sleep, she announced to the nation that she was going to die because of hospital waiting lists.

In that phone call, Rosie became a landmark. It was stuck-to-the-car-seat radio. All around the country, citizens listened, petrified. Doctors were getting calls from colleagues and from home telling them to stop whatever they were doing and turn on the radio. She was telling how she had had to wait seven months for a colonoscopy after the request was made by her GP, how a delayed diagnosis of bowel cancer could be lethal, how the cancer had permeated her bowel and become incurable by the time she had the test, how she, a public patient, had sat beside the partner of a private patient with the same disease in a hospital room and heard how he had undergone the colonoscopy within three days of referral, and she was going to die.

Her eloquence and dignity and courage were spellbinding. An avalanche of letters swept through her letterbox in the days and weeks that followed. "Rosie, County Kilkenny", most of the envelopes were addressed. Somehow, they reached her. Thank you, they said in ballpoints weeping the personal tragedies of a myriad strangers. It was as if her bleak story had, at last, given an accessible narrative to the chaos and the callous unfairness impinging on hundreds of other patients and their families too.

Only one letter dissented. Waterford-postmarked, it read: "Who do you think you are, making the people working in the hospital look like they don't do a good job? I suppose, when you die, Joe Duffy will play the interview again on the show."

"It upset me – for five minutes," says Susie Long.

A long peal of ebullient laughter erupts from the chair where she sits propped up with a pillow behind her back. Her skin is glowing and without a line; the short, auburn hair luxuriant. You can tell by the way her fatigued body refuses to cooperate with the vitality of her words that she is very sick. She sits now beside a different bed, in a room of Our Lady's Hospice in Harold's Cross, where she moved to from Callan five weeks ago.

In response to a question about what gives her the unextinguishable valour that made her phone *Liveline*, she points to a photograph on her dressing table. It is a freeze-frame of her family's history, taken 19 years ago. Sitting in the foreground is Susie Long from Ohio with her newborn daughter, Áine, snuggling in her arms. Ranged behind them are Susie's mother, who suffered violence from her husband and died in a car crash 10 years ago, Susie's grandmother, who used to admonish her for trailing coal through the house after scrambling her motorbike on the fuel mountains at the local power station with her deceased brother, and Susie's great-grandmother.

"I suppose she's what made me what I am," she says, indicating Sis Coyle, the oldest of the matriarchs, a second-generation Irish-American who died at the age of 91. "She was a Wobbly. She voted for Eugene Debs who founded the Industrial Workers of the World (and was a five-time socialist candidate for the US presidency). She was strong."

Since Susie was diagnosed with terminal bowel cancer in March 2006, she has been treated with two different forms of chemotherapy and with antibodies, as well as undergoing three abdominal operations. "I had to try every option to prolong life," she explains, "but, unhappily, it didn't work. The disease has spread very rapidly. I will die within the next couple of months. I was hoping to live until my son finished school in three years, but it didn't work out."

There is no self-pity in her voice and her eyes never brim with threatened tears, but the leaden tone of sadness is unmissable. If there is one thing Susie Long can say without contradiction it is that she has taken life by the scruff of the neck and lived it, virtually since the day she was born, 24 February 1966.

Now life is leaving her and she is "trying not to be angry". She asks rhetorically: "What can you do? You have to accept it. I am angry, though I don't rage. I've never had the poor-me syndrome. People get cancer and that's all there is to it. I'm in the sadness stage. I don't want to leave my children and my husband but I know that there is nothing that can be done for me. The closer I get to death, the sadder I am because I want more time with Conor and the kids. I live every day at a time. I'm grateful for every day because I know that today isn't the day."

At 18, she upped sticks and left her dull, midwest American home town, equipped with a literary map drawn from the Irish history books and the Jennifer Johnston novels she devoured in her teens, pitching up in Dublin in search of excitement in 1984. She sold jewellery from a street stall and worked as a waitress in The Living Room behind Trinity College. At 20, she fell in love with Conor MacLiam, a secondary school teacher from Rathmines, and they were married.

They were twin souls with an unshakeable allegiance to the ideal of social justice. "We thought it was wrong to skip queues," she replies when asked why they, a middle-class couple, did not have private health insurance. "We thought our tax should pay for our health system and everyone should be treated equally. When someone presents with obvious symptoms of cancer, they should be seen right away."

"If you could go back in time, would you go private?"

"No," she says, closing her eyes as if to concentrate on her words. "It's wrong."

After her *Liveline* interview, the recently unseated socialist TD Joe Higgins invited Susie to Dáil Eireann to witness a debate on the nation's cancer services. She brought her 14-year-old son, Fergus, with her after he pleaded to be allowed go. Together, they sat in the public gallery, separated by security plate glass from the politicians below and, as they sat there, Susie watched her youngest child grow angrier and angrier.

"He was disgusted. We were up high and we could see that Mary Harney was texting on her phone under the desk during the debate. Fergus is a very inquisitive boy. He questions everything."

Her babies were healthy from birth; Áine weighing in at eight pounds, her baby brother seven ounces heavier when he arrived five years later. Their mother "puked for the first three months with both of them" but it did not deter her from embarking on her first fight with the Department of Health. Having given birth to Áine at home, in the house of her parents-in-law while she and Conor still resided in Dublin, she was determined her second child would start life in the same way. By then, the family had settled in Callan, led to the rural idyll by proselytising friend-of-the-earth Susie. In 1988, Kilkenny did not have a homebirth policy then, and still does not today.

"I couldn't get a midwife. I fought the health board then too," she says, emitting another spirited laugh. "In the end, Fergus was also born in his grandparents' house in Dublin. I don't like confrontation. No, really, I don't like causing trouble, but I always end up doing it. I knew I was going to raise my kids to question everything and to speak out when they saw injustice against the underdog. That's how I am."

A member of Amnesty International, a member of Earth Watch, an advocate for the Home Birth Association, Susie was a project worker with the Women's Refuge in Kilkenny (and running discos in her spare time to raise funds), until her illness made it no longer tenable. In a lifetime of striving to make a difference, it was her cancer that caused her to make her most significant and lasting contribution to the homeland she adopted at 18. She has never regretted choosing Ireland. "This country has been good to me," she says. "I've made loads of friends and it's never been boring. Ireland has been the best country in the world in the last 20 years."

She was outraged on discovering the reason for the seven-month delay in her diagnosis was a shortage of day beds in St Luke's Hospital and that the hospital staff had spent years beseeching the Department of Health for more day beds. Last

May, she delivered a speech – watched by Conor, Áine and Fergus – at a formal presentation in St Luke's of architects' plans for its new 24-bed Day Services Unit, which was given the initial nod by health minister Mary Harney, after Susie's Liveline interview. Within the last fortnight, the HSE has approved 100% funding for the €5m building, which will accommodate two procedure rooms.

"I was delighted that day, because something good has come out of a tragic situation. Getting cancer is tragic. Hopefully, other people might live because of what I did. The hospital had been asking for a new unit for 16 years. The one that's there has six or eight trolleys. There isn't even a toilet. I'm glad I did what I did. The new unit will cut down on the waiting list and I hope that what happened to me won't happen to other people. But the health service shouldn't be delivered by the media. It should be planned, state-of-the-art, focused on needs. People deserve the best care but you're not going to get it unless you fight for it. I'd love to see the unit completed, but that's not going to happen."

The day after the presentation, some of the nurses asked Susie if she would like to join the annual Ossory pilgrimage to Lourdes, after someone cancelled at the last moment. A devout Catholic when she arrived in Ireland 23 years ago only to have her faith eroded by Church scandals, she thought: "I'd love to go to France." Áine went with her and, after politely attending the Ossory mass in Lourdes, they left the "holy trail for the tourist trail". Mother and daughter took a train up the Pyrenees to stroll around the mountains and drink in the fragrant May air, lingering in companionable quietude at café tables. "We had two good days, and then I got sick."

At four o'clock on the morning of the third day, Susie came downstairs from her hotel room and requested the night porter to call a taxi to take her to hospital. "I was in a lot of pain," she recalls. "Within four hours, I was seen, had an MRI scan and was diagnosed. The tumour had spread to my uterus. The people in the hospital in France were lovely.

"The people who work in the Irish health service are wonderful too. I have been hearing about the errors in diagnosing breast cancer in the past week and I would be very slow to blame anyone because you don't know what kind of conditions their work is done in. I feel sorry for health service workers who are put under such strain to do a good job just because they are under-funded or there is a cock-up in how the service is organised. I would hate for one or two people to be made scapegoats when it's the system that failed."

On her return from France in May she had surgery to drain her uterus and lapsed into a coma. She remained unconscious in Waterford Regional Hospital for several weeks. "I woke up in the ICU unit thinking we had all been in a car crash and I was so afraid for the children and Conor."

Being without a religious faith, she finds, makes dying harder. "I would love to have a belief in religion because it makes you feel safe but, unfortunately, I just don't. I like the community of belonging to a church. I love Christmas and Christmas carols. I used to love singing them to my children. I've told Conor I want to be cremated and, maybe a week later, there would be a memorial service. I was a very strong Catholic until I moved to Ireland," she laughs that rich laugh again, appreciating the irony. "I'm full of contradictions. That's what they said about Johnny Cash – 'partly truth, partly fiction, a walking contradiction'. Kris Kristofferson wrote that about him."

"You're a fan of Johnny Cash?"

She nods. "I've a tattoo of him on my back. Do you want to see?" and she slips her pyjama jacket off one shoulder to reveal an inky portrait of the country/rock star from Arkansas. "I had it done in Waterford," she adds proudly.

Susie can no longer cook. It used to be a labour of love, involving lots of healthy "wholegrain this and wholegrain that". (She was overweight before the cancer, but never smoked). Nor can she read the standard type size in novels any more – the great enduring passion of her life – since the medication started affecting her eyesight. But, in Our Lady's Hospice, where, she says, "I was lucky to get in," she is learning about new pleasures. "A woman comes around every Monday giving manicures. I've always been a tomboy because boys' stuff was so much more fun – but look at my nails," she flashes all 10, each immaculately varnished in warm plum. "I've got girly nails for the first time in my life."

Her spacious, sunlit room pulsates with this extraordinary woman's joie de vivre. It visibly enlivens those around her. The banter of the hospice employee who comes to clean her en suite is full of affection for her. The dinner lady is joyous when Susie asks for pudding. The nurse who comes in to administer an injection, whispers discreetly: "Did the earlier medicine help?" When the nurse leaves, Susie admits, under cross-examination, that she had been feeling unwell before the interview but that she had "popped a pill and felt much better".

"I just can't praise this place enough," she says. "I feel safer here because help is at the end of a buzzer. When I was at home I had the homecare team and they were wonderful but it wasn't enough for what I needed. Conor has been so amazing. He looked after me so well when I came home from Waterford Hospital and I couldn't dress myself or bathe myself. He dressed and bathed me. Since I came here, he's been coming up every weekend. Now he's going to take leave from work so that he can be in Dublin all the time. I worry about Fergus. He's in second year in school. I want to spend as much time as I can with my kids but that's going to mean that he'll miss a lot of school. Áine is starting an arts degree in history and English in UCD. She's moving into her grandparents' place; the house where she was born. She's very quiet and very strong."

Then it is Susie's turn to stop talking. She listens without a hint of vainglory trespassing her demeanour to the news that a commemorative plaque in her memory is being planned for the new Day Services Unit in St Luke's. Her eyes are closed, as she listens.

"Your children must be proud of you," her visitor suggests.

She opens her eyes. They are undimmed. And she says: "I hope so."

"The thing about Susie is she is so positive. She's dying, clearly, but everything about her is so positive. She's quite stunning," says Dr Garry Courtney, consultant physician at St Luke's Hospital, Kilkenny.

"She was very committed to making sure that the delay she encountered in having a colonoscopy, which was done under the National Treatment Purchase Fund, wouldn't happen again. I would very definitely say that, because of what she has done, it is less likely to happen to someone else.

"The Department of Health sets a target that 50% of work

in every hospital should be done on the basis of day care but, of the 317 beds in St Luke's Hospital, there are only six day care beds. Obviously, we failed Susie.

"The new unit will be state of the art with 24 couches or day beds, two procedure rooms, showers and toilets and consultation facilities. Susie gave a great speech the day the plans were presented last May. There were over a hundred people in the room, including her family and friends. 'Humbling' is a hackneyed word these days but it's the only one I can use to describe her. After the speeches, Susie visited the site in the grounds of St Luke's, studying the proposed facilities that she will never see.

"The design team for the building work is being appointed this month but from the outset it is planned to commemorate Susie in the building, with a plaque or, perhaps, a painting. She will not be forgotten in St Luke's."

'My dream was to swim.
He ruined my life.'

In 2007 the *Tribune* tracked alleged child rapist George Gibney to Orange County, Florida. Here, one of his alleged victim talks about how he ruined her life.

Sunday Tribune, 18 March 2007

After the detectives came to break the news, she walked to a field in the grounds of a religious order's house and hung herself from a tree with her scarf. Inside, she felt dead already. For years, the prospect of seeing the man who raped her being convicted by a court of the land and sent to jail had kept her engaged in living. The gardaí were optimistic.

Three other girls had sworn statements that he had sexually abused them too. These crimes were much more recent than the seven alleged rapes he had got away with in 1994 when the Supreme Court had ruled that they were so old he could not adequately defend himself against the charges. This second case file was watertight. The gardaí had worked assiduously, ever since she first went to them in 1997. They were talking about having him extradited from the US. Her counselling sessions were concentrated on getting her psychologically prepared for the ordeal of being cross-examined.

At first, after the guards sat with heavy surrender in her living room and told her that the state had decided not to apply for

George Gibney's extradition, all she felt was relief. She would not have to go to court after all. Would not have to see his face ever again. Would not have to recount to an audience of strangers the intense details of that day he raped her in a hotel room in Florida when she was just seventeen.

It was a priest who cut her down from the tree two years ago. Her parents got the call from a hospital emergency room. They were sorrowfully practised in the drill.

The hospital calls had become part of their lives. Often she would get up and leave the house in the middle of the night and wander aimlessly abroad. Sometimes she was admitted to A&E bleeding copiously after cutting her body indiscriminately with a knife or blades. Other times it would be an overdose of pills.

She had never tried to hang herself before, though.

It was the anger, she explains in a leaden voice. The raging anger that boiled inside her once the initial relief receded and which she could not express. She was left to drift like flotsam after a catastrophe in the sea. She who was once a future Olympic swimmer. The girl who cut through the water so fast that bystanders on the bank turned to one another and asked what was her name. A name to watch out for in the future, they would nod. That name lost to her now as she reluctantly chooses anonymity for a veil of armour. As if to compensate, she only ever alludes to George Gibney by his surname.

'I think he saw a vulnerability in me,' she agrees.

Her destiny was decided when she was five, after her mother was taken to Peamount Hospital with TB and remained there for six months. While her father would visit his wife at the hospital, the child would be sent to the house three doors down, where other little girls about her own age were minded by their live-in grandfather. 'If you tell anybody, your mother will die and it'll be all your fault,' the grandfather threatened her after the first time he sexually abused her, aged five-and-a-half.

The abuse was a regular occurrence, becoming increasingly severe and rough. Once, when she was seven, she came home with scrapes and bruises and had to make excuses to her parents. When she was nine, her parents, worried about her psychological withdrawal, brought her to Temple Street Children's Hospital. It was supposed that her symptoms were a natural response to her mother's prolonged absence from home.

Her parents hired a private tutor to come to the house because she had fallen behind academically in school. All the while, the abuse continued, not stopping until she was eleven, when the other family moved away from the locality.

When a swimming pool opened in her neighbourhood and she went there for the first time, she discovered a means of escape. 'It felt like I was flying,' she remembers. 'Like I'd been freed. I put everything into it. I really focused. It happened so quickly. One year, I wasn't able to swim. Within a year, I was breaking Irish records. People were wondering who I was.'

One day, a swimming coach phoned her parents after seeing her swim and told them she had the potential to be a great champion. Trojans Swimming Club in Blackrock was recommended, the citation eulogising its founder, George Gibney, the Irish Amateur Swimming Association's national coach when she joined in 1990 and Olympic coach to the Irish team in Seoul two years earlier. In 1990, most of the club's most accomplished swimmers left Trojans, their puzzling departure barely whispered in swimming circles. (It has since emerged that, in 1990, a male swimmer informed a senior swimming official that George Gibney had raped him when he was eleven.) Even though the pool was eighteen miles from their home, she and her father rose from bed at four o'clock every morning to be at the pool by 5.15 a.m., as stipulated. While her father slept outside in the car, she was swimming her heart out inside.

"I was so driven. All I wanted to do was to go to the Olympics at any cost. That was my dream."

Gibney showered her with attention. Promised her he would make her a star. Gave her swimming togs and tracksuits and hats and goggles. Hugged her every time she swam well. That year, at the national championships, she streaked home first in the 50 m freestyle, the 100 m freestyle, the 100 m breaststroke and the 100 m butterfly. She was sixteen years old, perfectly poised to be selected for the next Olympic games in Barcelona in 1992.

Then the sun went in. She was competing in Holland with the club. After one of the swim meets, she returned to her hotel room to dress for a disco that was part of the swimmers' itinerary. 'Gibney came to the room and started saying how bad I was and that I was never going to go anywhere. Suddenly, he jumped on me. He pushed me down on the bed and then left the room. After that he completely ignored me for a couple of weeks. I was wondering what did I do wrong. Back home, at training, he'd act as if I wasn't there. I felt all this guilt. I was swimming my hardest, training extra hard to get his attention.'

In 1991 Trojans organised a training camp in Tampa, Florida, to prepare for the National Championships in Belfast, where swimmers would be selected for the Olympics. The swimmers were assigned to host families, returning for a daily siesta to their houses after morning training and before the afternoon session. One day, her host family was away and she remained at the poolside with another girl after everyone dispersed.

"Gibney appeared out of nowhere and said, 'Come on, we'll go for breakfast.' The three of us went for breakfast. Then he drove us to a hotel that I didn't know. He brought me to a room and said, 'You, get in there,' and he went off with the other girl. I don't know where he brought her.

"He comes back and starts ranting and raving that I was so bad at swimming and how disappointed in me he was. I was sitting on a double bed. He jumped on me and raped me, there on the bed. He said if I told anybody, he would sue my family and nobody would believe me because he was George Gibney and he would bankrupt my family. Then he left.

"When he was gone, I just sat on the floor in the room. I couldn't leave because I didn't know where I was. He came back about three hours later with his wife and loads of kids and said: 'Come on you, we're going swimming now.'

"People saw me crying but nobody came near me. None of the swimming managers who were there approached me. My host family asked me what was wrong and I said I was homesick. I rang home and I told my mother that Gibney locked me in a room but I didn't tell her he raped me."

At the National Championships in Belfast that year, her legs shook so much standing on the starting block that she could not swim.

"Even then, I kept crying all the time. I couldn't stop."

Finally, in 1994, her trauma reached crisis point. She feigned an injury to get out of swimming in a competition and was referred to a doctor appointed by the Olympic Council of Ireland. The dam burst. She told the doctor about the prolonged abuse by the grandfather when she was a child and about being raped by Gibney.

She made a statement to gardaí about the first series of abuse. Two other females came forward and alleged that they had also been abused by the man. He fought the prosecution through the courts, seeking a judicial review but finally pleaded guilty in 1999. He was sentenced to five years' jail on conviction of seven charges of child sexual abuse of the three girls. The man is dead now. She heard he died in prison of natural causes. In passing sentence, the judge remarked that it was probably no coincidence that one of the girls was later abused by her swimming coach.

"I felt I got a bit of justice," she says. "It wasn't my imagination. It wasn't me going mad. It wasn't all in my head."

That experience encouraged her to make a statement against Gibney. He had eluded seven rape charges on the technicality that they were too old to defend. Yet, most of the Gibney charges pertained to the same years (or post-dated them) as the charges against the convicted grandfather.

The explanation she was given for the DPP's decision not to seek Gibney's extradition on foot of the second investigation was that he was entitled to insist on having each of the four complainants' cases tried separately. Again, this had not arisen in the case of the grandfather or in the vast majority of sexual-abuse prosecutions.

"The guards were absolutely brilliant. They couldn't have done enough," she says.

She is pursuing a civil action for damages against the Irish Amateur Swimming Association, the Olympic Council of Ireland and George Gibney. (This journalist has seen the legal statement of claim lodged in court, despite a denial by Swim Ireland that any such legal action exists.) Meanwhile, she is left to cope with the devastation. She takes six pills for her mental well-being every night, attends a psychiatrist every week and a cognitive counsellor twice a week. She does not socialise and has never had a proper romantic relationship. She has suffered from anorexia, dropping to under five-and-half stone at one stage though she stands 5ft 10" tall, and has had surgery for the scars left by her self-mutilation.

She is too embarrassed by the cut marks on her skin (the most recent episode was last November) to ever swim again.

"I'm sorry to say this," says her mother, sitting beside her on the couch, holding her hand and looking searchingly into her daughter's empty eyes, "but, sometimes, she's like the living dead."

They didn't rescue me

When Kelly Fitzgerald was dying from neglect, she asked her sister Geraldine to tell their story. Most parents comfort a child after a nightmare; the Fitzgeralds' parents were their nightmare.

Sunday Tribune, 3 June 2007

The last time Kelly spoke to Geraldine – maybe the last time she spoke to anybody – she said she was going to die soon. The children were sitting on the ground at the back of the house in Carracastle. They looked like Dickensian urchins; Kelly (15) and Geraldine (12), skeletal and shivering in their nighties while the rest of the family wallowed in the ample glow indoors on a winter's night in the West of Ireland.

"She was saying about death. She asked me to promise if anything happened to her to tell what was going on," Geraldine remembers, dry-eyed. "She was so calm about it."

After that bleak conversation, Kelly stopped talking. 'One minute, I noticed she had diarrhoea and she was sick. The next minute, she was whacking her head off the wall. It was like she couldn't help it. That's all she did, day after day after day. I can hear her head whacking against the wall. She was doing it and she was crying. One day, my father caught her and said: "Right, if you want to whack your head, I'll whack it for you."

"He brought her into the house and started whacking her head against the wall. He was whacking her head inside. She was whacking it outside. She didn't shake, didn't scream, nothing. When I looked in her eyes, it was blackness. It was like she was gone. Not even blinking. Just dead. The next day, I went to school. I was very upset. I told the social workers and they went to the house and asked to see Kelly but my father said she was in bed sick. They left soon afterwards.

"My father rang Uncle Gary in England and he said to put Kelly on the first plane to London. The night before she went, my father brought her in to eat. She couldn't lift her arms or hold herself up. Tears were streaming down her face. Everybody else went with her to the airport the next day but I was sent to school.

"That's my last memory of Kelly. Looking into her eyes and seeing nothing. Nothing. I don't think I'll ever get over her dying. Every time I think about it, I feel the same pain I felt then. I have to deal with that and live with that for the rest of my life and nobody has any idea how that feels and nobody gives a shit.'

On the table, as she speaks, lies the only possession of Kelly's that Geraldine managed to salvage from her sister's life. It is a child's miniature diary with tiny blank pages and the title 'Zoe Zebra' printed on its little plastic cover. She keeps it on a green string in her handbag, always. The written entries are sparse. On the first page, Geraldine has recorded: "Kelly RIP February 4, '93". Page two reads: "Better by far you should forget and smile, than you should remember and be sad."

The only other entry is for 13 June next. It says: "Kelly's thirtieth birthday today ... if she wasn't killed by our parents. I will always love you."

The life and death of Kelly Fitzgerald was described in Dáil

Éireann by the former Minister for Justice Maire Geoghegan-Quinn, as 'the most horrific abuse case in the history of the State". Kelly died, aged fifteen, in a London hospital from blood poisoning, triggering an avalanche of recriminations, much of it aimed at the Irish welfare authorities who had been alerted by their English counterparts that she was officially registered as at 'high risk' by Lambeth Council before the family came to live in rural Co. Mayo in 1990. The first indication of her maltreatment had been recorded when she was four months old and admitted to a London hospital in a state of emaciation and dehydration. After Kelly died, her parents Des and Sue Fitzgerald pleaded guilty in Castlebar Circuit Court to a charge of wilful neglect and were sentenced to eighteen months' imprisonment.

Lambeth Council had warned that another child in the Fitzgerald family was also on the at-risk register. The official minutes of a case conference at St Thomas' Hospital in London in March 1990 described this second child as "withdrawn, losing weight, marks noticed on her when doing PE, eating excessively, reluctant to go home from school at the end of the day, clingy, wants affection, pale, ghostlike eyes, sad and scared". She was the Fitzgeralds' third-born child, Geraldine, three years younger than Kelly and already stealing sandwiches from her classmates' lunch boxes at Larkhall School at the age of nine. Preparatory notes for a Western Health Board case conference about Kelly and Geraldine on 5 February 1993, under the heading 'Suspected Neglect', noted that at school in Scoíl Iosa, Carracastle, "both had a frightened look about them". In the welter of media coverage following Kelly's shocking death, Geraldine was obliquely mentioned in reports but never identified and then, wraith-like, she receded from the public's mind and ultimately vanished.

Fifteen years on, she is still underweight and riddled with bad health. Her lungs have collapsed twice and she has undergone surgery for a life-threatening condition classified as spontaneous pneumothorax. She has bad eyesight and suffers from asthma, migraines, irritable bowel syndrome and occasional kidney infections. She takes Valium and sees a psychologist every week. She believes her illnesses are associated with the trauma she has suffered throughout her life. She still bears scars on her back from the ritual beatings she says her father administered every day when she was aged ten, eleven and twelve.

Alienated from her parents, who remain in Carracastle, she lives in the West of Ireland with her husband Wade Thompson, a South African who has lived in Ireland for fourteen years and whom she married in September 2001. That was before she finally severed the communication cord with her parents. Initially, after their release from Mountjoy Prison she kept in touch, primarily to maintain contact with her siblings, including her baby sister who was born while Sue Fitzgerald was serving her jail sentence.

Geraldine invited her parents to her wedding reception in a hotel in Castlebar. Her father arrived late, dressed in mechanic's overalls, and told the bride: "You look like shit."

She is intelligent, attractive, distrustful, dignified, angry and strong-willed. She has no qualifications to pursue a career, having dropped out of secondary school when she went into 'self-destruction mode' while in care. She receives €185-a-week disability allowance and Wade receives the same amount in job seeker's allowance. Community Welfare contributes €74.50 to the couple's €150 weekly rent. They have fallen behind in repayments to the credit union for the loan they got to buy a car so that Geraldine could keep her appointments with the psychologist every week. "I've asked Community Welfare for money for clothing and food but, apart from once, they haven't given it to us. The rent allowance we get keeps going up and down. At one stage, we slept in the car for three nights. We'll soon be in serious debt."

Her dearth of knowledge about officialdom's dealings with her own case and with Kelly's is deeply disturbing, despite amassing a file of official documentation under the Freedom of Information Act, largely emanating from the Western Health Board. To date, she has failed to acquire her medical records from either Castlebar Hospital or St Thomas' in London and only discovered eight weeks ago that a Western-Health-Board-commissioned report exists, entitled "Kelly Fitzgerald: A Child Is Dead". Last Tuesday, she learned for the first time that the London coroner had formally concluded that Kelly died "from natural causes". It is as if Geraldine Fitzgerald has lived in a twilight zone all her life.

"I've got dreams. I've got ambitions,' she says, 'but my life hasn't changed. I'm doing this [interview] in the hope that my life can change. I'm twenty-seven years old and I feel my life is over, not beginning. I'm so sick and tired of it. I think I deserve something and I think she [Kelly] deserves something. I've fought so hard to be here all these years and what have I achieved?

'I am literally tired from the amount of times over the years that I've appealed to people to help me. I explain to them who

I am and what I'm going through and it still doesn't make a difference. The way I see life: you get born, you get f**ked, and then you die."

"She believes the reason she was singled out for what she describes as torture by her parents, from the age of five, was because she used to play with Kelly. "My father told us not to talk to Kelly, to pretend she didn't exist, because she'd been bold. Me and Kelly were separated from the others [there were three other siblings at that time]. We weren't allowed talk to them or play with them. We didn't get the treats they got."

At first, when they moved to Carracastle from London, Kelly stayed behind, residing with her grandparents and thriving for the time being. In Mayo, Geraldine was isolated. At night she was put outside the back door in her nightdress to sleep on the step with the dogs, until the dogs grew raucous with the cold and were brought inside. After her parents were informed that Geraldine had been breaking into neighbours' houses in the middle of the night, wrapped in a blanket, to steal bread, they put her to sleep in the bathroom with the door locked from the outside.

"Most of the time, I wasn't allowed into the house," she recalls. "While the rest of them would be having breakfast, I would be cleaning out the cowshed, restacking the turf and clearing up after the dogs. I had to walk the dogs every morning in my nightie – wind, rain or snow. I was never given anything extra to wear, except if somebody came to the house. I had to pick up the dog poop with my bare hands. If I missed any, my mother would take off her shoe and hit me on the head with it and then I'd have to clean and dry the shoes of the person who had stepped in it.

"When the chores were done, my father would make me do press-ups and run around the house.

"He used to stamp on my bare feet and hit me if the others fell over or hurt themselves. Sometimes, to make him stop hitting me, she (her mother) would slap me to make me cry.

"I never sat with the family for a meal. When they were eating, I was left outside. The only time I would be with them at mealtime would be when my father would tell me to stay and watch them eat. He'd offer me something on a plate but, when I went to take it, he would either put it down for the dogs or else throw it on the floor and tell me to eat it off the floor. Sometimes he made porridge and put a whole bag of salt in it or gave me dog-food and held my nose and forced me to eat it.' A teacher in Scoíl Iosa, noticing that Geraldine was coming to school with no lunch, apportioned some of her brother's lunchbox to the girl but Sue Fitzgerald went to the school and instructed the teacher to stop.

"My mother and father brought me to the bathroom every day and told me to take off all my clothes and he would beat me with his belt. The more I cried, the more he beat me. These beatings happened every day for three years."

(In a Health Board document outlining beatings suffered by Kelly at the hands of her father, it is repeatedly noted as "worrying" that Des Fitzgerald admitted he was sexually aroused during these beatings.)

"He hit me with a black pipe he used to have for the cows," Geraldine continues. "He said he hated me and I was a bitch. He said it was in the Bible that a father could take the rod to his child and that I made him do it. I was always warned by my parents to keep my socks up at school to hide the marks on my legs. Sometimes, after beating me, he'd fill the bath with water and put me into it and hold my head down under the water.

"On the school bus one day, I was crying and a girl in my class asked me what was wrong. I said I was afraid to go home but my parents found out and my father beat me with his belt.

"When the child psychologist used to call to the school, my father coached me in what to say to her. Sometimes, when I couldn't walk, I was kept home from school. I tried telling the neighbour, Mrs Duffy – she's dead now – and my parents beat me again.

"My brother, Rory (seven years younger than Geraldine), used to ask my mother for biscuits and he would bring them out to me but I was frightened for him. I used to be nice like that to Kelly and I got beaten for it and I couldn't let that happen to him. I told him not to play with me or talk to me."

After a fortnight away from the family, Kelly returned to live with them in Mayo for five months, until she was put on a plane at Knock Airport in a wheelchair and sent back to England.

"The social workers came to the house one day after that and we were all told to take ourselves off while they talked to my parents," Geraldine recalls. "My parents were really strange that day.

"They were really nice, and that wasn't good. I got to sleep in a bed and have food. In the middle of the night, the phone rang. My mother answered it and she started crying and I knew. I could feel it in the air. I asked my mother: 'What's wrong with you?' She just said: 'Kelly's dead.' The following day, we were taken into care.

"We were brought to the hospital in Castlebar. We were all in the same ward. We wanted to torment the doctors. One of us would put two others on a trolley and go wild, crashing into doors.

"It was the first time I felt like a child, happy. The social workers said we would be going into care and I said I'd rather go home and be beaten because that was what I knew. It didn't feel right at first, not being beaten. They said there was something wrong with me to feel like that.

"I went to a family in Tubbercurry with my younger brother, Rory. I had clothes and I had food and I had hugs whenever I wanted them. I had friends. I got my ears pierced. But the social workers said I should be upset because my sister had died. Everybody kept talking about Kelly and everybody was feeling sorry for my parents.

"When I tried to talk about me, they [her parents] said I was an attention seeker, that I was trying to take the attention away from Kelly. Nobody gave a continental about me. I started taking overdoses. I took a lot of them. If they had listened to me, I wouldn't have done that." She has not harmed herself since meeting her husband, Wade.

Geraldine and Rory were split up and sent to different families and, in her words, she 'went out of control'. She started smoking and drinking, self-harming and missing school. For most of the following six years, she stayed from Monday to Friday at St Anne's, a residential centre in Galway for children with psychological, behavioural and emotional problems. Her weekends were spent at another children's centre, Aiglish House, in Castlebar.

"In 1996 I tried to make a complaint [to bring charges against her parents for the abuse]," she says. "I was in fear of my family but they were allowed have contact with me and I ran away from Aiglish." A Health Board note of this time records that it was "no surprise" that she withdrew her complaint, following contacts with members of her family. What was surprising was that, as the garda investigation of her parents was underway, Geraldine and her siblings returned to the family home for three days that Christmas.

"We went to visit them once a month in Mountjoy. The social workers hired a mini-van and we would go up to Dublin and go back to Mayo in one day. My parents would say hello to everyone – 'How's it going? How's school?' – but they wouldn't want to know anything about me. While they were talking in one corner, I'd be sitting in another corner.

"An extra visit was arranged because it was my birthday. They were getting a cake and soft drinks and presents. I approached my mother for a hug and she said: 'Oh, I saw you the other day.'"

The agenda for a social workers' meeting about Geraldine, dated 3 March 1997, four years after Kelly's death, records: "Geraldine continues to be abused by her parents. While we have been able to protect Geraldine from the physical abuse that she experienced at home, we have been unable to protect her from the power and domination of her parents, particularly her father." The Health Board files attest to "the visible, ongoing rejection" of Geraldine by her parents on access visits.

"They didn't rescue me," she insists. "It was only when Kelly died that I was taken out of there. Even when I was in care, nothing was done without the consent of my parents. When the social workers wanted me to go to court to give evidence about what was done to Kelly, my father refused to give his permission.

"Even if it kills me, I am going to have my say now. The reason I didn't do it before was I thought I was to blame. People say that if you have been abused, you become an abuser yourself. I want people to know I'm not like that. I'm embarrassed; I'm ashamed of my life. People will say, 'Why is she doing this to her parents?' But the only thing I can think of is a voice saying: 'Please, Daddy, don't hurt me.'"

Ireland needs a new political party

A friend phoned with news of the revolution. "Ireland's going to become ungovernable," he predicted. "You won't see blood on the streets but there'll be more protests, more crime, more strikes and more tax evasion. Trust has broken down."

Sunday Tribune, 3 May 2009

That was the day the bus drivers abandoned their depots to strike in Dublin. Taxi drivers were clogging up Dublin city centre again with a rally outside the Dáil. The Revenue had warned about a re-emerging black economy. And between headlines about money-mad politicians commemorating the Easter Rising there was a press report that house burglaries are on the increase. Citizens are turning against each other: thieving and inconveniencing and begrudging fellow victims of a dysfunctional ruling class.

My friend was never one for hysterics. The conversation reminded me of another a few weeks ago with a hospital doctor who is admired by his colleagues for his bolshie advocacy on behalf of his patients. "I'm so full of anger," the doctor had confessed while deploring the inefficiencies of the HSE. "There's nothing more I can do. Nothing. They've all the power. I'm beginning to think I can't actually change anything."

His despair was temporary. The happy news is that normal service has resumed, judging by leaked accounts of the good doctor's fulminations on his patients' behalf as he keeps endeavouring to save lives. All the same, it was a worrying glitch.

The more we give into defeat, the greater the threat to our collective well-being. Abdicating our individual investment in society is the road to ruination, as our senior citizens are demonstrating. Radicalised by the government's withdrawal of medical cards for the over-70s last October and the discovery of their own political potency, they have founded the Senior Solidarity Party to contest June's local elections. It's a bracingly bold initiative by a section of the community the government had deemed electorally dispensable. There is such sweet symbiosis as the party's conception coincides with the demise of the PDs, who contributed disproportionately to the culture of individualism and greed exacerbating our present predicament. Protagonists of "grey power" teach the rest of us a lesson. Our problems do not stem from the sole fact that a small coterie of arrogant incompetents hold all the power, but that the many others motivated by principled goals are willing to surrender that power to them.

Abdicating our individual duty to help shape the nation can no longer be an option. A worrying vacuum exists in national politics. Government by Fianna Fáil and the Greens is an unfunny comedy of errors. The alternative offered by Fine Gael, despite Richard Bruton's impressiveness, is hardly reassuring. Eamon Gilmore and Joan Burton talk the people's language but Labour baulks at the prospect of fighting a general election without a Plan B coalition arrangement. Ultimately, it will always be amenable to getting into bed with Fianna Fáil. There are undecided voters who never wavered in their lives before now and for them, Declan Ganley, champion of capitalism and orthodox Catholicism, comes riding to the rescue. There are, indeed, worse indicators of poverty than a plummeting GDP.

Ireland needs a new political party; one that reflects the sweeping reassessments that have taken place in the past six months, ever since the old order started to disintegrate. The traditional left-right pigeonholes of politics have been brushed aside by those events, as have the divides tracing the fault lines of social class. No more are you a bleeding heart, pinko liberal if you decry injustice, political favouritism, unaccountability, mé-féinism, cronyism and inequality. There is a hunger for the new creed that the common good supercedes all else. Yet politicians still think they own the power. Ibec still thinks it owns the economy. And both of them think the rest of us so gullible that, if they tweak a few rules and banish a few faces from the boardroom, the people will be pacified.

One popular, coherent movement is what is required. This is not a time to repeat the mistakes of the last recession when single-issue candidates protesting against potholes and hospital closures exploited the big parties' hunger for power at any price.

One former politician who grew ever more disillusioned the more he listened to his colleagues and knew their utterances to be half-truths and untruths still believes that politics can achieve the impossible. I told him about the phone call with the despairing doctor who felt he could not really change anything but the politician said change was in the hands of all of us.

To my friend who called with news of the revolution, he would say: The time has come for the armchair analysts to stand up and be counted.

Your country needs you.

Just because Teflon is invisible when it is wrapped around the golden circle doesn't mean it is a figment of our imagination

One of Roald Dahl's stories is about an emperor so cruel his tailors trick him into believing their invisible cloth will insulate him against the most extreme Arctic cold. The emperor dons the cloth for a spot of skiing, and freezes to death. Once upon a time, I read that story and thought, "gullible fool".

Sunday Tribune, 19 April 2009

Nowadays, I read stories in the newspapers and think "what sort of fools are we?" They are stories like Dahl's. They are about illusionary things that we convince ourselves are real. Things like politicians' promises. Things like corporate ethics and fiscal justice and the same law applying to everyone equally. Things like the apostasy of crony capitalism and political nepotism.

There is a reason why Ireland boasts a world-beating body count of Nobel laureate writers. It's because we dwell contentedly in our imaginations. Our leaders tell us that, though we cannot see the hairshirts they are wearing, theirs are the same as ours. And we think how fetching they look in them. Blind faith has never been as unshakeable as it is in post-Catholic, post-boom Ireland.

Eight days after the finance minister said unequivocally in his budget speech that TDs would no longer receive long service increments we learn that, actually, they're still getting them. In the same breath, he said the income levies would be doubled from 1 May. Now they're being back-dated to 1 January. In the white glare of enlightenment, nobody mentions the word "dishonest".

This is a strange omission in a time of consensus that public trust must be restored after remorseless revelations of deceit in the Golden Circle. Is our complicity in this travesty motivated by a genetic inability to face the truth? Or is it that we are so utterly demoralised we feel we do not deserve to be told the truth? Those photographs of Bertie Ahern swanning around Fairyhouse with his "dig-out" buddy Joe Burke, while bar-room chatter across the land talks up "Whiparound"-Bertie-for-President, evoked Pearse's verdict when he decried: "The fools, the fools, the fools ..."

Another of the illusionary stories in the newspapers the other day was about Cromane Pier in Kerry. It seems politicians have been promising the pier since the 19th century and still they say it's coming. And still people will go out and vote for the politicians who keep promising the pier, just as did their parents and grandparents and their long-dead antecedents.

Our leaders know our appetite for fairytales is insatiable. So they feed us a steady supply, peppered with hypnotic words like "transparency" and "accountability". A current favourite is that crony capitalism, with its greedy, elitist cross-over directorships, is a thing of the past. Cronyism, we are told, is over.

Well, check this out for a game of musical chairs. Seanie Fitz quits Anglo Irish Bank in disgrace. His seat is taken by Donal O'Connor, chairman of Dublin Docklands Development Authority, where Seanie and his fellow Anglo director, Lar Bradshaw, previously reigned. O'Connor's DDDA seat, in turn, is taken by Gerry McCaughey, a poster boy of the builder brigade who brought us to the gates of Hades. McCaughey resigns a fortnight later when it emerges that he denied the exchequer €4.7m via a tax-avoidance scheme. When Bank of Ireland needs a new chief executive, it appoints Richie Boucher who, it turns out, advised Sean Dunne on the financing for his Ballsbridge site and urged Dublin City Council to grant it planning permission.

Now the state is setting up a half-way house to detoxify the banks' and builders' debts. Nama, this love child of incestuous market greed, is the brainchild of the economist, Peter Bacon.

Dr Bacon looks pleasant enough. He might be the most decent man you could meet. But he should not be dictating the bailout of the banks' development liabilities. Up to last summer, he sat on the board of Ballymore Properties, Ireland's biggest developer and winner of the controversial U2 Tower project in Dublin's docklands. Ballymore is reported to have borrowed up to a billion euro from the nationalised Anglo Irish Bank. The company's boss, Sean Mulryan, has been a regular development partner of Sean Dunne (whose Ballsbridge site is exempt from Nama's remit because the financier, Ulster Bank, is a non-national).

Apologists for Bacon's pivotal role in structuring Nama argue that he was Ballymore's European director and, therefore, uncontaminated by the company's liaisons in Ireland. What they do not mention is that, in Britain, for instance, Michael Fingleton's Irish Nationwide, which is seeking to extend the state guarantee scheme to pay €2.2bn it owes to overseas lenders, has partnered Ballymore in development projects. Ballymore and Irish Nationwide have a joint venture company registered in Oxford called Clearstorm to which Bacon was appointed a director in 2003.

Just because Teflon is invisible when it is wrapped around the Golden Circle doesn't mean it is a figment of our imagination.

The rest of it, though, you just couldn't make up.

Perhaps Our Lady might materialise on a slice of toast in the Four Seasons Hotel

When the moving statue of Ballinspittle kick-started a blitz of holy visions around the country during the last recession, some ill-advised workmen cleared a Marian shrine on the Cork-Dublin road for a spot of spring-cleaning. In the absence of the Blessed Virgin's plaster likeness, an anonymous joker stuck a sign on her pedestal, announcing: "Gone to Lunch".

Sunday Tribune, 12 July 2009

It's easy to scoff at the visionaries flocking to Rathkeale this past week to recite the rosary around a tree stump. Even the canonical responses to the screamingly dodgy phenomenon cannot keep the smirk off their statements. Yet, some of the pilgrims have exhibited a ruthlessly honest assessment of their own states of mind, such as the lady who confessed: "My eyes are showing me what my heart wants to see." Time and again, people descending on the west Limerick town, eager to tap into reliable, old-fashioned religious ecstasy, have marvelled at how it has brought the disparate together. Young and old, they say, are united in prayer. Believers and non-believers. Settled folk and members of the Travelling community; a tangible beneficence in a town where the ethnic tensions are sometimes palpable. The word 'sharing' peppers their testimonies like an essential ingredient.

One can only hope that Our Lady will soon make a personal appearance in or around Government Buildings and in the vicinity of Ibec's parallel planet on Baggot Street. Perhaps she might materialise on a slice of toast in the Four Seasons Hotel while the ruling elite power-breakfast over their list of demands for self-preservation. Or her silhouette might become imprinted on the cufflinks of a strutting banker as a shock deterrent from the road to perdition. Our Lady of Nama, help us.

For we are desperately, woegeously slow learners. Nine months ago, we were Paul heading for Damascus, awaking to the catastrophic madness of rampant, greed-driven capitalism. We were wrapped in a charismatic renewal, rejecting the deadly sins of self-interest, avarice, profit-worship, arrogance, nepotism, vulgar display and lording it over the fellow with the smaller house and the Citroen Saxa. When the over-70s rebelled in the Westland Row church against the hijacking of their medical cards and Sean FitzPatrick was exposed as a hypocrite and a cheat, we were converted en masse to the creed of everyone-pulling-together.

Well, actually, no. That was an illusion too.

A Nobel Prize-winning economist from Harvard told an audience in Trinity College on Thursday night that it is time to find "a new capitalism". Professor Amartya Sen said we need to develop "a sharing ethic". He's right, of course, but there is little point in preaching to the converted. Was Tom Parlon, who called electricians deprived of their rightful pay "lunatics", in the professor's audience? Were Brian Cowen, Mary Coughlan and Brian Lenihan there, blushing at their high-handedness in spending fortunes we do not have to shore up the banks while depriving the poor of their Christmas bonuses and keeping An Bord Snip Nua's tough medicine a secret from the beleaguered taxpayer? Was Bertie Ahern, who encouraged those who advised caution to commit suicide, listening? Or his buddy, Sean "Baron of Ballsbridge" Dunne, he who calls economists who foretold the downward plunge "hyenas".

The establishment's consensus last week that the electricians were the anti-patriots putting the entire economy at risk was proof that all the talk of turning our backs on liberal capitalism was no more than empty words. Employers who withheld the pay they agreed two years ago for work done cast themselves in the role of the well-intentioned wronged. So indoctrinated is the establishment in the capitalist gospel that scarcely anyone demurred. Never mind that it was the construction industry that pulled the rug from under the economy. Never mind that we now have to find countless billions to buy builders' and developers' debts to rescue the banks. Never mind that 62% of construction employers inspected last year by the National Employment Rights Authority had breached employment rules.

In the stand-off with the electricians, employers have argued that everyone knew the economy was up the Swannee in 2007, when the new pay rates were agreed. Come again? I seem to recall a certain Mr Parlon advising all and sundry in the springtime of 2008 that there was never a better time to buy a house. Already, the establishment is wriggling out of its promises to find a better way than the cosy capitalism that created our old fools' paradise, the Celtic Tiger. That is because, deep down inside, it does not believe in the concept of sharing.

Bring on the moving statues, I say.

He recalled his parents drunken violence, their piercing words

Peter Fitzsimons was a household name in Irish fashion when we met. I expected him to be suave and as big as his reputation. He wasn't. He was small with a half-hearted beard and a Dublin accent. He was a maverick. He used to hire models to come over from London for photo-shoots of his new-season collections, having been sent one too many Irish girls with "no chin, I swear – no chin". One such was Catherine Dyer, a gazelle of a creature who would soon be the new Mrs David Bailey. Peter took Catherine and me to dinner. Their shop gossip was scandalous and strictly off-the-record. I marvelled at how relaxed Peter was in the company of Catherine's other-worldliness.

Sunday Tribune, 9 June 2009

Later, we met by chance in town one morning. Peter asked what story I was writing for the paper. Before I could answer, he said he had a better one. Tears ran down his face as, there in Grafton Street, he told me that he grew up neglected and battered by his parents. The term "child abuse" was still Ireland's little secret in those twilight years of the 1980s. He said he wanted his story written in the paper. He wanted to be named and photographed for it. He was adamant. We arranged to meet another day for a proper interview. He recalled his parents' drunken violence, their piercing words, the names they called him, the menial jobs they made him do from when he was a tiny fellow, lugging coal up the stairs to their flat, how they beat him so badly he was seldom free of bruises.

Looking back, what is extraordinary is that there was no reaction to the article. No threatening letters came from lawyers. No scrawled, vitriolic missives from indignant fundamentalists. No opening of the floodgates for other victims to tell their stories. It was as if Peter's story was so aberrant it warranted no discussion.

Peter had no regrets. He was attending a psychiatrist, trying to cope with his memories. He went on making beautiful clothes. Each Christmas, he arrived in the office with a garment he had made for me. One year there was a gorgeous parachute silk coat which, he instructed, should never be belted. Another Christmas, he brought a black-and-white polka-dot summer skirt full of pleats and promises. That was the year he succeeded in dying.

In the years afterwards, the other stories came out. Andrew Madden told of being sexually abused as an altar boy by Fr Ivan Payne. Colm O'Gorman told of his abuse by Fr Saan Fortune. There was the Kilkenny incest case. The Kelly Fitzgerald case. Each one was regarded in isolation. Even the Ferns report cataloguing child abuse by more than 20 priests, was treated as something confined to frustrated celibates. Ditto the Cloyne report. Now we have the Ryan report. Each time, we compartmentalise it. We render the horror containable by a process of labelling. We put it in a box marked "Church" or "Schools" or "Incest" or "Institutions". And so we hot-house the climate in which the abuse of children flourishes.

It is the same instinct that caused us to brag infinitely that Ireland was the best country in the world for bringing up children. The land of leprechauns and saints and scholars was an Arcadian wonderland for children. Nobody challenged it. Babies were exported to America for adoption. Those kept behind were viciously beaten in school and at home and the poorer children were carted off to bleak institutions. When the Celtic Tiger came, our child-loving nation built more golf courses than playgrounds. A High Court judge had to threaten a government minister with jail to secure accommodation for children at risk. We have spasms of debate about a children's referendum but it never happens. Children suffering mental ill health are either ignored or dumped in adult hospitals. The children's ombudsman has to issue public threats to get the HSE to cooperate with her investigation of child-protection procedures. Wards are being shut down in Crumlin children's hospital. The DPP keeps sending back garda files on child abuse with orders that no charges be brought.

People ask why Ireland has such a diabolical history of child abuse. Perhaps the endemic casual disrespect for our child fellow citizens has something to do with it. We need to acknowledge that before we go hammering commemorative plaques into the edifice of the state as a gesture to survivors.

Peter never gave up on Ireland. He loved his country. But, as Laurence Durrell put it, he hated it creatively too. He may have complained that our models lacked chin, but he believed in our backbone. We owe it to him and all the others to display it now.

To suggest disbanding the children's office just two months after the Ryan report on institutional abuse is beyond belief

Of all the images used in news coverage of the Leas Cross report, the saddest was a television close-up of somebody's mottled, aged feet. It spoke volumes. These were feet that had lived. Once upon a time, they would have skipped to school. Later, they might have danced a waltz or a jive or a three-hand reel. Maybe they played footsie under a table and walked up a church aisle to stand beside a forever love and ran through summer meadows and trudged through rain to get home, safe, and curled up on a child's bed to read a night-time story.

Sunday Tribune, 19 July 2009

The camera operator's trick to convey the humanity at the heart of the Leas Cross scandal while preserving the dignity of the owner of those feet stirred something ineffably poignant. Those feet will not dance or skip again. They have lost their independence. They depend on others now to get them from A to B. From bed to the armchair to the dining table. What was once taken for granted requires the exertions of others, maybe strangers. The old givens of mobility and self-reliance, of freedom of choice and a personally determined routine have been substituted by something that requires the utmost trust in other human beings.

That is what is so inexpressibly painful.

To reach the end of your life and discover you cannot place your trust in others must be frightening. To be thrown like a sack or left sitting in an uncomfortable position, maybe smelling your own urine, to be ignored when you try to attract someone's attention, to realise in what might be rare lucid moments you are no longer to be treated as part of the human race.

There was as much symbiosis as there was choreography in the release of Diarmuid O'Donovan's report last Thursday; the same day the government published Colm McCarthy's Bord Snip Nua proposals for €5.3bn state savings. While the O'Donovan report chronicled the chilling story of what happens when basic human sensitivities are consistently insulted, the McCarthy report was entirely constructed in a desert of human considerations. Most everyone said that was proper and correct. After all, McCarthy deals in the cold science of economics. His job was simply to enumerate all the possibilities. It is up to politicians to choose from his litany of Hobson's choices. For, as someone once said, if you laid all the economists in the world end to end they still would not reach a conclusion.

Finance ministers do not have the luxury of confining their decisions to the realm of the balance sheet. They have to think about the political consequences of whatever measures they adopt. Unfortunately for the citizen, the political exigencies do not always equate with the best interests of a society. That is why McCarthy's proposition that the office of the Children's Ombudsman be disbanded is deeply disturbing. On whom can we rely to uphold one of our society's most flaunted values, our commitment to cherishing children?

To economists, children are an expense to be pruned. To politicians, they are not a constituency, unlike farmers or trade unionists or even – as they learned to their cost last October – older people. The establishment has shown over and over again how dispensable it regards the rights and status of children to be in the greater scale of political coordinates.

That anybody could suggest eroding the children's office just two months after tales of the most unimaginable horrors poured out of the Ryan report on institutional abuse is beyond belief. The overriding text of that report was society's failure to listen to children, to believe them and to protect them. They had nobody to turn too. When Emily Logan was appointed the inaugural Children's Ombudsman in December 2003, it followed a recruitment process that involved children interviewing candidates for the job. That was a marvellous gesture of empowerment by a country that has shed an ocean of crocodile tears for children over the decades.

Logan's office is not perfect. But it is a harbour with a beacon and it only costs about €2m a year to run, godammit. Its staff comprises former nurses, social workers and teachers; people with special insights into the world of children. How are they to fit into a generic ombudsman's office along with the information commissioner and the data protection commissioner?

Contrary to the consensus that Colm McCarthy's recommendations will prove politically unpalatable to the cabinet paymasters, there are elements of the state who would shed no tears over the abolition of the Children's Ombudsman's office. Logan is currently investigating the incarceration of children in St Patrick's prison, deaths of children in the care of the state, the HSE's handling of the Catholic Church audit of child sexual abuse complaints and the non-implementation of the 'Children First' guidelines.

Commentators agree Ireland will be impoverished if it does not slash and burn, as prescribed by McCarthy. But we will be an even poorer nation if we lock the door on those of our citizens who are only learning to skip and run and dance and live.

History is full of accidental heroes

Sheila Cloney left instructions that no eulogy was to be delivered at her funeral. She must have known it would be a brave soul who would defy her wishes, even after she had departed this world. Anyway, who could find words for her?

Sunday Tribune, 5 July 2009

A friend of Sheila and Seán tells me there was so much more to her than the Fethard boycott that publicly pigeon-holed her. She loved opera. In later years, she played Lyric FM day and night. She was a fine horsewoman. She was a loyal friend. She didn't trust people easily. She was petite and didn't dye her hair when it turned grey. When she was a girl, her father, Tommy Kelly, was a well-to-do cattle dealer who was wont to bundle up his children's perfectly good clothes for poor children he encountered around Wexford's Hook. Sheila would be despatched on horseback to deliver them. Matters of conscience never were optional in the Kellys' DNA.

When she told Fr Stafford to take a flying jump with his 'ne temere' diktat that her daughters receive a Roman Catholic education, she would have been acting on moral instinct. She wasn't planning to change the world. Nor did she intend her father's cattle business to be sacrificed, as it was, along with other prosperous Protestant businesses in the locality. She didn't plan for a movie to be made about it one day; a film she would never watch. Because she spent the rest of her life shunning publicity, most of us imagine Orla Brady, the actress who played her in *A Love Divided*, when we hear Sheila Cloney mentioned. Even upon her death, no pictures of her appeared in the newspapers.

When the movie was released in the US eight years ago, the League of Decency sneered that it was "based on an allegedly true story" and that "cruel caricatures of the Catholic clergy abound". The league's president, a William Donohue, denounced it as "an anti-Catholic film" whereas it was an anti-demagoguery movie with a wardrobe left over from *The Thornbirds*. When Sheila Cloney fled with her daughters to Belfast and onward to the Orkney Islands to escape the Catholic Church's proprietorial clutches, she was to the holy, patriarchical Ireland of 1957 what the witches were to Salem. Whatever about eluding the Catholic Church, a young, strong-willed Protestant woman taking on the establishment of a repressed society had no hope of evading history.

She was feisty. She and Seán had a tempestuous marriage. She once told someone close to her that she loved her husband from the day she met him until the day he died. That will be 10 years ago next October. Seán Cloney spent his last years in a wheelchair, following a motor accident and botched surgery. He too was a champion, pursuing justice for people who had been sexually abused as children by priests in the diocese of Ferns. He reposes in the Catholic graveyard in Templetown alongside an uncle who was a Catholic canon. One of their three daughters, Mary, who died a year before him, is buried in the Church of Ireland graveyard in Fethard-on-Sea. For herself, Sheila chose cremation.

As in life, the Cloneys' love may appear divided but it still triumphs. How fitting that, in the week Sheila died, it was reported that civil marriage ceremonies will soon outnumber their church cousins. Whether she liked it or not, it is her legacy that couples tying the knot these days recognise wedlock as a tough enough challenge without the encumbrance of a procreation-for-Rome decree. A religious ceremony is joyous and meaningful for many couples and it is to be encouraged when appropriate but what Sheila Cloney taught Ireland is that making personal choices is what being grown up is all about.

A Protestant woman I know married a Catholic man in 1979. They chose to have a ceremony in her church, officiated by ministers of both persuasions. After the bride-to-be declined to sign the 'ne temere' pledge to bring their offspring up as Catholics, there were unaccountable delays in acquiring the dispensation from his church which the groom required to marry his Protestant girlfriend. It eventually arrived one week before the wedding, adding to the stress of an already stressful time. The husband has never since entered a Catholic church, other than for funerals.

History is full of accidental heroes because it is in the most prosaic choices that the most seismic shifts occur. As Seán Cloney said in his last recorded interview, God chooses his most humble people to instigate the greatest changes. While Éamon de Valera was praised in the Seanad last week for his intervention in the Fethard boycott, Sheila Cloney went to her resting place without a church eulogy. Can you get more humble?

Gerald Barry was allowed say what he wanted about the girl he murdered ... lies now imprinted on the nation's record

He swore she wanted it. He said they lay down together on that scrubby patch of wasteground on the shortcut into Galway city and made love. He said she died in a post-coital freak accident. He made it sound tender.

Sunday Tribune, 31 May 2009

Anywhere you went during those days while he was in the witness box, snatches of his story blared out from radios and televisions. If you had been following the trial, you might have realised how outlandish it was. When you got into a taxi, or wandered into your own kitchen or queued for your lunch sandwich or boarded the bus going home and it was already bellowing out the latest radio bulletin, it might have seemed plausible. Most people are sceptical rather than cynical and sceptics are as inclined to believe as to disbelieve. The medium of reporting gave his words a veneer of credibility. You might have thought: "Maybe he's telling the truth. She was 17 and away from the watchful eye of home. She was a continental girl after all, presumably with liberated continental ideas. Maybe she did want it, like he says."

Gerald Barry was allowed say whatever he wanted about the girl he murdered. His despicable lies are now imprinted on the nation's record. Manuela Riedo had no voice. He traduced her virtue. He said she was the sort of girl who would meet a stranger on wasteground on a dark night and lie down there and then and have sex with him. He was unanimously found guilty of murdering her. He was given the mandatory life sentence. He got another five years each for stealing her phone and her camera. He went unpunished for raping her. That he had terrorised her and invaded her before killing her was not treated as a significant matter in the administration of justice. Nor was he penalised for grotesquely trampling on the memory of her; all that was left to her heartbroken parents, Arlette and Hans-Peter Riedo, as they sat in that courtroom and listened to his lies about their only child.

The jury in the murder trial was not permitted to know that Barry had already killed a man, blinded another man and raped a young woman. Yet he was given carte blanche to denigrate Manuela Riedo. Had he raped her and not murdered her and the case had proceeded to trial and he had pleaded guilty, he would have qualified for a more lenient sentence for saving her the distress of testifying. In either scenario, he gets rewarded for her enforced silence. That is a savage injustice. To the contrary, the law should increase his punishment for compounding his crime by lying about his victim on oath. His lawyers – even if impervious to how far-fetched his defence sounded – could warn him he would stay in jail longer if he usurped his position to defame his victim. As it is, he will be out by the time he is 40.

By a twisted coincidence, on the same day that Barry was convicted of raping a 21-year-old French woman just two months before he murdered Manuela, elsewhere in the Four Courts, another murder victim was being denied a voice. The brother and sister of Finbarr Dennehy wanted the *Irish Daily Star* to be prosecuted for criminal libel for wrongly reporting that his death was caused by a bizarre sex game. His siblings' application last Thursday was refused in the High Court because, the judge explained, you cannot libel the dead.

For all our pious breast-beating since the publication of the Ryan report, events in our criminal courts last week indicate that, as a society, we still harbour an unquestioned ambivalence about sexual crimes. Remember the C Case? It plunged the country into paroxysms of moral outrage in 1997 when a 13-year-old girl became pregnant. Anti-abortionists swooped into the girl's neighbourhood in a convoy of four-wheel drives to persuade her guardians she should be made to give birth to her rapist's baby. The rapist, Simon McGinley, was back in court last week, convicted of raping an 86-year-old woman with Alzheimer's disease in her home. It turns out he had only served five years of his 12-year sentence for "unlawful carnal knowledge" of the 13-year-old girl.

Why did McGinley only do five years for raping a child? Why was Barry free to murder Manuela when he had killed one man, blinded another and raped a woman? And why, Minister Dermot Ahern, do you think victims of child abuse will troop into garda stations around the country with evidence to convict their torturers in industrial schools?

Why, oh why, oh why do we insist that the victims do our donkey work for us when we cannot even safeguard their dignity in a courtroom? Even when they are dead?

At long last, we're getting our sense of humour back

Sunday Tribune, 15 March 2009

"I'm going to tell you a joke," said this elderly lady I know who perennially wears daffodil yellow and enters rooms like sunshine. "Are you ready?"

"Ready," said I.

"What's the difference between an Irish banker and a pigeon?"

I give up. What's the difference?

"A pigeon can still put a deposit on a Beemer," she erupted in gales of glee. "I heard it on the radio. Good isn't it? You get tired of all the bad news."

I recycled it, as one is obliged to do with jokes. Everyone laughed, even if some groaned too, for theatrical effect. It spread little rays of relief over our bleak socio-economic landscape. In return, someone enlightened me as to the definition of optimism – "A banker ironing five shirts on Sunday night".

The two Brians tell us it's our patriotic duty to take this recession seriously, but they're wrong. What the country needs is lots of laughter.

An attitudes survey last week discovered that the thing that makes us happiest to be Irish is our sense of humour. If it is possible to generalise about the characteristics of a people, Irish wit is waspish and deadly. It can slice a sacred cow in two with a single punchline.

But we've got a little bit rusty lately. We've been much too busy playing po-faced rich westerners marooned in our traffic jams and the exurbs. That joke about the difference between Iceland and Ireland – I promise I won't repeat it! – seems to have reawakened our appetite for a good, spine-chillingly funny joke. It's free and it's legal.

In the bad old days before the Celtic Tiger, witticisms proliferated. Back then, Michael Smurfit gave Dublin a fountain to grace O'Connell Street. It was slinky and modern, representing a prostrate woman with mermaid tresses, and it was called Anna Livia, but not for long. Dubliners christened her the Floozie in the Jacuzzi.

When the life-size bronze statue of Molly Malone and her wheelbarrow materialised at the bottom of Grafton Street, she was dubbed the Tart with the Cart. The two sculpted housewives sitting on a bench beside the Ha'penny Bridge, their shopping at their feet, were never known as anything other than the Hags with the Bags. Charlie Haughey's vanity refurbishment project on Government Buildings became Chateau Charlemagne.

Those were the days of The Flynnstones and Mar-A! on Scrap Saturday when the country ground to a stop every week for its fix of scathing satire. It's no coincidence that Newstalk began airing its own version yesterday in the guise of The Emergency.

We haven't needed to laugh at ourselves this much since the time the Olympic shot-putter demolished the net, twice. Sure, if you didn't laugh, you'd cry. It's therapy.

As Joseph O'Connor, the guru of humour who has the nation in stitches every week with his radio column, prescribes "We're a shook-up, mixed up post-Tiger nation/Somewhat in need of consolation."

There are signs that our sense of humour is returning. There was an ad on the radio recently for a "pre-boom" sale in a tile shop that made me want to renovate the bathroom in gratitude for the joke.

In Eddie Rockets, I ordered cheese fries on the side after reading the disclaimer running along the bottom of the new menu: "We are not responsible for lost or stolen articles, bad punctuation, the recession, mispeled words or the weather!"

Finally, a special word of thanks is due to Mr Prawo Jazdy, the most wanted driver in Ireland, better known as Mr Driving Licence (but lost in translation to the gardaí), for teaching us that it's good to be able to laugh at ourselves again.

The 2010s

Women kneel to church that relies on their subservience

It felt like *Father Ted* on tour on the number seven bus last week. Each morning, it picked up possses of pilgrims and disgorged them at Dublin's RDS for the International Eucharistic Congress. Women massively outnumbered men, their cheerfulness contagious.

The Sunday Times, 17 June 2012

One morning, a Colombian pilgrim sitting beside me asked if I'd like to come to today's mass in Croke Park. "But aren't all the tickets sold?" I said. No, said she, they had been urged at the congress to bring along anyone they met. Little did I think as a schoolchild learning about Irish missionaries proselytising in the jungle that I'd be targeted for conversion aboard a double-decker on the Rock Road.

That same morning, a Canadian boarded at Booterstown and sat beside a tiny old lady. "How're you doing?" boomed the Canadian, companionably. "I had my last cigarette this morning," replied the elderly Irish woman. She was getting fit, she explained, for a beach holiday in Spain. The Canadian shook with laughter.

Another day, as the bus trundled past a church with an outdoor sculptural depiction of the crucifixion, two pilgrims were photographing each other kissing Jesus's feet. Inside the bus, a country woman was assuring someone on the phone that she was praying for them and that the congress was jammers with cardinals.

Each morning, after they disembarked at the RDS, silence engulfed the number seven. Gone were the women with their laughter and their enthusiastic godliness; these pillars who launder the altar cloths and fix the flowers, who keep house for the priests and rouse sullen families for mass and who are forever stoking the fires of faith. A colleague who visited the congress told me she saw women queuing like groupies to kiss the cardinals' rings.

Sometimes you see Muslim women attired like walking tents and you wonder why on earth they collude in their own oppression. All week I watched these Catholic women on the bus and I wondered the same. For all their devoted sunniness, it is because of women like these that the Church authorities feel they can go on treating half the population as simpletons.

It is also why, despite decades of awakening to the abuse of children under the eye of the Church, Irish society has never acknowledged the systemic abuse of women by a church-indoctrinated state.

While the pilgrims flock to kiss cardinals' rings, there are 164 Irish women known to be living with the chronic after-effects of symphysiotomy, a barbarous Catholic-endorsed procedure whereby the pelvis was surgically unhinged during childbirth. Should they have wished to, many of them would have been incapable of attending the congress because of incessant pain, incontinence and immobility.

This is the same Church that demanded women submit to

"churching" purification ceremonies each time they engaged in the filthy business of childbirth. It is the same Church that wrenched children from their mothers and had them exported to America for adoption, in cahoots with the state's airline, Aer Lingus. The same Church that incarcerated women in Magdalene Laundries where they skivvied for their sins. The same Church that deems women unfit to be priests or even lowly deacons and which, just this year, produced a gender-cleansing version of the liturgy that eradicates seditious female pronouns.

The women at last week's congress were reciting responses day after day that are designed to deny their very existence. Good as they are, I wanted to shake them and say it's this ingrained subservience that allows the Irish state to take the Church by the hand and dance all over women's human rights.

Were it men who had their reproductive organs routinely ripped out by Michael Neary, would the surgeon who worked for nuns at Our Lady of Lourdes hospital in Drogheda have got off scot-free from the criminal law? If Miss X and Miss C had been teenage boys instead of teenage girls, would the state have forced them to give life to their rapists' offspring? If men could get pregnant, would the state expect them to carry their anencephalic babies to full term only to watch them die horribly within hours of birth, or would the state force men to travel abroad for terminations when they get cancer and need life-saving treatment? If the survival of the species meant men had wombs, would our whole society keep schtum about the scandal that every hospital in the state refuses to perform abortions made legally permissible by a 20-year-old judgment of the Supreme Court?

No, because men would not stand for it. Women, conditioned by generations of servitude, are our own worst enemies.

Devout Catholic females are not, by definition, stupid; just encumbered with an irrational optimism. Women of proven intelligence were invited to speak at workshops during the congress – though none who has ever expressed a subversive sentiment in the public square. Mary McAleese, the former president and former pro-vice chancellor of Queen's University Belfast, a professor of criminal law and a canon lawyer, towers intellectually over many of the hierarchy, yet she is unfit to run an office in the Holy See.

As winds of decline blow through the Catholic Church in America and Europe, acquiescent women are the glue holding the facade together. There are signs that it's starting to come unstuck.

Last Tuesday two American nuns, Sisters Pat Farrell and Janet Mock of the Leadership Conference of Women Religious, were summoned to meet Cardinal William Levada in the Vatican. Levada's Congregation for the Doctrine of the Faith has accused American nuns of going rogue with talk of "radical feminism" when they should be warning against the evils of abortion and same-sex marriage. Nuns across America are unrepentant.

In Ireland, the American nuns have a burgeoning support group. Their counterparts here, who run schools and hospitals with Fortune 500 efficiency, are formidable women. Imagine what might happen if they joined forces with the Association of Catholic Priests (ACP) and told Rome they will no longer tolerate being treated as underlings.

The ACP has demonstrated that it is up to the ordained religious to give a lead to a blindly orthodox laity. The slogan on one pilgrim's recyclable bag said it all on Thursday morning as she stepped off the bus at the RDS. "Use me again and again," it said.

So now we know that Quinn was stupid as well as greedy

What do you expect to get when you order a €100,000 wedding cake, as did Seán Quinn's family? Marilyn Monroe leaping out of its snowy vastness in a slashed whiter-than-the-bride frock to huskily sing "I want to be loved by you"? Men in white coats, more like.

The Sunday Times, 7 October 2012

The Quinnasty had the cake flown in "fresh" from New York for daughter Ciara's nuptials in 2007, and sent the tab to the Quinn Group for payment. According to the newly published property register, you could buy 12 houses in south Roscommon for the same price. I wonder were the 400 guests informed of the price of their gateau, and did they choke on it? Did Ireland's patriots turn in their graves when Seán Quinn, that great Irishman who selflessly made himself the 164th richest human on earth so he could give his neighbours jobs, deemed Tea Time Express beneath him?

The revelation that the cake stood a towering six-feet tall, consisted of nutty meringue and was adorned with cascading flowers that each took an hour to sculpt cannot explain what the Quinnasty could have possibly thought justified the exorbitant price. Its creator, Sylvia Weinstock, has disclosed that she is in the habit of instructing airline pilots not to brake suddenly when she is escorting one of her cakes. That surely trumps all other metaphors for the prevailing cultural ethos.

Once upon a time, Seán Quinn belonged to an elite called "wealth creators". In Celtic Tiger Ireland, wealth creators were messiahs, endowed with supernatural powers.

They could look at a field of nettles in Bally-go-backwards and see the next Taj Mahal, complete with roulette tables and high-rollers in tuxedos. Wealth creators had vision and chutzpah and nerves of steel. They were the cleverest of the tribe.

Buying a €100,000 cake isn't clever. It's stupid. Anybody who has ever planned a wedding knows the cake is only a prop for the photographs. Ten supermodels would have provided a backdrop for the same price. Wedding cake is designed for feasting the eyes; not for eating after the beef wellington and baked alaska. Unattached females might liberate a wedge to place under their pillows and dream of George Clooney cooing "I do", but that's about the height of its usefulness.

Ciara Quinn's cake has taken its place in the iconography of Ireland's boom-time excess. It's up there with Johnny Ronan's flight from Enniskerry to Marrakesh for an after-hours drink with a former Miss World. Seán Mulryan flew Debbie Harry, the singer with 1980s band Blondie, to sing for him at his Co Kildare stud farm on his 50th birthday. Seán Dunne hired Aristotle Onassis's yacht for his wedding reception.

Diarmuid Martin, the Archbishop of Dublin, said last week that children's first holy communions should be simple affairs, not extravagant displays of spending. The same philosophy should apply to their parents' weddings. Isn't gluttony a sin? Spending €250 on a slice of cake when there are children starving in the world is not just stupidity. It is unconscionable stupidity.

It beggars belief that, despite what we now know about the purportedly modest-living Seán Quinn, there are people who still regard him as a victim of greed, not the epitome of it. So indignant are they at the supposed injustice being perpetrated against Ireland's once richest man, his supporters are giving him €2m to take his victimhood case to the courts, the same courts for which he has shown nothing but contempt.

Defenders of ostentatious acquisitiveness à la the Quinnasty argue that the rich have a duty to spend their wealth. Think of the damage to the environment, if nothing else, caused by cakes flying across the Atlantic and pub crawls stretching from Wicklow to Morrocco.

A story flourished on the grapevine back in the days of plenty that one multimillionaire couple instructed their household staff to keep the engines continually running in their garaged supercars so that the interiors would be balmy when they climbed in. You think that's far-fetched? I recently read a review of a book about conspicuous consumption that recounted the daftness of one rich man's ambition. So badly did he want to be known as the man who paid the highest price for a painting that he bid for it twice – against himself.

It's tempting to scoff at the Quinnasty's crassness. For all their wealth when they had it, they were pathologically lacking in self-esteem. Why else would they have bought a €100,000 cake other than to flaunt their capacity to spend money? These, after all, are people who pride themselves on knowing the prices of things, and bargaining them down. Stephen Kelly, one of Seán Quinn's sons-in-law, once swapped a €380 laptop for a €9.8m building in Russia.

Capitalism needs stupidity in order to work. If people didn't behave idioticially and go shopping for frightfully expensive things they don't actually need, the rich wouldn't keep getting richer. It's precisely because money buys status in a society of commodities that we have phenomena such as gated communities on the one hand, and ghettos on the other. It is oxymoronic to buy a €100,000 cake and call yourself a republican; moronic being the operative part of the word.

The luxury goods market is predicated on producing things people don't need. Walk down the Croisette in Cannes and you will see diamond-studded mobile phones selling for the price of capacious homes in some Central American countries. Rich people spend astronomical amounts of money on art, then lock it away in bank vaults and hang imitations on their walls.

This is the attitude that inspired former tycoons to buy acres of land, iconic hotels, golf courses, trophy properties and whole streets during the boom. The governing theory is that there is no such thing as enough.

For the two minutes Ireland considered itself rich at the start of this millennium, we showed the world how to spend because, as everybody knows, you'll never beat the Irish. Some people who have become household names became champions of inane expenditure, the bread-and-butter of the capitalist model.

Encouraging stupid behaviour in order to create market demand is big business. Its beneficiaries are often its best exponents, which means that the cleverest of the tribe can be the most stupid, too.

This is no utopia for children but it can be a better place

March 1, 1993 was an inhospitable night. I remember it well because I spent most of it in a photographer's car, searching scattered rural villages for a young woman whose name we did not know. The editor of my then newspaper had sent us on what seemed a wild-goose chase. "Find the girl in the Kilkenny incest case," he had instructed us. We did not even know what part of the county she came from.

The Sunday Times, 16 September 2012

As we lurched from one village to the next, the car radio poured forth details of the case. That day, the girl's father had been jailed for seven years after pleading guilty in the Central Criminal Court to six sample charges of rape, incest and assault. Over the years, his daughter had accumulated broken bones, urological and gynaecological injuries, a dislocated finger, chronic leg pain and a loss of vision in her right eye. At 15, she conceived a child by her father. After the birth, her mother accompanied her to a clinic to obtain contraceptives. It was a real-life horror story in an Ireland of unquestioned happy families.

We stopped at a chipper in either the fourth or fifth village. On hearing of our quest, the girl behind the counter told us to wait and she left the shop. A few minutes later, she returned. Her friend was willing to meet us, she said. We were directed to a dour building down the street. We climbed a rickety staircase all the way to the top. At the back of the building, beneath the eaves, we found the two of them. The girl was a huddled, washed-out spectre in the crepuscular light. Her son was slumbering under a bundle of thin blankets. She told us he had learnt that day that his grandfather was his father.

Judge Catherine McGuinness published her report on the Kilkenny incest case in 1993 and introduced Ireland to the reality that all families – good and wicked alike – are protected by a constitutional padlock.

"We believe the very high emphasis on the rights of the family in the constitution may, consciously or unconsciously, be interpreted as giving a higher value to the rights of parents than to the rights of children," she wrote. She referred to "ambivalence towards family violence [that] goes right across the community" and recommended an amendment to enshrine children's rights.

We did not know that night in Kilkenny that another child had died the month before on the other side of Ireland, as a result of what Máire Geoghegan-Quinn, then the minister for justice, described as "the most horrific abuse case in the history of the state".

On her death bed, Kelly Fitzgerald's battered, bruised and skeletal body bore witness to a lifetime of torture at the hands of her parents, Des and Susan Fitzgerald, who lived in Carracastle, Co. Mayo. In 1996, a report on the case by Owen Keenan, a former chief executive of Barnardos, reiterated McGuinness's recommendation for a referendum. Their calls have been echoed in a chorus of similar reports down through the years.

In the 2006 Baby Ann adoption case, McGuinness observed in her Supreme Court judgment that the biological parents, who sought the return of their two-year-old child from her foster parents, had married eight months earlier after receiving legal advice that to do so would strengthen their position.

She "reluctantly" consented to the application, having noted that the only person in the case whose interests and rights were not represented by lawyers or a guardian ad litem was the child.

Next year will be the 20th anniversary of the Kilkenny incest report. By then, the referendum promised for 20 years will have been and gone but there is no guarantee that it will have been carried.

As referendum day looms, what once seemed a cause of consensus and good sense is eliciting entrenched resistance. Often, those opposed preface their objections with: "I'm all in favour of children's rights but ..."

The spine of opposition is a conservative Catholic constituency whose mission is to defend the marital family. Oddly, some of these voices are the same ones who criticise media coverage of the Church's failure to protect children from predatory priests because, they rightly asserted, most abuse occurs within the family. This is the same sort of disjointed compassion evinced by the apparent lack of interest among absolutist anti-abortion activists in the creaking conditions of the National Maternity Hospital.

Campaigners for this referendum are braced for the predictable pro-family arguments but, last week, a big(ish) gun fired an unexpected salvo. Hugh O'Flaherty, who resigned as a Supreme Court judge after it was revealed he interfered in a fatal drunk and dangerous driving case, declared that children's rights could be copperfastened by statute without need of a constitutional amendment. The following day in a district court, a man charged with neglecting his children and sexually abusing one of them asked a judge to change his bail terms, permitting him to see his children before the trial.

You can expect to hear another Supreme Court judge being disingenuously quoted by the anti-referendum side in the coming months. In his judgment in the Baby Ann case, Judge Adrian Hardiman stated that parents had no greater rights in the constitution than children did.

Hardiman's statement does not contradict McGuinness's position. Her concern is that, while a perception exists that parents have greater rights, it may deter child-welfare services from resorting to the foibles and expense of law.

The constitution, after all, hinges on its interpretation. As long as any ambiguity exists, no argument against an amendment is sustainable.

Ireland has deluded itself long enough that this is a children's utopia, even though it remains legal to "spank" children, contrary to the Convention on the Rights of the Child, which this country ratified a year before Kelly Fitzgerald died. A recent survey by Newstalk found that almost half of Irish people think it acceptable to hit a child.

What is it about children being treated by the state as equal citizens that so scares the grown-ups? Let's gather our courage and not be seduced by legal sophistry into abandoning any more children to the padlocked horror of the presumptively perfect Irish family.

Deliver us from the evil of these hypocritical Holy Joes

When Pádraig "Pee" Flynn was a European commissioner, he would emerge from his white Mercedes outside the Catholic church in Castlebar on Sunday mornings and lead his family to the front pew. From there, he would ascend the altar and read the epistle to the chosen people.

The Sunday Times, 1 April 2012

Pee, a self-styled "Messiah", is piety incarnate. Before the 1985 divorce referendum, he proclaimed: "Introducing divorce would give respectability to actions totally at variance with Christian ethics. Those who facilitate actions that offend that ethic must share in the consequences for society afterwards."

With one hand, saintly Pee was fending off divorce and abortion in referendums. With the other, we now know thanks to the Mahon tribunal, he was stuffing his pockets with the IR£50,000 (€63,500) he corruptly solicited from the developer Tom Gilmartin.

Pee was in exalted company. Ray Burke, his cabinet colleague, inherited his Dáil seat from his father, Paddy, who was known as Bishop Burke, such was his ubiquity at constituents' funeral masses. When Rambo, as Burke junior came to be known, was the minister for justice, he promised to decriminalise homosexual sex but never quite got around to it. Maybe he was too busy collecting corrupt payments from Joseph Murphy Structural Engineers (JMSE) and Century Radio, not to mention his house, Briargate, which he received compliments of Brennan and McGowan builders. While Rambo did his bribery rounds, men who made love to other men risked being sent to jail.

Flynn and Burke were mere handmaidens in the piety pecking order compared with Don Lydon. The former senator collected enough papal knighthoods and brown envelopes to wallpaper Rambo's house. Mahon found that the Knight of the Order of Malta and Knight Grand Cross of the Equestrian Order of the Holy Sepulchre of Jerusalem took corrupt payments from developers, connected with lands at Quarryvale and Cherrywood in Dublin.

Lydon was wont to hold forth in the Seanad on matters of private morality. When a Fianna Fáil government was forced by the European Court of Human Rights to decriminalise homosexual sex, he demanded to know: "What are we going to legalise here? ... Are we going to legalise holding hands, which nobody would object to, gentle kissing, caressing? Are we going to legalise mutual masturbation or fellatio? Are we going to legalise the insertion of a penis into somebody's anus, which is buggery or sodomy in my book, and I believe to be an act against nature? ... Promoting something which we believe to be inherently wrong [means] we are one more step towards a society which loses all moral standards."

The most ostentatious Holy Joe of them all was Bertie Ahern. Every advent, he forswore the beer. Every Ash Wednesday, he arrived in the Dáil with the ritual Catholic smudge on his forehead. He named the house that the businessman Micheál Wall gave him 'All Hallows', which means everything that's good and holy. He did his utmost to get God name-checked in the EU constitution, and the Church gave him a knighthood for his endeavours.

He squared his apparent hypocrisy as a prominent member of an anti-divorce party by never divorcing his estranged wife or proposing marriage to his "life partner". Nor did his conscience appear troubled by any concealment of his assets from his wife when he eschewed owning a bank account during their legal separation proceedings. Little wonder that, 14 years later, Ahern could bring himself to lie to the Mahon tribunal.

How did Ireland let itself be suckered by so many Holy Joes chasing brown envelopes? Des O'Malley, a former Fianna Fáil minister, gave a clue in an interview on Newstalk last week. He recalled his local bishop in Limerick, the late Jeremiah Newman, warning him before a Dáil vote in 1985 on the proposed liberalisation of condom sales that the TD's first duty was to Catholic teaching. "In other words, he was saying, 'You take your orders from me,'" he said, pointing out that, until then, condoms were only available on doctors' prescriptions. "As if a condom could cure an illness."

O'Malley considered the vote a matter of conscience. He abstained. For that sin, Fianna Fáil expelled him from the parliamentary party by 73 votes to nine for "conduct unbecoming". Charlie Haughey, as the Fianna Fáil leader, instigated the move. Haughey had a mistress, a mansion home, a yacht, an island and off-shore bank accounts. The Moriarty tribunal calculated he was paid more than IR£8m between 1979 and 1986 by various businessmen. Among those who voted to expel O'Malley were Burke, Ahern, Flynn and Albert Reynolds, who, Mahon found, abused his power by asking businessmen for donations.

What a twisted land we inhabit. Politicians' pervy obsession with sex and women's bodies inflicted hardship, tragedy and, sometimes, death on citizens. In a dissenting judgment on David Norris's homosexuality challenge in the Supreme Court in 1984, the late, great Judge Niall McCarthy observed that gay men were subject to sanctions never applied to "the venal, the dishonest, the corrupt and the like". Sex was the only sin.

There has been a disconcerting silence from Catholic bishops since the Mahon report was published. Another missed opportunity to make themselves relevant.

It seems that politicians who lie, steal, importune, withhold tax, take bribes and banish their neighbours to a concrete wilderness in return for a builder's 30 pieces of silver are above episcopal condemnation. Save it for a girl made pregnant by a rapist.

In his most famous judgment, McCarthy said in the X case on abortion: "The failure of the legislature to enact the appropriate legislation is no longer just unfortunate; it is inexcusable." Two decades later, it still has not been done.

The decade when Haughey, Burke, Ahern, Flynn et al got their toehold in Ireland was when Eileen Flynn was sacked as a school teacher for living with a separated man; Joanne Hayes was viciously cross-examined at a state tribunal about her out-of-wedlock pregnancy; Anne Lovett died, aged 15, at a holy grotto in Granard with her new-born baby; Irish editions of *Cosmopolitan* contained blank pages where advertisements for abortion clinics appeared in the British editions; Tens of thousands of women and girls stole across the Irish Sea for abortions.

And surely be to God, looking down from heaven at the rank hypocrisy, Jesus wept.

Parents on the edge

Una Butler is campaigning for reforms to the Mental Health Act after her late husband John killed himself and their two daughters.

The Sunday Times, 25 November 2012

Last weekend marked the second anniversary of John Butler's death. He had placed a container of petrol in his car boot and driven the vehicle into a wall near his east Cork home. Earlier, the 43-year-old crane driver had prepared breakfast for his two children and, while they watched television, he strangled Zoe, 6, and smothered Ella, 2.

Una Butler, their mother and the family's sole survivor, attended mass in Cobh cathedral last Sunday for the anniversary. "To see their cousins there was heart-breaking. Zoe and Ella should be there too," she said, surrounded by photographs of her daughters and vases of anniversary lilies in a house she rents in Ballycotton. (She lives there because she cannot bear to return to the home where her children died.) "It is so hard to live without my girls. Sometimes, I wonder if I can," she said.

The following day, an inquest by the Dublin city coroner heard how the body of Anna Byrne, 35, from Dunboyne in Co Meath, was found last March at the bottom of cliffs at Howth summit. She had been 8½ months pregnant and was due to give birth to twin boys by caesarean section in three weeks. A mother of two sons, she told her husband she loved him in a final phone call and left a farewell note in her car, which was parked nearby.

The inquest heard that Byrne had been taking Seroxat anti-depressants for 10 years but stopped during the pregnancy. When she was informed at 20 weeks that she was carrying male twins, she said she felt devastated and overwhelmed at the prospect of having four sons.

A note in her records in mid-February described her as "anxious". Her GP had prescribed Sertraline, an anti-depressant used during pregnancy, and the dosage had been doubled by Dr John Sheehan, a psychiatrist at the Rotunda maternity hospital. Byrne said she felt "part of her life was missing" because she did not have a daughter and she had planned the pregnancy in the hope of having a girl. The inquest returned an open verdict.

Down in the seaside village of Ballycotton, Butler heard the story of Byrne's death and said: "That's another one; three more people dead."

Butler is campaigning for reforms in mental health treatment to provide for mandatory risk assessments of patients' families. She also wants the Mental Health Act to be amended to allow for the involvement of patients' families in their treatment, without breaching patient confidentiality.

According to statistics she has compiled, there have been 24 cases of "filicide", when parents kill their children, since 2000 in Ireland. In all, 34 children have died. Most recently Bernadette Scully, a doctor from Tullamore, and Emily, her 11-year-old daughter who was severely disabled, were found unconscious in their home last September. Emily subsequently died.

This Tuesday, Safe Ireland, a network of 40 domestic violence frontline services, will release figures showing 3,066 children received support from such services last year. While not not all filicide cases are linked to domestic violence, this is the highest number since national statistics were first collected in 2007. Last year, 2,141 children were admitted to family refuges.

Adele King, the entertainer known as Twink, has disclosed in her autobiography, *Twink Unzipped*, that she contemplated taking the lives of her children after her marriage collapsed.

"I had hit rock bottom," she said on *The Late Late Show*. "I picked them up from the Billie Barry school of dance. Frances Black's song, 'All the lies that you told me, all the tears that I cried', was on the radio. I couldn't see a future for myself and my children in the picture I was presented with and I thought I couldn't go and leave them here. I would like me and my babies to be together somewhere else and that [meant] taking their lives."

Butler said: "Filicide isn't as rare as people think but it's hard to get people who can talk about it because they're either in psychiatric hospitals or in prison or dead."

She remembers waking to the news in April 2007 that an entire family had died in Monageer, Co Wexford. Adrian Dunne, 29, had taken his life after killing his wife Ciara, 24, and their daughters Lean, 5, and Shania, 3. The family had visited an undertaker together to order their coffins.

"I remember hearing about Monageer and thinking 'My God, how could that happen?'" Butler said.

A 2009 inquiry report on Monageer, which was extensively redacted for legal reasons, concluded that Adrian Dunne was the driving force in the deaths. It said he had repeatedly given misleading information to service providers.

Butler suspects her husband downplayed his illness to his

mental health carers. "I think he minimised his symptoms," she said. "Had they heard my story rather than just hearing what John wanted them to hear maybe he and Zoe and Ella would still be alive. They didn't get the full story of what it was like to live with John.

"When he was good, he was very, very good and when he was bad, he was very bad. He was a street angel and a house devil.

"He was never physically violent to me or Ella and Zoe but he was extremely emotionally abusive to me. I was onto Women's Aid a lot. I thought of leaving on numerous occasions.

"Call me old-fashioned, but I did what I thought was right. I knew John was a good person. I always hoped he would come back to normal.

"I did meet his psychiatrist on two occasions but John was there as well. When we went home, I got John saying, 'What did you tell her that for?' I think it would help the professionals if I could have met them maybe for 10 minutes once a week so I could tell them what was going on at home. I think they could have educated me too about his illness and what I could do."

The Butlers were married in the summer of 2000. He was quiet with dark good looks and a talent for football and road bowling. "I adored the ground he walked on," Una said. Six weeks after the wedding, John had an accident at Irish Steel where he was employed as a crane operator. He spent two years out of work with a back injury and developed post-traumatic stress disorder. In November 2009, gardaí were alerted when John disappeared overnight. After he returned, he said he had driven to Wexford with thoughts of killing himself.

About a year later, on November 16, 2010, he woke his wife at 7.30am and rubbed her back before she left for work with the Revenue Commissioners in Cork city. The roads were thick with ice. "I asked him would I stay home? I can't remember what he said, that's the thing, I can't remember."

When he failed to answer her phone calls from work, she decided to return home. Near the village, a garda stopped her and said there had been a road accident ahead; there was just one person in the car. He told her it was John. "Where's Ella?" Una asked, assuming Zoe was in school.

By then, the two-days-a-week child-minder and Una's sister had found the children dead in the house, after smashing a window to gain entry. John had broken the key in the lock of the front door, delaying the discovery. The post mortem examination recorded he died of smoke and gas inhalation and burns.

Una wants an inquiry into the deaths of her children and her husband.

"I will never forgive John for what he did to my girls because living without them is a nightmare," she said, "but I don't think John – the good John – would expect me to. The demons took him over that morning.

"When I got his case notes after he died, the first paragraph insinuated that John and I did not know if we wanted our relationship to continue. I was never asked about it. I could have told them he wasn't taking his medication.

"I met Kathleen Lynch [the junior minister for mental health] in July. She said the HSE was doing a serious incident report. I got the report in October. It was one A4 page, basically. It's as if my girls didn't matter." A spokesman for Lynch said that "the role of family members in the recovery process" was recognised and there were provisions for family involvement in patients' treatment.

"However, in the case of adults, the involvement should normally be with the individual's consent," the spokesman said. "The Medical Council's guidance on professional conduct and ethics requires such consent, except in extreme circumstances where there is a serious risk of death or harm to the patient or others ... However, prediction of events such as those in this case is very difficult, if not impossible."

Noreen Murphy from Bantry, Co. Cork, believes there were unmissable signposts that she and her children were at risk from her mentally ill husband, but she could not get anybody to listen to her.

On September 9, 2007, Donal Murphy was found dead in his car beside the GAA pitch where he excelled at football. The 39-year-old had previously attempted to take his life in January 2007.

"He had repeatedly threatened to take the family with him. He said he would burn the house down," said Noreen. "I spent nearly two years going to the hospital every day but they ignored me. I passed on suicide notes he wrote at different times but they weren't in his file after he died.

"The [three] children used to sleep in their clothes and I would keep the car keys close to get away. Eventually I took the children to live with my mother. The reason we survived was because I took his threats seriously. I had the clothes line taken down and the knives and the garden hoses removed but, in the end, he got the pipe of a Hoover. He wasn't a bad man. They take who they love."

In her empty house facing the lighthouse in Ballycotton, Butler said: "I'll go on campaigning for these changes so this doesn't happen to other families. I used to wonder all the time why John didn't take me too. It would have been much easier for me. Then I believe I must be left here for a reason. I want my girls to count."

Read this and weep for the abused girl let down by all

I first met the girl nearly 15 years ago. She sat between her mother and her father in their living room. Her eyes were empty, her speech mechanical. "She's like the living dead," her mother said.

The Sunday Times, 25 February 2012

The girl told me her story. When she was five, an elderly neighbour began sexually assaulting her. He was the grandfather of children who lived nearby. When her mother was hospitalised for six months, the girl was looked after by the grandfather. He warned her that if she told anyone, her mother would die. She told nobody. The abuse stopped when she was 11, when the grandfather's family left the neighbourhood.

She struggled in school and became withdrawn at home. Her parents brought her to a doctor who said she was reacting to her mother's prolonged absence from home. Her parents hired a tutor to help her catch up at school.

After the abuse ended, a local swimming pool opened. When she swam, she felt happy. "I felt like I was flying," she said.

She streaked through the water. Bystanders asked who she was. A swim coach advised her parents to take her to George Gibney, the national and Olympic coach. Gibney took the girl under his wing. He told her he would make her a star. Soon she was breaking records. Gibney gave her gifts of togs and tracksuits and hugged her every time she climbed out of the pool to accept another medal. He said she would swim in the 1992 Olympics in Barcelona.

"That was my dream," she said. She woke at 4am each day to train. Her father slept outside in his car while, inside, she swam. Unknown to them, Gibney's secret criminal life was starting to crumble. Chalkie White, another coach, alleged to Gary O'Toole, a world silver medallist, that Gibney had abused him from the age of 11. As he listened, O'Toole recalled warding off an attempted assault by Gibney when he too was 11.

White and O'Toole eventually unmasked Gibney as a rampant child sex abuser, but not in time to save the girl. In Holland for a competition, Gibney came to her hotel room, jumped on her and pushed her onto the bed. He left as abruptly.

Back in Dublin, he shunned her. The harder she trained, the more he ignored her. At a training camp in Tampa, Florida in 1991, he drove her to a hotel and, she claims, raped her. He said if she told anyone, he would sue and impoverish her parents. She told nobody.

The girl made her first suicide attempt while Gibney was fighting 27 counts of sexually abusing seven other swimmers. She was referred to Dr Moira O'Brien, the honorary medical adviser to the Irish Amateur Swimming Association (IASA – now Swim Ireland) and Ireland's doctor at the three preceding Olympic Games. The girl's secrets erupted.

Gardaí began to investigate the first man who abused her. Two other girls came forward. He was convicted on seven charges and jailed for five years. Sentencing him, the judge commented it probably was no coincidence that one of the girls was subsequently abused by her swim coach.

Buoyed, the girl made a statement to gardaí that Gibney raped her in Florida. By then, Gibney had eluded the first charges when the High Court ruled the delay since the alleged incidents disadvantaged his defence. He fled to Florida.

In 1997, the girl instructed a solicitor, Timothy Ryan, then with Hughes, Murphy & Co in Dublin, to sue both her abusers, along with the IASA and the Olympic Council of Ireland (OCI). She underwent counselling to prepare herself to testify at Gibney's criminal trial.

In 2004, two gardaí visited and informed her that the Director of Public Prosecutions had decided not to apply for Gibney's extradition from America. That night she hanged herself from a tree in the grounds of a priests' order house. One of the priests found her in time.

By this time, the girl was anorexic and frequently self-harming. She could no longer hold down a job. She gradually became dependent on her ageing parents. She has developed an addiction to cough medicine, drinking two bottles a day. She is often put on suicide watch in hospital.

With her permission, I used to phone her solicitor (who had by then moved to a different firm) to check how the civil case was progressing. When he did not return calls I became suspicious and checked the Courts Service records. They showed that, though he had issued proceedings as instructed, he had never served them. The case had been dormant for nearly a decade.

I told the girl's mother. She feared the news could kill her daughter so we agreed not to tell her. The mother knew my husband was a solicitor. She asked me to request him to take on the case. I protested that it would be a conflict of interest for me, but she said that she did not know another solicitor. I asked my husband. He took on the case and issued proceedings against Ryan.

In January 2009, my husband retired and another solicitor took over the case. That July, the 1997 proceedings against IASA and the OCI were revived by a High Court order. Both bodies applied to have them struck out. In December 2010, the High Court acquiesced, saying the delay was "inexcusable and inordinate". IOC and IASA were granted costs.

Last December, the girl reached an out-of-court settlement with Ryan's insurers, having rejected an earlier offer of €100,000. The two sports organisations have pursued her for €95,000 costs. After I emailed the OCI asking Pat Hickey, its president, whether he considered this pursuit morally justified, I received a phone call from the organisation's solicitor. He asked if I thought it appropriate, in light of my husband's involvement in the case, that I write about it. He advised me to be very careful, "from your personal point of view".

One day last November, the girl phoned me from a psychiatric hospital. She was harrowingly distressed. While she was on the phone, she left the hospital, bought a bottle of vodka and boarded a bus. She said she could no longer bear being alive. She said goodbye. Hours later, a stranger found her in a shopping-centre toilet with her wrists slashed.

As I write, she is back in hospital.

Half told tale blinds us to best – and worst – of Haughey legacy

A boy I used to know went trick-or-treating to Charlie Haughey's house one Hallowe'en. He donned a cape and a Scream mask and fearlessly headed for the famous mansion. When he came home, he was clutching IR£100 in his dimpled little fist.

The Sunday Times, 3 November 2013

Easy to be generous with Ben Dunne's largesse, you may scoff, but Haughey didn't have to be kind. He was long retired by then. Lurid accounts of his kept-man extravagances were pouring like boiling oil from the payments-to-politicians tribunal at Dublin Castle. He was a pariah.

When he allowed me to visit him in Abbeville seven years after his retirement from Dáil Éireann with the pompous valediction "I have done the state some service", he cut a pathetic figure. His housekeeper, the last of the staff, had retired the previous Friday. It was Maureen, his wife, who carried the rattling tea tray to the study. An April snowfall had settled upon the gardens; a sculpture of Cuchulainn wrapped in a sheet of white, as if awaiting the removal men.

I had written to Haughey asking for his assistance with a biography of Mary McAleese that I was writing and he had phoned weeks later, asking: "Why should I help you after what you've been writing about me?" But he did help and some time after my visit, a large envelope arrived with documents he had promised. In the meantime, Terry Keane, his gossip-columnist mistress, had fetched up on *The Late Late Show* to reveal their open secret of an affair. When I phoned to thank him for the documents, he told me he would never speak to her again.

A great yoke had been lifted off Irish journalists by then. After decades of timorous caution, the media had carte blanche to report the truth about this man who had emerged from the Arms Trial trailing cordite, bullet-proofed by draconian defamation laws and his intimidating personality. I once witnessed him tell an English journalist who dared question him about the economy during the 1987 general election to "f*** off".

His reputation was pulverised when the Moriarty tribunal established he got nearly €11m from 16 wealthy businessmen and companies in 17 years. After a hailstorm of revelations about Haughey's monogrammed Charvet shirts and nights drinking Cristal champagne in the Coq Hardi restaurant, lawyers advised editors it was now virtually impossible to defame him.

Being a journalist in the Haughey era was exhilarating. There weren't enough adjectives in the dictionary to describe him – narcissistic, power-hungry, treacherous, sybaritic, unnerving, charismatic, pretentious, erudite. When he wasn't the Boss, he was the Squire, or Il Duce, or Sweetie. Sebastian Barry, who wrote a play about him, said he embodied Ireland.

Journalists could never be objective about Haughey, something that puts a greater onus on historians. He dominated a macho world of mohair-suited men. He was full of edge in a country always on the brink of bedlam with the bloodshed of the Troubles, frequent general elections, emigrant planes, dole queues, vicious abortion and divorce referendums, insularity and isolation.

There have been many recent reminders of those days. Not least are the spine-tingling photographs of Aiden Gillen – and his startling hairline – playing Haughey in RTÉ's forthcoming drama. Alarmed by the advance publicity, some Haughey apologists have set up a website to trumpet his achievements.

Amid reports that Abbeville has, at last, been sold – to Chinese buyers, the rumour goes – two figures synonymous with the Haughey era were laid to rest last week. Denis Foley, a former Fianna Fáil TD in Kerry, is best remembered for his outing as an Ansbacher man, part of a golden circle of offshore tax evaders. John Byrne, another Kerryman who put IR£17.5m through Ansbacher bank's tax laundry, died a day later. The multimillionaire developer told Moriarty that Haughey, his insatiably materialistic pal of 40 years, never importuned as much as a penny from him.

These new truths about Haughey were not the whole truth. Sam Smyth relates a story in his book, *Thanks a Million Big Fella*, about the day Haughey was booed as he left the Moriarty tribunal. A woman told the author she had taken the bus from Raheny, Haughey's bailiwick, to Dublin Castle that morning. The bus driver had his transistor on and was listening to the news about Haughey's impending appearance as a witness. The passengers asked him to turn up the volume. When Charlie Bird breathlessly reported on *Morning Ireland* that Houdini had eluded the waiting media by arriving inordinately early, a cheer went up on the 42A.

Looking back, it is amazing to see not how much has changed, but how little. While Haughey reigned, the banks were laughing. Irish Permanent flagrantly advertised non-resident accounts in Aer Lingus's in-flight magazine. The state made the citizens bail out the Insurance Corporation of Ireland after bankers paid €90m for the white elephant. Allied Irish Banks' (AIB) bosses had Faldor, their own British Virgin Islands tax-dodging fund, a gilt-edged perk which Pat Rabbitte, then the Labour leader, likened to "the key to the executive loo". At the Dirt inquiry by the Dáil's public accounts committee, banker after banker swore he "knew nothing".

Following a Revenue investigation on foot of that inquiry, AIB paid €90m to the exchequer. Nobody was charged with anything. Nobody was sacked. Nobody resigned. And, as we know from what happened next, nobody learnt any lessons.

While the unleashing of the media by the tribunal disclosures about Haughey allowed the truth to emerge, it also distorted it. So fixated has the analysis of his personal greed become, it has obscured much of this complex man and his complex times. Was taking money from rich businessmen worse, for instance, than calling a general election in 1989 to avoid paying IR£400,000 to haemophiliacs fatally infected by state-supplied blood?

It's time to end our orgy of despising Haughey for his feeble vanities, and for our own gratification. It exonerates him of other transgressions, ignores his achievements and precludes any honest assessment from which Ireland can learn. He did good too and he did other things that were more venal than living off the fat of rich friends.

Haughey told *The Daily Telegraph* in 1988: "Ireland is where strange tales begin and happy endings are possible." But no ending is possible when only half the story is told.

How the constitution brought heartbreak on Christmas Eve

At 10 minutes to midday on Christmas Eve, not long before Father Christmas cracked his great whip and set out from the North Pole, a child's voice echoed around the vast emptiness of Dublin's Four Courts. The sound wended its way along deserted corridors and eerie courtrooms, past judges' chambers and the slumbering law library. It swirled around the soaring, silent round hall and came in under the door of Court Four.

The Sunday Times, 28 December 2014

Nobody in the room let on to have noticed. Nobody betrayed puzzlement that a young child would be spending the final hours before Santa's visit in the land's loftiest courthouse. Least of all did the three judges sitting on their high bench, as they listened to Conor Dignam, the senior counsel for the interests of the unborn. At the moment the child's call reverberated, Dignam was arguing that the Irish language version of article 40.3.3 in the constitution gives foetuses greater protection than does the English language one. Furthermore, he said, article 25.6 contains a requirement that, whenever the two versions come into conflict, the Irish language one takes precedence.

The difference between the two versions of article 40.3.3 is that the English one undertakes to vindicate, as far as is "practicable", the unborn's right to life whereas the Irish one says it must be vindicated as far as is "possible". Could it be true that Irish law has less respect for the majority of people who based their voting decisions in the eighth amendment referendum on the English version?

"Can you tell me the Irish word for practicable?" asked Judge Nicholas Kearns. No alternative word was offered. If it wasn't all so utterly barbaric, it would make for searing satire.

The previous day, three judges, 17 lawyers, 19 journalists and a widowed father whose deceased only child was being kept artificially functioning in a hospital, heard seven medical consultants give evidence about her deteriorating condition and her foetus's "almost negligible" chances of survival. Having clarified that the woman was beyond feeling anything, Peter McKenna, a former master of the Rotunda Maternity Hospital, was asked if the unborn could sense something. "It would not be unaware. It would not be unaffected," he replied.

What the medical consultants told the court was gruesome. Lawyers and reporters who have witnessed disturbing murder trials, and even some of the doctors themselves, discreetly wiped away their tears.

"This should be televised live," whispered the reporter beside me, "so that the people defending article 40.3.3 know exactly what its consequences are."

Out of consideration for the dead woman's father and for the younger man sitting beside him – the woman's partner and the father of her unborn – some of the doctors' most harrowing descriptions have not been reported in the media. It is, alas, too late to save those two haunted-looking men from the horror.

It began on November 27, when the woman, aged in her mid-twenties and a mother of two young children, was admitted to her local hospital. She was almost 15 weeks pregnant and was complaining of severe headaches and vomiting. On the evening of November 29, she lost her balance and fell in the bathroom. At 10pm that night, she had "a severe turn" and was "incoherent with pain". At around midnight, she was taken from the hospital and transferred to Dublin. The neurosurgeon who attended her there believes she "was probably gone by the time she arrived". She was declared clinically dead at 5.20pm on December 3 but kept ventilated because clinicians could not "figure out the 8th amendment".

Dressed in mourning black, her next of kin sat in the courtroom while obstetricians, intensive care consultants and neurologists testified that the woman is dead, she cannot be brought back to life, and her foetus, if it were, miraculously, to be born alive, would have a case against the state in time to come for its appalling birth deformities.

It should be sufficient for defenders of article 40.3.3 to know that, in this case, its barbarous consequence is that a father had to go to the High Court on Christmas Eve to ask permission to have his only child taken off a hospital ventilator so that her family can bury her with dignity. Some absolutist anti- abortion campaigners have cavilled that the case "has nothing to do with abortion"; nor has it. Yet article 40.3.3 caused this barbarism.

The court handled the tragedy as kindly as it could. The distress in the room was palpable, just as it must have been among the doctors and nurses who have cared for the woman in hospital. These are not the people who need convincing that article 40.3.3 is pernicious and vile. Its defenders who were, perhaps, last-minute shopping or wrapping gifts or singing

Christmas carols during Tuesday and Wednesday's hearings, are the ones who need to know the cruel facts.

There is, for instance, the Lazarus phenomenon. This was explained by Dr Frances Colreavy, an intensive care consultant. In circumstances of somatic support, a spontaneous spinal reaction can cause an arm or a leg to suddenly move. Apologising to the family for what she was about to say, Colreavy added that the phenomenon can be so dramatic "the patient can seem to sit up in bed".

When she visited the woman the previous day, "the deceased in the bed", she said , bore little resemblance to the "very pretty" woman in a photo on the window sill. There was a tube through her nose providing nutrition. Pressure sores were a problem. Her temperature had risen to 38.5 degrees and the foetus's could be 40 degrees. The woman's body was showing signs of pneumonia. Her abdomen was striped blue, red and purple. She was being given antibiotics for MRSA and other toxic medicines not licensed for pregnant women. There was an open surgical wound on her head, where fungus was growing. When Colreavy looked in, she could see the brain was rotting. Nurses had applied eye shadow in advance of a visit by her little daughter but, because her eyes were swollen and a "gelatinous material" was coming out of them, they could not close.

In conveying these details, there is a danger of stooping to the same level as the gratuitous disseminators of pictures of aborted foetuses. But, if the woman's own loved ones had to sit and listen to this catalogue of horror those who foisted it on them should hear it too.

She and her partner had chosen names for their expected child. She had told her children they were going to have a little brother or sister. All their lives have been irreversibly damaged because of article 40.3.3.

Leaving the Four Courts on Christmas Eve, there came again the sound of a child's voice. From around the corner appeared a woman all dressed in black. She was holding two small children by the hand. They looked to be the same age as the deceased woman's children. They had her father's colouring. They were smiling, oblivious as yet to the obscenity their country had visited upon them.

Law reform is useless while cute hoorism stays in high regard

Ireland has more ethical backbone as it emerges
from economic woe. But only on paper.

The Sunday Times, 20 September 2015

They're back, just as we knew they would be. They are the born-again builders. One of the most egregious pitched up in O'Brien's pub on Leeson Street in Dublin about 10 days ago. Seán "the Dunner" Dunne had lost none of his cockiness, despite being bankrupt on two continents.

He arrived into the bar leading by the hand his wife, Gayle Killilea, a former gossip columnist and grocer who became the overnight proprietor of a property empire. The pair had alighted from an Aer Lingus flight from Heathrow during evening rush hour, exuding an aura of wealth. She wore a leather-belted camel coat and staggeringly high-heeled boots. His complexion had a crinkle-free sheen that belied his 60 years.

The couple's fairytale finances have perplexed courts from Ireland to America to South Africa. Dunne claims that, before he went bust, he gave Gayle €100m in return for her love, having their children and because "she washed the odd shirt too".

Dunne owes about €200m to NAMA, the state's bespoke lifeboat for developers. His total debts exceed €700m. He is in breach of his legal obligations under bankruptcy legislation to declare fully his financial affairs, an arrestable offence.

Ten years ago, around the corner in Ballsbridge, he spent €379m on two hotels that set a record land price of €54m an acre. Not one to rest on his laurels, he then made Dublin house prices the craziest in Europe with the €58m purchase of Walford, a shabby period house on Shrewsbury Road. As has become his leitmotif, Dunne vehemently denied any involvement in the purchase and threatened journalists with High Court writs if they wrote otherwise. To those who argue that property developers were innocent victims of the economic crash, I give you the Dunner.

In the bar that night, he regaled fellow patrons with accounts of his salubrious life in America. Two customers got short shrift when they berated him for the damage he inflicted on Ireland, and the burden of his continuing cat-and-mouse games with NAMA and Chris Lehane, the official assignee in bankruptcy.

The Dunnes' visit coincided with the annual ritual of political parties' think-ins before the commencement of the Dáil's autumn term. This is likely to be the last full term before the general election. Down in prettily thatched Adare, Fine Gael was trumpeting its adroitness in steering the banjaxed economy into recovery mode and demanding that voters return the party to power so that nobody will banjax it again. Meanwhile, in the Glen of the Downs, the Labour Party was pumping out a pre-election message that, in government, it had effected administrative reforms to ensure the capitalist cronyism that lay at the heart of the 2008 crash would not happen again.

Fine Gael's claim to posterity is rather dubious, as the government inherited a troika bailout which prescribed the austerity measures it was required to implement. Labour's boast has more merit. Brendan Howlin, as the minister for public expenditure and reform, has expanded the remit of the Freedom of Information Act, introduced a lobbyists' register and provided legislative protection for whistleblowers.

On paper, Ireland has more ethical backbone as it emerges from the economic doldrums. But only on paper.

It will take more than legislative reform to stamp out the ruling class's sneaking regard for the cute hoor, be it in politics or business. Our Taoiseach is a dab hand at it himself – a talent he demonstrated when the Fennelly report on the retirement of former garda commissioner Martin Callinan was published. The normally media-shy Enda Kenny did a star turn on RTÉ's *Six One* news that day, claiming the report had vindicated him. The problem for his interviewer, Bryan Dobson, was that he had little time to digest the report, which the government released just before the programme went on air.

Time will show the true extent of Kenny's talent for kicking political banana skins up the road, and out of his way. In the future, students of scandal management may be required to dissect his handling of the Siteserv controversy as an object lesson.

It emerged last April that Department of Finance officials were concerned about the sale of Siteserv, an IBRC-indebted company, to the billionaire tax exile Denis O'Brien, involving a €119m writedown. Initially, the government denied there was any need for an investigation. Then it said there would be an inquiry handled by Kieran Wallace, IBRC's liquidator, who had also been an adviser to Siteserv. In response to objections that Wallace might have a conflict of interest, Iarfhlaith O'Neill, a retired High Court judge, was appointed to adjudicate if any arose.

When it became clear even to the government that this quasi-self-examination by Wallace was politically untenable, it announced on June 3 the establishment of a Commission of Investigation under the auspices of the Department of An Taoiseach.

Daniel O'Keeffe, a retired High Court judge, was appointed to chair the commission and a deadline of December 31 was set for the publication of its report. O'Keeffe's selection surprised many lawyers, who pointed out he was already the chairman of the Standards in Public Office Commission and a member of the Central Bank's investigations committee. On July 9, a month after the Dáil approved the commission's terms of reference, O'Keeffe announced he was stepping down for personal reasons.

A third judge was then appointed to take his place. However, when Brian Cregan took the reins, no offices had even been allocated to the commission. Last week, the Irish edition of *The Times* revealed that the commission has not yet completed its preparatory work, and there is little likelihood it will report until after the general election.

The delayed commission amounts to another masterstroke of scandal management. By acquiescing in the establishment of an inquiry, after protracted reluctance, the government removed the Siteserv controversy from the national conversation. It, literally, changed the subject. By setting an unrealistic deadline, it ensured there will be no damaging report before the parties go to the hustings.

Some politicians, even on opposition benches, are sanguine

about the delay, arguing it is the report that counts, not the timing. There is, however, something even more important at stake – the rigorousness of Ireland's new-found embrace of accountability and transparency.

Kenny's calling card as Taoiseach has been to make Ireland the best small country in the world in which to do business, but few things are as damaging to a country's business as a reputation for cutting corners, patronage and golden circles. It may be in the government's best interests to put the IBRC report on the long finger but it is in the worst interests of the state and, ergo, of the people.

It is counterproductive to introduce legislative reforms with one hand while pulling political strokes with the other. If Kenny expects the electorate to entrust the economic recovery to him, the Taoiseach will have to give up all the ould sins.

Forget our footballers, let's give three cheers for the Green Army

The fellowship of the Green Army is the essence of what the Rising was all about.

The Sunday Times, 19 June 2016

Have you heard the one about the Irish football fans who went to Paris and taught the French the meaning of their own language? Seldom has the City of Light witnessed such joie de vivre and bonhomie as the Green Army has brought to its boulevards. The Buzzfeed France site has already deemed the Irish "winners of Euro 2016", and even the fusty *Daily Telegraph* declared in a headline: "Irish fans prove why they are the best fans". The newspaper's website has a video of an elderly Parisian being cheered by crowds of Irish each time he emerged onto his second-floor balcony.

Schmaltzy it may be, but I find it impossible not to feel choked with love for my country when I watch the numerous videos of Irish fans partying in France. One, recorded from an open-top Paris tour bus and capturing millipedes of singing green shirts undulating beneath a night sky, epitomises the unthreatening exuberance they have brought to Euro 2016. In a world that increasingly seems on the edge of apocalypse due to genocidal partisanship, they have shown how patriotism can be as much a force for good as for war-mongering evil. Their rendition of

Abba's 'Dancing Queen' with their Swedish counterparts was a cameo of two neutral countries failing abysmally to behave as sworn enemies.

Some residents of arrondissements where the spontaneous Irish choirs descended have complained about traffic disruption, late-night noise and side streets being used as giant pissoirs, but these are minor inconveniences in a state where water cannon and stun grenades have been deployed against other countries' fans and against France's striking public-sector workers. When a nation opts to host the Euros, it must expect to suffer some aggravation.

The curmudgeons appear outnumbered by French citizens tweeting their enjoyment of the Irish fans' celebrations. Stay-at-home Irish cynics may ascribe their compatriots' endearing boisterousness to a mass PR job by Paddys desperate to be loved, but I suspect there is also a fraternal motivation to lighten the mood for France after its recent horrors.

A video recorded in the small hours of Thursday showed a group of Irish fans picking up their empty bottles and cans in a Bordeaux street while singing: "Clean up for the boys in green". Another showed five lads in green shirts coming to the aid of an elderly couple with a flat tyre in Paris. That sense of kinship was echoed in the Stade de France when the Republic's fans sang "stand up for the Ulsterman" during last Monday's match in tribute to Darren Rodgers, a young Northern Ireland fan who had died in Nice.

A story is told that a crowd singing The Fields of Athenry in downtown Paris after Monday's match stopped abruptly when a Frenchman among them fell to the ground. Irish fans went to help him back up. When the Frenchman smiled and raised

his beer can to his mouth, the singing erupted once more. Joe.
ie reports that when three Swedish brothers called Nordström
wandered into Quigley's Point bar in Paris before last Monday's
match, they became involved in an Irish sing-song. One of the
brothers, Joakim – who turned out to be an ice hockey star in
America – bought drinks for all the Irish in the pub as a thank-
you for being so welcoming.

Milan Kundera, the Czech-born author of *The Unbearable
Lightness of Being* who became a French citizen, had a
theory that the patriotism of small countries was more soft-
hearted than that of big countries "buoyed by their glory, their
importance, their universal mission". Could Ireland's preferred
position as the perpetual underdog explain these displays of
patriotism described by Kundera as small territories' "enormous
compassion for their country"?

All the edifying images from France remind us that our
country is nicer than our state. While the partying goes on
in France, more people are sleeping on Irish streets. Lawyers,
landlords, hoteliers and insurers are still fleecing citizens, and
criminals are still murdering each other on their neighbours'
doorsteps. Graffiti newly scrawled on hoarding near Leinster
House proclaims: "Same damn government". The disconnect
between the state and its people is a counterpoint to the jubilant
unity of Irish fans in France.

Of course, there is a dark underbelly. Excessive drinking is
a common sub-theme of Ireland's Euro odyssey and statistics
have repeatedly shown that incidents of domestic violence
increase during such competitions. WB Yeats could have been
talking about these football jamborees when he said the abiding
Irish sense of tragedy sustains us "through temporary periods

of joy". There is always the danger that something horrible could happen yet in France, since it only takes a few, but the good that has been done cannot be undone.

There was something profoundly appropriate about the seven fans who travelled to the Euros from Cork with the names of the executed 1916 rebellion leaders on their backs, instead of footballers' names. The fellowship and kindred spirit of the Green Army is the essence of what the Easter Rising was all about. If Yeats came back from the dead, he might acknowledge that Ireland really has changed, changed utterly.

For one thing, it is unselfconsciously post-Catholic. A scene on a French train, caught by one of the videos, shows that, while Ireland's fans have proven a unifying force in a riven, Brexit-trembling Europe, they remain different and separate. When a nun, dressed in veil and habit, enters a carriage occupied by green-clad men and women, they burst into a word-perfect performance of the Our Father hymn. It was neither irreverent nor pious; just a cultural reference by an unrepressed generation.

The same mischievous irony inspired the "Angela Merkel thinks we're at work" banner paraded by Limerick University students at Euro 2012 in Poland. The flag, which was featured on the cover of *Bild* magazine, was later sold for €15,800 at a charity auction in aid of a three-year-old boy being treated for cancer in Belfast.

The post-Troubles generation may still treat England as the main foe, but the rivalry is confined to the playing field. Off it, they have reversed roles. The day after police in Marseilles battled street riots by English fans, a video was shot in Paris of about 30 Irish supporters encountering half a dozen men in English shirts sitting outside a bar. The Irish debuted a new anthem for the occasion. "Please don't start a riot, please don't start a riot, di-dah-di-dah, di-dah-di-dah," they sang. Yeats would hardly believe this terrible beauty.

The 70,000 or so Irish fans who have travelled to France have lifted up this country after a long, dark period of emigration, unemployment, economic inequality and the temporary loss of sovereignty. They are not the plucky losers we Irish love to despise. They are proud carriers of the Irish flag. And we owe them a party when they come home.

I idolised my big sister, but society cast her out when she got pregnant

She was my big sister and I idolised her. She was wild, beautiful and wilful, with the elocution of a diva. "My name is Berenice," she would insist, emphasising the polysyllables. "Ber-e-nice".

The Sunday Times, 19 March 2017

Having her to myself on the country bus from Cork city one evening, after her day's work as a beauty therapist, was thrilling. She talked to me as though I were grown up too. Modernity oozed from her, in a grey Revlon uniform, the vivid pink of her bri-nylon polo-neck matching the colour on her lips, but I felt an unnameable dread when I noticed her sticking-out tummy.

That night, raised voices came from the kitchen – a rare event in our all-female household – followed by the slam of the front door, and silence. Somehow, we knew we should not ask.

Soon after that night, my other two sisters and I went back to boarding school in the city, where the Ursuline nuns dedicated themselves to moulding "young ladies". Our mother visited us every Sunday, as she did religiously for 13 years, sitting in the car for hours under a canopy of ever weeping trees. Only decades later did Adrienne, Gina and I realise that each of us had felt cast down by the shadow of Bessborough, the nearby mother and baby home.

Gina, the youngest and the athlete, remembers running past the dour place every Wednesday for her cross-country training and how it "gave me the heebie-jeebies". Sometimes, from the basketball courts, you could see bent shapes in the far distance, working in the fields. When I wrote in this newspaper some years ago that a nun had instructed me not to look at those women, I received a vexed letter from the convent branding it "a lie".

It is no lie. Bessborough was a parable for any female tempted to sin, or be sinned against. Just as the Bon Secours nuns were asked to run Tuam's mother and baby home, Cork's Bishop Cohalan had invited the Sisters of the Sacred Heart of Jesus and Mary from France in 1922 to cater for the new state's "fallen women". As is now known, Bessborough was temporarily shut down by the Department of Health in the 1940s after 100 babies died out of the 180 born there in one year. As is also now known, children in Bessborough were used for vaccine trials while their mothers were sent out to cut the lawn by hand, on their knees. This was the Ireland of 98% Catholics, 90% of whom went to mass every week.

In 1974, the Taoiseach Liam Cosgrave voted against his own government's defeated bill to allow married couples to buy contraceptives. In Seanad Éireann, a papal encyclical banning contraceptives, Humanae Vitae, was reverentially read into the record. Cork's formidable bishop Cornelius Lucey declared that no Catholic had the right to disagree with the Church's teachings. There was not a single day-nursery in the whole of Co Cork, Ireland's biggest county.

That year, too, our mother stopped visiting for weeks on end. Later, we learnt her absence was because she had gone to stay with Berenice in England, where she was waiting out her pregnancy while privately arranging to have the child adopted. Berenice never lived in Ireland again after that. One Sunday, our mother told us in the car under the weeping trees that she had gone to South Africa. I felt my heart break, imagining her alone in a steaming jungle full of prowling beasts, and thinking I would never see her again.

Our mother made these plans out of love for the four of us. She had lost her husband, the love of her life, 10 years before when God's invisible hand reached down and squeezed his heart in a vice grip, snatching him from this world. Widowed at 39 with four daughters, aged from 10 to one, she knew the shame awaiting us once tongues started wagging. So she chose the second option on a particularly Irish menu: either send Berenice to a mother and baby home or to England, so that she could come home a virgin once again. Except she didn't come home and our family was splintered forever.

For the next 38 years, my mother kept a photograph of the baby in her purse. She had written his name on the back in her careful hand, and the legend "one week old". She never stopped pining for her firstborn grandchild. My sisters and I never saw our nephew. A shroud of secrecy hung over us all.

Six years ago I received an email. "Forgive me if you're not who I think you are," it began, "but I think your sister is my mother." His name was Duncan Carr – Duncan McCarthy Carr, Ber-e-nice's child. Adrienne, Gina and I spoke to him on the phone that Sunday, our joy dimmed only by having to tell him it was too late; his mother had died three days after her 51st birthday. He said he would come to Dublin the next Sunday.

Adrienne and I drove to the nursing home where our mother was living with Alzheimer's, confined to a wheelchair and unable to speak. We told her Duncan had found us, that he sounded lovely and that he'd had a good life so far. "Isn't it wonderful, mum?" said Adrienne,

"It is," our mother said, uttering her only words in two years. Less than 48 hours later, she was admitted to hospital and started to die.

Last week on RTÉ Radio, a man said it was the children in the mother and baby homes he felt sorry for, because the mothers just had to deal with gossip and shame whereas the babies died.

Regardless of the fact that many mothers lost their lives too, there were different kinds of deaths caused by society's reduction of love to a filthy, four-letter word. Judgmentalism killed families.

I told Duncan I would not write this column if that were his wish. He said, in a crystal-clear English accent, that I must. "Other than my two children, I'd never met anyone who was me until I met my aunts."

When he came to Ireland, he brought a letter Berenice had written him when he was born, to be opened on his 18th birthday. She said she loved him, she was sorry, and she hoped he would understand one day.

I knew her lost child understood better than many of us in this country when Duncan said to me last week: "Why can we be so cruel to those most in need of a trusting hand?"

We owe it to America to deny Trump welcome

Time to make a stand against the inflammatory behaviour of the US president.

The Sunday Times, 20 August 2017

I admit, Donald Trump brings out the snob in me. But that doesn't make me wrong about him. And it doesn't make him any the less a vulgar, inarticulate, sleazy, self-obsessed, lying Twitter boot boy.

I don't believe I am alone in wanting to hurl petty insults at his effeminate, circle-making fingers and those glow-in-the-dark teeth, not to mention the sulky puss on him. The deeply shallow have a way of bringing others down to their own superficial level of judging a book by its cover, saving them the trouble of ever actually reading it. How else do you engage with somebody who boasts he has never read a whole book, despite purporting to have written one?

America's president considers himself an arbiter extraordinaire of such trivia as a woman's looks and a man's anatomical measurements. Nothing will dissuade me that the most urgent reason he fired 6ft 8in James Comey as the FBI's director was that Trump couldn't bear to not be the tallest man in the room. When he declares Angelina Jolie isn't beautiful but statues celebrating slavery are, quelling the inner snob is quite the challenge. It isn't eased by Trump's repeated tweets revelling in fantasies of killing journalists.

Yet, if there is to be any hope of getting rid of the creep-in-chief, Trump's critics have to resist snooty disdain, because that is the last hostage available to his apologists. Sneering at Trump bolsters the PR fallacy that the billionaire, who has never had to depend on a bus timetable or a beans-on-toast budget, is seen as the antithesis of "Washington elites" and pontificating "liberals". You insult Trump, they say, and you're insulting everyone who voted for him. In the same breath, faux anti-establishmentarians and inverted-liberals, bending over backwards to be tolerant, insist we must respect the presidency, even if the president doesn't. How did Trump's "birther" campaign against President Barack Obama square with respect for the office? When the office-holder treats the office as a Snow White-style mirror for his vanity, it becomes difficult to distinguish one from the other.

Almost all the fears about a President Trump are coming true. He's building the Mexican wall. He's intent on banning Muslims from entering America. He has reneged on climate change undertakings. He has withdrawn funding for abortion services. He ogles other leaders' wives. He baited North Korea into a nuclear stand-off and is taunting Iran too. When he couldn't stop investigations into his links with Russia by sacking his appointed officials, he checked if he had the power to pardon himself. Instead of uniting the alienated peoples of his country, he has driven them further apart, especially in the past week. The thank-you he got from David Duke, a Holocaust-denying former "imperial wizard" of the Ku Klux Klan, crystallised on which side of the widening chasm the president stands.

By equally blaming white supremacists and those who

oppose them for the violence in Charlottesville, Virginia, Trump insinuated that Heather Heyer was partly responsible for her own murder when the human rights activist was run down by a car driven amok by a Nazi-sympathiser. Trump's pathetic attempt to make amends subsequently was to tweet that she was "beautiful". Then he tweeted that Confederate statues are beautiful too. The Daily Stormer, a Nazi propaganda website, called Heyer a "fat, childless slut", which sounded more like the things Trump is wont to say about women with minds of their own, and bodies he will never possess.

His apologists argue that slavery is part of American history and is legitimately memorialised in public places. Does Germany have statues to Hitler, Goering or Himmler? Did you hear American fascists objecting to the destruction of Saddam Hussein's statue in Baghdad after the 2003 invasion of Iraq?

The most troubling aspect of Trump's reign is the needling mystery as to why Vladimir Putin wanted him ensconced in the Oval Office. Various foreign policy theories abound but, if it was simply to cause chaos, thus creating the conditions for political destabilisation, both domestic and global, the odious plot is rapidly paying off.

Which brings us to the latest dilemma. Is America, the world pioneer of regime change in foreign lands, now in need of one itself? Ought we not help the vast majority of Americans to escape Trump's megalomaniacal and increasingly ominous power-hold? The majority of voters in last year's presidential election did not vote for him and, since then, his popularity has plunged. By last week, nearly two in every three Americans didn't want him as their president.

Trump's arrival in the White House has changed the rules of engagement. According to US intelligence agencies, Russia helped put him there by subverting American democracy; a trick picked up by ex-KGB agent Putin, one supposes, from studying CIA interventions from Nicaragua to the Persian Gulf.

America is the world's superpower. Nuclear armament, human migration and climate damage are global issues, likely to have a more direct and enduring impact on sub-Saharan Africa or the Middle East than downtown Kansas. Trump's contempt for the planet, his megaphone jeering at Pyongyang and Tehran and his fanning of racism make his occupancy of the White House a worldwide concern.

Ireland sees itself as a friend of America, and so it should act as one: by withdrawing the welcome mat rolled out to Trump. Enda Kenny invited him here during his last visit to the White House as Taoiseach in March. That invitation hangs now like the sword of Damocles over Leo Varadkar's head and the heads of everyone in Ireland who deplores his hate-spreading utterances. Greg Stanton, the mayor of Phoenix, has said Trump should stay away from his city, where he is scheduled to appear on Tuesday, following the comments he made about Charlottesville.

It took guts for Stanton to send that message to the world's most powerful political leader. How much easier it would be for Americans to take a stand if whole countries, such as Ireland, told Trump too: we don't want you here.

Critics may occasionally succumb to the urge to jeer Trump's hair-set and too-long neckties out of an overwhelming feeling of powerlessness to do anything about what really worries us: his power. Yet, until we withdraw our welcome to him, his welcome for himself will cast a long shadow across our planet.

I'll vote yes to make this a fairer country

Informed opinion leaves no option but to back repeal of eighth amendment.

The Sunday Times, 20 May 2018

The pain of childbirth is the most excruciating pain you will ever have in your lives, my mother used to tell us, her daughters. Coming from someone who likened the exquisite ecstasy of her first kiss with our father to that rare delight of "being hit by a combine harvester", this was rather alarming.

She was a woman who believed it best to be prepared for eventualities, arming herself with what, in today's parlance, would be called informed opinions. She was a woman overflowing with love, too, which is probably why she suffered the agony of childbirth four times.

The first time I got pregnant, I bought a card depicting a baby and wrote inside: "Hello daddy. Looking forward to seeing you in nine months." My husband discovered it propped against his dinner plate that night. He looked at me speechless with happiness. I looked back, braced for the body-ripping pain. It did not come. Into week 12 of the pregnancy, there was blood.

On my walk to work, I took a detour to the National

Maternity Hospital in Holles Street. "So terribly sorry," I was told, gently. "It's over." I was taken to theatre for a D&C (dilation and curettage) to clear out my womb. That night, a doctor drew a curtain around my bed and talked to my husband and me so kindly that I cried for the first time since walking into the hospital that morning.

I cried for weeks afterwards, on and off. I cried at home in the dark. I cried at work in front of embarrassed colleagues. I cried, not because I had lost a child – because I knew, deep in my marrow, that I had not. I was crying for our shattered dream; for the family that, for a while, we were going to be. Then I stopped crying. Life resumed and I got pregnant again. This time the pregnancy lasted eight weeks. No surgical procedure was necessary. The kind doctor told us miscarriage was normal; that about one in four pregnancies end that way.

Recently, an irate male reader wrote to me asking "by what divine inspiration did you choose yourself" to adjudicate on the facts of abortion when there are many others with opinions "much more informed than yours". While he was at it, he demanded to know why did I "continue to quote" Peter Boylan, the chairman of the Institute of Obstetricians and Gynaecologists, who has been campaigning for the repeal of article 40.3.3?

I did not tell that reader why, but I will now. I quote Boylan because I trust him. I trusted him when he pulled that curtain around my bed and talked so softly to my husband and me after the first miscarriage. I trusted him throughout my third-time-lucky pregnancy and when, after our child was born, he seemed nearly as happy as we were. And I trusted him when, clearly devastated, he testified on Christmas Eve 2014 in the

NP case, about a pregnant young mother being grotesquely kept breathing by machines after being declared clinically dead, in a vain attempt to save her 15-week foetus.

Boylan is one of 1,323 doctors who had signed up by Friday morning to the pro-repeal cause. As a former master of Holles Street, his word carries great authority. He has been targeted for being a prophet in his own land. The low point came during Monday night's RTÉ television debate when John Monaghan, a fellow retired obstetrician, called what was done to NP "noble" and suggested Boylan "go back to school" to learn about the foetus.

Mostly, the current debate has been less vicious than the 1983 one, bar the magnified bloodlust images paraded outside the National Maternity Hospital. What has not gone away is the undercurrent that women who argue for abortion provision are fundamentally bad mothers. The heavily Sellotaped, anonymous pronouncements that "your punishment awaits in hell" still arrive. Some years ago, I received a letter, signed by a woman and bearing a printed residential address in Dublin. She said she had heard me discuss abortion on a radio programme and that I was "a hypocrite".

Her letters kept coming, a whole series of them culminating in one saying she had reported me to gardai for having had an abortion in a named Irish hospital, having gotten pregnant by my supposed lover, a named – and happily married – businessman. I reported it to gardaí.

Two nice officers visited the woman, adjudging her to be "not mentally ill". She made them tea and said she could not remember how she had heard about me, the businessman and the abortion. They told her what she had written was untrue and that it had upset me. They asked her not to write to me again. She promised. The letters stopped coming.

That's the thing about being female, you see. Your anatomy is public property. Your womb is the country's moral bear pit. Your body is not your own. You, who spend nearly 40 years dealing with periods and missed periods, could not possibly be as "informed" as others, including the sort of men who avoid eye contact with tampons in a supermarket aisle.

Right now, servants of the state are trying to justify having withheld information from women about their own bodies in the cervical cancer controversy. Their predicament was precipitated by the heroism of Vicky Phelan, who has shared the most intimate details of her life in pursuit of justice. In its laws and in its practices, our state treats women as imbeciles. It treats raped, pregnant children as incubators. Yet it treats barely there embryos as fully fledged persons.

These embryos enjoy the protection of the same constitution that enshrines the relic of a woman's place in the home. When I was young, a pregnant woman was said to be expecting a baby; not carrying an unborn child. A first-time expectant girl or woman was pregnant.

Now she is "a mother", conjuring up a sweet-scented meringue of joy. It allows no acknowledgment of "the anxiety of reproduction, the oddness of it, and how it feels like dying, pulled inside out", as Anne Enright described it in *Making Babies: Stumbling into Motherhood*, the most beautiful ode to anything that I have ever read. Next Friday, when I go to vote, I will stand beside Vicky Phelan, Savita Halappanavar, Ms X, Ms Y, Ms D, Brigid McCole, the "fallen women" of the Magdalene

Laundries, the women who underwent symphysiotomy without their consent, and men who sacrifice their own cosy world for the greater good, men like Peter Boylan.

Most people who will vote yes are not in favour of abortion per se. Many will do so reluctantly, because an informed opinion leaves no option. I will stand beside these people to make the future a fairer country for all the children yet to be born, including, I hope, the future children of my own miracle baby.

If parties really cared, there'd be no homelessness

Dáil never challenges constitutional property rights' reign over human need.

The Sunday Times, 30 September 2018

Roddy Doyle does not trade in cheap sentimentality. That is why *Rosie*, his film about a Dublin family's rapid descent into rough sleeping, is so upsetting. There are no gimmicks. He could have set it in a snow storm or juxtaposed the family's nomadic desperation with oblivious well-heeled folk in the salubrious seaside suburbs but Doyle, being a gifted writer, knows homelessness needs no exaggeration.

At the end of the film's European premiere in Dublin's Light House Cinema on Tuesday night, the applause was truncated and tentative; not because it is a bad film but because it is so harrowing that clapping felt inappropriate. Outside the cinema, others were sliding down the same greasy pole towards dislocation and despair. Four families a day are becoming homeless now.

Across the Liffey in Leinster House that night, the government was fighting a motion of no confidence in the housing minister Eoghan Murphy. It would have been a better use of their time if the cabinet had decamped to the cinema and watched what being homeless actually entails. Since he became Taoiseach last year, Leo Varadkar has repeatedly told the opposition that his party's empathy is as big as theirs. If that is true, it just goes to prove to the Taoiseach, who says protests do not build houses, that empathy does not build them either.

Inside, I have recoiled from the "posh boy" tag the left-wing opposition has pinned on Murphy, believing it to be as unfair as calling someone "poor boy" or judging anybody by how they speak or where they live or went to school. I have changed my mind. Watching *Rosie*, I realised that Murphy is a posh boy, and I'm a posh girl, and Fine Gael is a posh party and that anyone who has never experienced or closely witnessed the grinding relentlessness of homelessness cannot truly understand how it eats you away. It unravels you and the people you love and, ultimately, it unravels society.

For Rosie Davis, who is played by Sarah Greene and was "inspired by too many true stories", according to Element Pictures, being homeless means draping a towel over the bedside light in a cramped hotel room to lull your children to sleep, your nostrils choked with the smell of the takeaway food containers from which you ate dinner. It means taking turns to brush your teeth in the toilets of a greasy spoon café. It means your children having nowhere to play. It means having no privacy to make love. It means going to house viewings and knowing the speculator loudly discussing the "space" with the estate agent already has the house bought. It means your child being late for school. It means having to go to a friend's house when your toddler needs to pee, now. It means you all fall out of society together, and land apart.

One day, Rosie's family was living in a house with a pet dog and a trampoline in the back garden. The next day, they were homeless because the landlord decided to sell up. Rosie and her children sit endlessly cooped up in the family's small car, the boot bulging with their belongings stuffed into refuse sacks. Her phone credit dwindles as hotel after hotel says there is no room at the inn as soon as she says she is on city council credit. As she tries to hold her family together, including her partner John Paul (Moe Dunford), who works in the kitchen of a fine restaurant, her eldest daughter struggles to do her school homework in the front passenger seat and the next daughter gets called "smelly Milly" in the school playground because Rosie has been unable to wash the child's tracksuit for PE.

In the film's most heartbreaking scene, Rosie's little son escapes into the back garden of their former home and bounces with delighted abandon on the trampoline. Rosie pulls him off it, tears washing her normally stoic face.

In all of this, there is a subtle message for the government. It says: "Watch out." People who are not homeless but who see others in that situation, and those who are peripherally affected by it, care deeply that their kin, friends and fellow citizens have been failed appallingly by the state.

Rosie is the beneficiary of many acts of kindness. Her hard-pressed friend does a laundry wash for her; John Paul's brother keeps the family dog and furniture in his own tiny home; the restaurant boss drops everything to help when Rosie's daughter goes missing. These kindnesses cannot triumph over the system, but those who perform them can punish those who preside over it.

Doyle has said there was a possibility, when he was writing

the screenplay, that homelessness would no longer be a problem in Ireland by the time the film came out. He said he wishes it had improved in the meantime. Over in the Dáil, property developer turned TD Mick Wallace was saying plenty of people are thrilled with homelessness, including builders, developers and speculators.

Politicians can cite all the statistics available, they can exorcise numbers from the official homeless figures, bicker about how long homelessness has been an issue and quote every report on the subject – but that's all just words. Empathy requires emotional understanding. If the government truly empathised, it would have devoted itself to eradicating the problem. It would challenge supposed constitutional property rights in the courts and not hand over state land to private developers while, as Wallace said, they sit on their own lands watching the value increase.

People have not forgotten how Michael Noonan, as finance minister in 2015, said the public should stop "scapegoating" property developers over the economic crash. That was the year the government halved the requirement for developers to include social and affordable housing in their estates. People see how the state never challenges the dogma that constitutional property rights reign supreme over human need. People see, as Wallace said, how the new Land Development Agency will invite developers to build homes on state-owned land while their own fallow lands grow in value.

In an RTÉ/Behaviour & Attitudes exit poll in the 2016 general election, 6% of voters said the homelessness situation was the biggest influence on their vote. That percentage would have been significantly higher in constituencies worst affected by the crisis. It will have increased concomitant with the deepening of the problem.

On Wednesday, there will be a Raise the Roof protest against homelessness outside Leinster House. It is likely to be big and angry. It may even prove that protests actually can build houses, when the state hasn't.

Let's not squander our golden moment

Level of debate in the campaign for the Áras is an insult to Irish progress.

The Sunday Times, 21 October 2018

Come to Ireland and feel the love. Britain's Prince Harry and Meghan did, and now they're expecting a baby. In case you hadn't noticed, Ireland is an Arcadian haven these days. Even the weather has been glorious. The whiff of coconut oil and after-work sea swimmers still lingers long after summer faded away. There are Michelin-starred dinners being served up in Ballydehob and Baltimore. Instead of pathetically whining our victimhood, we find ourselves pitying British citizens for having such nincompoop politicians who presume they are entitled to Irish passports and that we all want to kill each other over here.

Our rugby men and hockey women are trouncing the world and we've another Booker-winning author to our bow. As for the championship hurling, did you see that match between Cork and Limerick? Beauty in Technicolor motion. Tourism Ireland should bottle whatever is in the air.

Come to Ireland to live and let live, might go the slogan. Since the bans on same-sex marriage and abortion were comprehensively voted out of Bunreacht na hÉireann and children's rights were enshrined, there is joy abroad in Ireland.

It springs from the country's escape from the old dictatorship of judgmentalism. No more self-righteous condemnation of the neighbours and telling them what to do. At long last, our rulers, our constitution and our statute books are starting to catch up with the people. Fraternity, the missing leg of our republic's three-legged stool, has been found. It was sheltering in the hearts of the majority all along.

Ireland deserves this golden moment. The country has emerged from decades of painful revelations about child abuse, women's abuse, institutionalised inequity and the betrayal of trust, all facilitated by a culture of secrecy. Keeping schtum was the cardinal rule. Speaking out and supporting one another is what dragged us to this happy place.

It's not perfect. The proliferation of human bodies bundled on doorsteps and languishing on hospital trolleys testifies to that, but there is an optimism now that, by standing united, the people's wish for fairness will triumph. Whatever you thought about the principle of water charges, the power of communities to get them abolished was a lesson in what standing together can do.

That spirit was mobilised again to repeal the eighth amendment and is active now in the Raise the Roof campaign. These movements do not happen by magic. They grow out of conversations. Whole armies cannot vanquish a people sharing informed opinions and solid information in order to crystallise their values.

Yet the absence of substantive discussion in the presidential election campaign has been an insult to a country that has found its voice after decades of damaging silence. The campaign has been shallow, obsessed with money matters and hijacked by asinine soundbites about dog-grooming and one man's age. Being a good president is hard work. The nebulousness of a role that is mostly symbolic requires a wise head – first, to divine the message that needs to be conveyed, and then figuring out how to convey it. The president is the people's touchstone. In choosing the holder of the office, the people establish their ideals. Anyone watching this campaign, however, would be forgiven for thinking Áras an Uachtaráin is the winner's podium in a race to the bottom.

When we dumb down the presidency we dumb ourselves down in the process. Incoherence, snide insinuations and hate-propagating stunts have no place in the Aras – unless, of course, that is how we want to see ourselves. Anti-intellectualism was the stick that was used to beat us into submission for most of the first century of this state's life. Can't we see that we toy with it at our peril?

The lovely Ireland we have now is a fragile shoot. It could start dying before we even recognise it. Sometimes you recognise it more in its absence than in its presence. *The Late Late Show*'s London edition was one such epiphany. All that "isn't Ireland great?" and "don't ya just love the place now?" palaver was a throwback to an Ireland that felt it had to convince the world it was lovable in order to convince itself. Now Ireland not only feels the love but wants to spread it by seeking a seat on the UN security council. Forelock-tugging is as redundant as Flurry Knox's top hat.

Ireland's narrative of lugubrious bar-stool rebels has been replaced by a polyglot rainbow taking responsibility for its own destiny. Lament has given way to hope; the soul-scrunching greyness has turned to yellow, red, pink, purple and a generous dollop of Farrow & Ball's Elephant's Breath. The question is: can it last?

Life goes on and nothing stays the same, but we can stretch this happy age by guarding it vigilantly. Ireland's tectonic plates are shifting. You can hear them groaning under the weight of climate destruction and the impending Brexit, with its concomitant fears about a fortress border and what violence might erupt that could lead to, or be caused by, reunification, should it happen.

Beyond this state, planet Earth is wobbling precariously. The most powerful country, America, has an unapologetic purveyor of hate at the helm. The second-most powerful country, Russia, has sent its spies to murder its citizens abroad and interfered in the democratic procedures of foreign states. One of the richest countries, Saudi Arabia, feels so invincible that it murders and dismembers a journalist in its embassy, apparently expecting no consequences for its actions.

On the other end of the scale, some of Earth's poorest countries are, literally, being eroded by ecological destruction motivated by the corporate credo that you can never have enough profit. In Donald Trump's world, where the worth of a man's life is measured against a $100bn arms deal, great leadership is badly needed. As the biggest, wealthiest and most powerful countries on the planet rip up the human rights code of conduct, the duty passes to smaller countries to keep guard.

Michael Collins, a founding father of this state, said the people should not look to their leaders but to themselves. "The strength of the nation will be the strength of the spirit of the whole people," he said. Ireland still has its own battles to fight, primarily the transfer of control of education and healthcare from the Catholic Church and the eradication of cronyism among the privileged. To achieve those goals, we must keep having meaningful conversations. By stretching our imaginations, we can stretch the borders of our minds.

Ireland knows its place – it's in the EU

Brexit-battered Britain is in no position to take a dig at its neighbours.

The Sunday Times, 23 December 2018

The Spectator magazine exudes a particularly English type of loftiness-for-toffs. If it were a human creature, blue blood would course through its cerebrum. Its fragrance would emit rose water and musty, high-brow volumes. Its readers, one imagines, first encountered each other while being propelled by their starched nannies in perambulators around Sloane Square. Subscribers to such a mind-broadening periodical would, no doubt, consider themselves well versed and cosmopolitan; people with standards.

So when *The Spectator* stoops to mud-slinging, you know Britannia has awoken to its dire straits. Time to find a whipping boy. "Leo Varadkar is being played like a fiddle by Brussels," went – as it turned out – the understated headline on a blog opinion piece last week by a contributor called Brendan O'Neill, who declared himself an Irishman. Accusing the Taoiseach of "meddling in British politics", and "his minions" of trying to "scupper" Brexit, O'Neill spluttered: "Who does he think he is?"

Describing the upstart Varadkar's utterances as being "motored by the elitist, practically imperial belief that what is good for his government – his foreign government – is more important than what the British people themselves, in their millions, voted for", it would be easier to score points finding holes in this assertion than by shooting fish in a barrel.

The article brings all the reliable stereotypes of the political ecosystem swimming to the surface. There are "cynical" Brussels oligarchs and "once plucky" – but always gullible, apparently – Ireland allowing itself to be used as their "patsy". At the risk of tedium, O'Neill and his ilk need reminding that Ireland is an independent, sovereign state with a Taoiseach whose constitutional duty is to his country and its people, not them next door. That's how it's been for nearly 99 years now.

Isn't it interesting, though, how the sputter of bilious indignation from across the water is just so many variations on the theme of role reversal? England's born-to-rulers keep harping on about inverted imperialism and how they are now the colonised ones, exposing a still deep-rooted assumption that the whole world considers imperial conquest to be the apogee of national superiority. Elitism is only undesirable if it does not come with a "made in Oxbridge" hallmark.

The Spectator is not alone; though it is the most lamentable. Examples are numerous. There was the Tory MP quoted anonymously by the BBC as saying: "The Irish should really know their place." There was Priti Patel, another Conservative MP, threatening a revisitation of an Gorta Mór. Last weekend, the *Mail on Sunday* newspaper reported that Theresa May "loathes" Varadkar and can barely bring herself to speak to him.

There could hardly be a starker contrast than that between the parliament beside the Thames blowing itself asunder over its self-made dilemma and the parliament beside the Liffey, which is phenomenally united in its belief that Brexit poses a real threat to peace and prosperity on this island. Even amid its chaotic cacophony, Britain still has plenty of voices of reason. One such is former prime minister John Major, who criticised the "breathtaking ignorance" of rigid Brexiteers about the vulnerability of the Irish border. Even former foreign secretary Boris Johnson, writing about a post-Brexit Mars Bar famine in *The Spectator*, where he was the editor for nine years, posits: "There may have been times in the last century when the government of Britain has looked more pathetic, but I can't think what they are."

The attacks on Varadkar revive memories of rank anti-Irishness during the Troubles, which hit its nadir when Robert Kilroy-Silk, a politician and television presenter, wrote in the *Daily Express* that Ireland was peopled by "peasants, priests and pixies". Frequent hate-inciting cartoons had Irish diplomats in London making the regular consternation commute to register complaints in the Foreign Office.

What a change it is that Ireland is now the one feeling sorry for all the good English people sucked into Brexit's doomed engine. When blindsided by your own short-sightedness it is difficult to recognise your friends from your enemies. Varadkar is no jingoistic, Brits-out opportunist plotting to stick a tricolour in Carson's upraised hand outside Stormont. His own political lineage is as blue as the Tories'. Home-rule enthusiast John Bruton, one of his predecessors as Fine Gael leader, was witheringly dubbed John "Unionist" by the late Albert Reynolds. Varadkar has even ventured in recent months that it is "not too far-fetched to imagine" someone from Carson's unionist tradition becoming Taoiseach in Dublin some day.

That said, our Taoiseach can come across as somewhat smug,

albeit the trait is not confined to his views on Brexit. He likes to remind his listeners that he is a doctor, that he is young, in touch with the cultural zeitgeist, and leader of a country that reflects his own fetching modernity. Indeed, he is a mirror. Smugness has become part of the new Ireland, since its reinvention as Europe's savvy, young, progressive state.

There is a temptation to wallow in Britain's undignified need to lash out at Ireland for having the cheek to wag the EU's tail. But fortunes change fast and who knows what will be the next *bête noir* of Brussels. Will they come looking for their pound of flesh in the form of corporate tax reform when Brexit is complete? Besides, where was their solidarity when the Irish had to bail out the bondholders?

This country has woes which give it no reason to be proud. Consider the ranks of people sleeping on the streets and lying for days on hospital trolleys. It is the worst European country for responding to climate damage and has been deemed a tax haven by reputable international bodies.

Neither is the EU perfect. It is building a military force right under our noses and, sometimes, Germany and France behave as if they own the whole alliance. Yet, we are better off within it. Women and others who suffered from institutionalised prejudice know this from experience. If the new Ireland is progressive, it is because the EU has made us so.

How it must rankle with Brexiteers when they look across the Irish Sea and realise that Ireland knows its place damned well – it's in the EU, buffered against big and hectoring neighbours. This is no reason to wallow in their predicament, however, much as we may pity them their poor political representation. Roles inevitably get reversed, eventually. And, besides, *schadenfreude* is not a word in the Irish language.

The 2020s

I have no troubles with honouring real heroes of Irish independence

Wrong to let fuss over Sinn Féin tweets cloud the sacrifices of our forebears.

The Sunday Times, 13 December 2020

A mid the furore over the Kilmichael ambush in Co Cork a century ago, and Sinn Féin TD Brian Stanley's tweet equating it with the Troubles in Northern Ireland, 10 men and women carrying mementoes and pots of Christmas cyclamen gathered in the Catholic church graveyard of my native town, Bandon. Without oration or fanfare, the group quietly recited a decade of the rosary at the republican plot gravesides of their forebears.

John Galvin, 18, James O'Donoghue, 18, and Joseph Begley, 24, were lured to their deaths in December 1920 by members of the Essex regiment of the British Army, which was garrisoned in the town. There is a small memorial to the three men beneath a tree on Laurel Walk, where the road heads for Dunmanway and where they breathed their last.

At the graveside this month, one man held the original photograph taken of the dead men in their open coffins the night before their funerals in St Patrick's Church, showing their corpses marked with mutilation. Copies of that photograph hung over mantelpieces in the three families' various homes throughout much of the 20th century.

John Galvin was my father's first cousin. The Galvins lived further up South Main Street in Bandon. John worked for my grandfather Jerome – his uncle – in the business house at No 77, which my father would eventually inherit and which became the family home for my three sisters and me.

Jerome grew up in the Rock, Ardgehane, Barryroe on the magnificent Seven Heads peninsula. When he died, aged 75, his obituary in the *Southern Star* newspaper described the business he ran as "a posting establishment", which we called "the bar", and to which he added undertaking, coffin-making and a saw mill. He and my grandmother Nora made quite the entrepreneurial partnership. While she looked after the business in Bandon, he worked as the farm steward more than 30 miles away at Drishane Castle, a convent and school run by a French order of nuns in Millstreet.

Our generation knows only the flimsiest threads of what happened to Jerome during the War of Independence. He was an elected member of Cork county council when he was arrested, for reasons unknown to us, and held first in Macroom Castle and then Cork City Gaol. From there, he was transported to Ballykinlar internment camp in Co Down, at the other end of Ireland, where he went on hunger strike. One of our family's treasured keepsakes is a letter Nora wrote to him there. With meticulous penship, she kept him abreast of their joint business affairs, the local economy and, in passing, the wellbeing of their two babies. She made no mention of her nightly escape by pony and trap with those babies to her own family home eight miles away in Kilbrittain, travelling dangerous country roads in pitch darkness.

It was only when I watched RTÉ's powerful documentary on the abuse of women in the War of Independence and the Civil War that I realised, with a jolt, why Nora must have made that journey: she was a young woman alone in a public house regularly plundered by drunken Black and Tans. As far as I know, the closest she came to talking about it was when my mother arrived in Bandon to begin her married life in No 77, and Nora brought her out to the back yard to show her the bullet marks still on the walls from those anarchic nights.

The story we grew up with about Jerome's internment in Ballykinlar was about the escape plan he concocted with his fellow internees to tunnel their way out under the barbed wire using teaspoons. Other internees have described Ballykinlar as "a hell hole". In the single year the camp operated, three prisoners were shot dead by their keepers and five more died of malnutrition.

After Jerome was released, the French nuns held a welcome-home party for him in Drishane. The new independent state awarded him one of those War of Independence medals with a metal bar, signifiying exceptional service. He took the anti-treaty side in the civil war, and was elected an independent member of Cork county council. His priority was to build houses for his impoverished home town, and his legacy is still visible in Bandon's bricks and mortar.

Jerome died of heart failure on a Sunday morning at the age of 75. The headstone at Timoleague Abbey, where he lies with his ancestors, dispenses with first names. "McCarthy, the Rock" is all it says.

I never met my grandfather but, from what I know, I do not believe he was motivated by prejudice. When commentators chant the revisionist hymn that west Cork was a hotbed of sectarian murders in 1920, it enrages me, because it is sweepingly unfair. I imagine Jerome's blood boiled, too, when he witnessed injustice.

When the *Skibbereen Eagle* – as the *Southern Star* was named back then – reported on Jerome's mother's funeral in November 1913, it observed that the mourners were "representative of all creeds and classes". Whatever her son did to earn his service medal, I do not believe she brought him up to murder Protestants just because they were Protestants. There were plenty of reasons to join the fight for national self-determination.

To revisionists contemplating their navels in their ivory towers south of the border, the IRA's murderous violence in the Troubles was utterly without justification. Easy for them to say from the top of the heap in their self-satisfied independent state. Not so easy for their fellow Irishmen and women left behind in a sectarian state where, to apply the words of President Michael D Higgins in a different context, they endured "deeply layered humiliation [and] loss of respect".

It is said the victors write history but there are no winners in war. It is a merciless spiral of tit-for-tat death in which nobody is all wrong and nobody is all right. Many critics of Sinn Féin's "selective" version of history have exhibited the same selectivity themselves, latching on to Higgins's warning against exploiting the past for contemporary insidious purposes.

Less attention has been given to his caution against amnesia. My grandfather and his contemporaries took on the might of an empire. To impute equivalence between the occupied population and the occupying force is inherently unjust. If there had been no rampant, unapologetic, systemic and institutionalised injustice in the first place, there would have been no cause for the fighting. For many people, this essential truth is what links the Troubles to the revolutionary period a century ago.

That is an aspect of the debate that is too important to surrender to the crude and incoherent witterings of Sinn Féin TDs on Twitter. Each of us has our part to play. Let none of us be ashamed to share our long-held stories, before they evaporate in the mists of time.

Why we need to talk about a united Ireland

'Don't frighten the horses' attitude does nobody any favours on this island.

The Sunday Times, 20 June 2021

If *Punch* magazine had done the united Ireland debate it might have portrayed a landscape of galumphing giants while, underfoot, little people squealed: "I'm sorry, it's entirely my fault for getting in your way," just before being squashed into eternal silence. Ireland's obsequious timidity about mentioning the U-word has gone way beyond pathetic. It has become downright dangerous.

On Tuesday, the second-most senior politician in this country told his party's ard fheis that he believed the state's constitutionally enshrined dream for the reunification of Ireland's isle and its people could happen in his lifetime. In his speech, the Tánaiste espoused nothing more than what 94.4 per cent of voters endorsed in the 1998 referendum replacing the territorial claim on Northern Ireland with an aspiration for peaceful reunification by consent. Such was the predictable outrage that a stranger to the debate might imagine Leo Varadkar had proposed marching on London and hoisting the tricolour in Westminster.

"Unhelpful and ill-advised," pronounced Brandon Lewis, the secretary of state for Northern Ireland, suggesting everyone should "dial down the rhetoric". So said the man who announced in the mother of parliaments that his government intended passing a bill to usurp international law and breach the Brexit withdrawal agreement when the ink was barely dry on its signatures. "Does @LeoVaradkar believe in the Belfast agreement's principle of consent for the people of Northern Ireland or not? Seems not," tweeted the former DUP leader Arlene Foster, giving a whole new meaning to the term non sequitur.

As usual, some of the most indignant reaction was voiced within the Republic, where little Irelanders, literally, branded any hint of a united-Ireland conversation as a threat to peace and progress. The double standard is breathtaking. Few of these critics voiced any concern when, in April, the UK prime minister Boris Johnson said in a BBC interview he could not envisage a referendum on reunification for "a very, very long time to come".

Irish citizens living in Northern Ireland have as much a right to hear their government discuss the state's constitutional position on reunification as have British citizens living there to hear their government uphold the current constitutional position. After Ireland was carved into two territories a century ago, Winston Churchill wrote: "Both Northern Ireland's Catholic nationalists, as well as the Protestants and unionists stranded in the south, must be left to stew in their own juice." And northern nationalists can go on stewing, as far as some people south of the border are concerned.

Last week, while appearing before a House of Lords

committee on the Ireland/Northern Ireland protocol in the Brexit agreement, Jonathan Powell, who was Britain's chief negotiator in the Good Friday agreement talks, accused London of "deliberately provoking" the Dublin government and of damaging the Anglo-Irish relationship. Imagine the rush to condemn in this Republic had those words, instead, been uttered by an Irish politician.

The theme of Fine Gael's ard fheis was "the future". To not have mentioned the prospect of unity would have been a case of *Hamlet* without the prince. The future is a different country now. Brexit has shaken the foundations of the UK. The pandemic has accentuated the folly of having separate health and public safety policies on this island. As a result, Ireland's constitutional future is no longer set in stone.

The "don't frighten the horses" mentality in the Republic's establishment is already endangering that future. Whenever there is an attempt to plan its design or even to imagine it, the Praetorian guard of little Irelanders shuts it down. Varadkar has been criticised for bad timing but when, pray tell, has there ever been a good time in the five fraught years since the Brexit referendum? As long as the debate stays stuck in the talking-about-talking-about-it rut, the risk increases that – just as happened with Brexit – Ireland will be perilously ill-prepared for reunification when it happens.

One such diversion is the accusation that the Fine Gael leader is playing party politics against the backdrop of a by-election in Dublin Bay South, where the ascendant Sinn Féin has a strong candidate in Lynn Boylan. Varadkar is capable of such a cunning plan but his record on Northern Ireland, including his pledge that no government in Dublin will ever again abandon its nationalist people, suggests he is a sincere united Irelander. Ditto in the case of Simon Coveney, his slightly older party deputy leader, who previously raised obsequious hackles by expressing the hope that Ireland would be united in his lifetime.

Unlike the mostly hidden work of the new Shared Island unit in the Department of the Taoiseach, Varadkar's ard fheis speech was an attempt at open, inclusive and stimulating discussion. "Unification must not be the annexation of Northern Ireland," he cautioned. "It means something more: a new state designed together, a new constitution and one that reflects the diversity of a bi-national or multinational state in which almost a million people are British. Like the new South Africa, a rainbow nation, not just orange and green."

He pointed out some of the dilemmas that we face. Will we be willing to change the state's titles and symbols for this new Ireland? What would be the role and status of the Irish language? Could devolution exist within the political structures? These are crucial issues that need to be discussed but the don't-frighten-the-horses brigade has succeeded, once again, in burying them under a pile of condemnation.

The enduring attitude that, in the Anglo-Irish relationship, one of us has got to be the grown-up and that one has always got to be Ireland is becoming farcical. On the night before Varadkar delivered his speech, Michael Portillo, a former Conservative Party MP, presented *Partition, 1921*, a television documentary. The thrust of his thesis was that the Tories and their former leader Andrew Bonar Law, by supporting threats of Ulster Volunteer Force rebellion in the north of Ireland, were the architects of the border a century ago. The case he made verged on party subversion, especially considering that Portillo won his parliamentary seat in a by-election caused by the death of Anthony Berry when the IRA blew up the Grand Hotel in Brighton during the Tories' 1984 conference.

Turning to face the camera at the end of the documentary, Portillo pondered Ireland's destiny. "It is to be hoped that, after so much bloodshed, the question of removing the border is to be approached with more wisdom and sensitivity than were evident at its creation," he said.

In a week of censorious shibboleths about the U-word, Portillo's acceptance of difficult realities, both in the past and in the future, and his willingness to learn from one in order to enhance the other, were impressive. He embodied just the sort of grown-up that Ireland needs to be.

I told my family to accept my wishes – but this is the way I want to die

Cervical cancer campaigner Vicky Phelan supports
the rights of the terminally ill to a dignified death.

The Sunday Times, 28 November 2021

The excruciating lengths to which Vicky Phelan has gone in her attempts to stay alive might have destroyed another person. At night, in the apartment where she was staying in Alexandria, north Virginia, in her last desperate shot at extending her life, she used to imagine her children asleep in Ireland, where the clocks were five hours ahead, and feel acutely alone.

She phoned them every evening before their bedtime, at six o'clock Pacific standard time. Amelia, 16, would chat away but sometimes Darragh, ten, refused to speak to her.

"Angry; punishment; 'because you're not here I'm not going to talk to you'," she recalls in that matter-of-fact way that is pure Vicky Phelan. "When I'd left, he didn't really realise I'd be gone for a long time. That went on for a good few days, when he wouldn't talk to you at all. But, sure, you have to go with it."

The familiar, lovely hair she once had is gone. Not so the trademark vitality, though. Dressed all in black and her face devoid of make-up, those big eyes still mirror a woman who relishes being alive. "I'm a young woman. I don't want to die," she says.

But, on her 47th birthday last month, she told her family she was stopping her fight to live on. When Phelan left Ireland in January on a mission to try to prolong her life, the plan was for the family to visit her in the US, but the Covid-19 pandemic halted international travel, stranding them on opposite sides of the Atlantic. Many nights stretched bleakly ahead during the nine months she spent on a phase two cancer drug trial at the National Institutes of Health (NIH), just over the state border in Maryland. To fill the empty hours, she would read the myriad messages from well-wishers on Facebook. "That affection kept me going on the days when it was hard."

She longed for Ireland and its people, who have, metaphorically, kept watch with her ever since the day, four years ago now, when she settled her High Court case against Clinical Pathology Laboratories in Texas for €2.5 million.

Having been told her cervical cancer was likely to kill her within six to 12 months, she had stood outside the Four Courts in Dublin and revealed that she had refused to sign a confidentiality undertaking. She said she did so because other women with the disease needed to know the authorities had withheld knowledge of their misread smear tests following their cancer diagnoses. "The Irish are great," she says with a smile, sitting in her kitchen where lists of hospital phone numbers are pinned to the wall behind her. "So many of them reached out to me on Facebook and Instagram when I went over there."

One evening, while renting an Airbnb apartment at the start of her stay, she visited O'Connell's Irish pub, where the staff told her the proprietor, John Brennan, was from her native town of Mooncoin, Co Kilkenny. The next day, Vicky's mother rang her, to say Brennan had called round to their house to offer her the use of his apartment, free of charge, in Alexandria's pretty suburb of Old Town. She gratefully accepted.

The trial she was on at the hospital was for an as yet unnamed immunotherapy drug designated M724, designed to help patients' bodies fight their cancer. It is the same principle underlining Pembrolizumab, the drug she began taking to great effect after the court case, though its benefits ultimately waned. Every three weeks in America, she underwent a scan to monitor the effectiveness of M724.

"Every time I'd sit in a waiting room over there, nobody spoke to each other, whereas here you'd be sitting in a waiting room and you'd be chatting away. I found that very isolating."

Eventually she asked her oncologist to put her in touch with somebody else on the trial. He gave her a woman's phone number and Phelan sent her a message. "She texted me once and said, 'Oh, yeah, I'd love to meet up for a coffee.' It never happened." Meanwhile, the scans were showing no change in Phelan's condition. Then they started showing the tumours were increasing. "I had the chat with my oncologist at the NIH. He was trying to convince me to go on another trial that he had going but it was only a phase one trial, and I said to him, 'No, I don't think so.'"

Instead, she opted for proton beam therapy, which is similar to radiotherapy, at the nearby Georgetown University Hospital. "I knew it wasn't going to do anything for me except maybe buy me some time."

After undergoing a plethora of medical assessments to establish whether she was suitable for the treatment, Phelan was referred for a PET scan. It was early on a Friday morning and she was alone in the Old Town apartment when her new oncologist phoned with the result. It was bad. Yet another tumour had appeared. Proton beam therapy, which would have cost Phelan $150,000 (€132,500), was not advisable. The time had come, the doctor said, to "ask yourself when you stop". The news, she says, was devastating.

"I literally got out of bed and said, 'Right, I have to go home.' I got on the laptop and booked a flight for the Monday."

An Irish friend came from New York to pack up her belongings in the apartment "because I was, I suppose, in shock, going, 'Shit, this is not good.' Because I knew at that stage I'm not coming home to anything but palliative [care]."

At the airport, Phelan reached the departure gate in a wheelchair. Ireland was still sleeping when she landed in the early hours of September 27, and was driven home to her still-slumbering family in Annacotty by her parents. She received her first, and final, dose of chemotherapy on October 18, becoming so unbearably sick that a nurse from Milford Hospice came every day to care for her.

"You think you'll be able to tolerate it but, Jesus, no. You get these terrible shooting pains going through your body from chemo. They go right through your bones."

Together with Jim, her husband from whom she had been separated but is now reunited – "we're a partnership" – they told Amelia that the quest to extend her mother's life had reached the end of the road.

"The first thing Amelia said – which blew me away – was, 'Well, you got four years, Mam,' which none of the adults said. That's exactly what I had been trying to say to them when they were all distraught and saying, 'You can't give up.' I understand where my family are coming from when they say, 'You have to try this and you have to try that.' I have to sit them down and say, 'You know, you're not the one going through all this. It's not your body having to put up with all this shit. Easy for you to say, and then f*** off home and not have to deal with the after-effects of all these drugs.' I said, 'No, I'm done.' I've had enough. I've put my body through torture. I have to accept it.

"After they saw how sick I was from the chemo, it made it much easier to talk about because I said, 'Now, do you want me to be like that and prolong the agony or are ye actually going to listen to me? Accept my wishes and the fact I don't want this, and my time will probably be shorter but this is the way I want to go.'" Telling Darragh was harder. "It was the first time we mentioned the word 'death' or that this might not end very well. He knew how sick I was. I said there are no drugs that are going to make me better. They're only going to keep me alive for another little while. He said, 'How long?' I said, 'I don't know, Darragh.' Yesterday [last Monday] he didn't go to school and I asked him why, was he sick? He said, 'No, I'm just sad.'"

Now back on Pembro, as she calls it, and with a scan due after Christmas, Phelan's thoughts have turned to the circumstances in which her life will end. She wants it to happen at the family holiday home, a bungalow from where they can see the sand dunes of Doughmore beach in Doonbeg.

"I think I'd rather die there than here [in their home] for the kids' sake. Dying here would be very hard for them. The memory of it." She has chosen cremation and a wicker casket. She wants no wake, to save her children from seeing strangers looking at her in the coffin.

She is planning a private funeral for family and close friends. Later, there will be a memorial service where she wants the Stunning and the Blizzards to perform her favourite songs, including Postcards from Heaven.

She has seen gold lockets on the crematorium website that she would like for Amelia, so that she can wear her mother's ashes around her neck, and a leather bracelet version for Darragh. She hopes Jim will meet someone else eventually.

Is she frightened?

"When I'm well, I'm not. When I'm sick, yes, because you worry about how it's going to end. At the moment my biggest worry is ending up with some complication that I would have to go to hospital for. If I end up in hospital, nobody can come in and I'm on my own again and I've already spent most of the f***ing year on my own.

"I'm a young woman. I've a strong heart. I was quite fit before I got cancer. I don't want to linger – for the kids – but, no matter how much you sedate someone, you still have to wait for the heart to go. The younger you are, the longer that's going to take, so I think I'd be lingering quite a while.

"What's the option? I'm not going to go to [an assisted-dying clinic in] Switzerland at this stage."

Gino Kenny, a People Before Profit TD whose unsuccessful right-to-die Dail bill she supported last year, has told her he intends introducing a new bill next year.

"I'm glad he's going to do it but Gino's bill is unlikely to be enacted in time for me. I don't know why we [Irish] won't talk about this. I mean, it's going to come to us all at the end of the day.

"It's about choice. We choose what way we want to live – when to have children, when to get married. Why should you not be able to choose what way want to die, particularly in a situation like mine?

"I'd never advocate euthanasia but, in conditions like mine, or motor neurone disease or multiple sclerosis where the end is not going to be nice, where people are going to deteriorate and going to die, there's no coming back from it when you're terminally ill. So why should you prolong the agony?"

Phelan has seen other cervical cancer campaigners and friends die, and knows what's ahead, but it is for her children that she worries. "I know it doesn't happen to everyone but that death rattle, you know, I did see it in one case and it frightened the life out of me. And I thought if it frightened me, what would it be like for my children if they had to witness that?

"I've spoken to some of the families afterwards and they're horrified, devastated, by the way their parent or sibling died. But after that happens they box it away and don't talk about it. It's too painful.

"We do wakes really well in this country and we do death really well – when a person is dead – but why don't we do that bit in the middle when a person is dying?"

Saying she is "more accepting now that this is coming", she leaves the kitchen to search for a picture in an adjoining room. The open door reveals a large first-aid box on the wall. Her reality is harshly omnipresent.

The following day, she texts "you were lucky to get me on a good day", adding that she had woken up violently ill.

Listening back to the recording of the interview, two traits stand out. One is an occasional dry cough that punctuates her unequivocally candid conversation. The other, amazingly, is how frequently she calls herself "lucky".

Grace has a voice at last, and our duty is to listen

This vulnerable woman has suffered negligence by a thousand cuts.

The Sunday Times, 10 October 2021

Most of us do not know her. We have never seen her. We do not even know her real name. Yet the woman pseudonymously known as Grace has hovered in our collective conscience as a spectral reminder of our imperfect state ever since her story emerged at the Dáil's public accounts committee more than four years ago.

Now, from the 800 pages of two "substantive interim" reports by Marjorie Farrelly, the senior counsel chairing a commission of investigation into the case, Grace comes alive in all her vulnerable humanity.

She was born to a 17-year-old resident of a mother and baby home in Cork nearly 43 years ago, arriving into this world with microcephaly, an under-developed brain, caused by asphyxia during delivery. She was destined never to speak and would need care for her entire life.

When Grace was five, a health board psychologist wrote that she was being fostered by Family A, who were "very fond of her" and wanted to adopt her; that the child was walking and running and sometimes rode a tricycle, could feed herself with a spoon and assist in dressing herself. Grace began attending a special needs school in Co Wicklow. On January 27, 1989, the sister in charge wrote: "She is a pretty 11-year-old [she was actually 10] who has long, fair hair and pale complexion ... She is good at dressing/undressing, cannot manage laces, fine zips and small buttons. Loves to help with the washing-up, set the table, do simple household skills, eg dusting and sweeping. Loves swimming ... climbing frame and indoor trampoline." The sister added: "[Couple A] deserve great praise and thanks for the love, care and time they have given to [Grace]."

Then calamity happened. Mr and Mrs A separated and Mrs A was subsequently hospitalised for a deteriorating health condition. Thus, Grace came to live with Family X in February 1989, sealing her fate for the next 20 years. The couple had returned from Manchester, where Irish-born Mrs X had minded children in her home. After the Xs settled in an isolated area in Co Waterford, the Brothers of Charity began placing children with them for periods of two weeks in the summer of 1984 on temporary boarding-out contracts.

When Kitty Greaney, the children's officer with the South Eastern Health Board (SEHB) who is now deceased, brought Grace to the Xs' home, she noted "there was a great welcome for her". The terms of the boarding contract provided for IR£34.50 weekly payments to Mrs X.

In her exhaustively detailed reports, Farrelly says that the commission could not ascertain if health board officials knew Mrs X had been convicted of larceny four months before Grace arrived in her home. The SEHB also seemed unaware that Mr X had two convictions, for larceny and theft. Nor did health officials seem aware that other people were living at the property, including Mrs X's nephew, who slept in a caravan behind the house, and the couple's daughter and one-year-old grandson.

These gaps in knowledge stem from the SEHB's failure to produce a report, as required by the regulations, on the suitability of the foster parents and the condition of their home. Nor did the board obtain a doctor's report on the foster parents' health, as the regulations also required. Despite a 1988 policy stipulation that garda clearance must be obtained, the commission found no evidence that an application had been made. Likewise, it found no evidence of any attempt to verify Mrs X's dubious claim that she was registered as a childminder in England.

For Grace, this was negligence by a thousand cuts. Though she would not attend school again until the age of 17, it seemed, at first, as if she had luckily escaped any ill-effects from the numerous failures by officialdom in placing her with Family X. In August 1989, six months after her arrival, a report described her as "a child with a happy and sunny disposition".

After six years with the Xs, Grace started to attend a day care centre. A month later there was concern about her stripping off on the school bus. On October 19, 1995 a staff member in the centre noticed bruises on Grace's left hip and both her elbows. It was assumed these had happened accidentally.

Six months later a letter postmarked March 8, 1996, arrived in the SEHB office from the mother of a girl with an intellectual disability who had stayed with the Xs for short periods ten years earlier. "To whom it may concern," she wrote. "This letter is concerning my daughter [EE] who is mentally retarded. I have just found out from her that while on holiday in [the Xs' home place] she was sexually molested by the husband of the woman she stayed with."

The SEHB resolved to remove Grace from the house, and secured a place for her in Clonmel. Gardaí were notified of the alleged sexual abuse but EE's mother refused to let her daughter be interviewed because of the trauma it would cause her, so the investigation went nowhere. When the Xs were informed Grace was being removed, their response was "over our dead bodies", or words to that effect. They were allowed to make representations to the SEHB at a meeting on May 17.

In August, Mr X wrote to Michael Noonan, then minister for health, with no mention of the abuse allegation but suggesting "for some obscure reason [the SEHB] are prepared to deny [Grace] this comfort and happiness". The Xs also got the local schoolmaster, who would have been unaware of the abuse claim, to write to Noonan on their behalf. Farrelly has found that Noonan sought a report but did not intervene.

According to evidence, Grace's situation remained in a "holding position" with the SEHB until a case conference in October decided to leave her with the Xs. This horrifying decision appears to have arisen, in large part, from a fear the SEHB could be sued for defamation if it mentioned that an abuse allegation had prompted her removal. Farrelly says the commission got "no satisfactory explanation" for the decision, and she observed that "a type of administrative paralysis took hold around the fact that the allegation had not been investigated and could not be substantiated".

Her report notes that not a single health board official had met Grace in the six months between the board getting the abuse complaint and deciding to leave her in the house.

Grace remained with the Xs for another 13 years. Farrelly's next report will deal with what happened next. In the meantime, these first two reports have, at last, given Grace her voice. The least we can do is listen, and learn.

State should disown baby home report

The censorship of witness testimonies renders
the investigation a travesty.

The Sunday Times, 13 June 2021

The Latin dictum "in vino veritas" is a model of brevity in explaining how wine loosens the tongue to allow the truth to come out. In the parlance of psychoanalysis it is that state of disinhibition when someone feels so at ease that all restraint is thrown to the wind. Alcohol is not always a prerequisite. Sometimes just being in your comfort zone can have a similar effect.

It seems to have been a case of "in academia veritas" when Mary Daly, an emeritus professor of history at UCD and one of the three members of the commission of investigation into mother and baby homes, addressed a seminar for postgraduate students at the University of Oxford on June 2. Until that day the three had maintained a Trappist-like silence since their seventh and final report was published in January, a report that caused consternation among survivors and campaigners.

Pure bewilderment greeted its conclusions that there was no evidence women and girls had been forced to enter the institutions, no evidence of harm caused to children used in vaccine trials, and no evidence of forced adoptions. People who had conveyed their personal experiences of quite the opposite in the homes under investigation were perplexed as to how the three wise commissioners – Daly, Yvonne Murphy and William Duncan – could have reached those conclusions.

Daly's acceptance of the invitation to speak at a college event outside of Ireland was appallingly insensitive to the feelings of survivors who were already pained at discovering their testimonies had been elided and distorted in the report's findings. It was disrespectful, too, to the Irish state and its people after the commission members had rejected repeated requests from the Oireachtas committee on children to come before it and answer questions about its work.

Once Daly started talking at the forum organised by the university which, she pointed out, was where she had done her graduate studies, she was on a roll. Her disclosures that the commission felt constrained by legal threats, its unwieldy terms of reference and the uncontested nature of the confidential committee running parallel to the investigative channel, have all caused ructions. There are calls for the government to repudiate the entire report, on the grounds that the legalistic impediments Daly enumerated have compromised its credibility.

While lawyers and academics may argue about the commission's methodology till the cows come home, there was something else Daly said at the seminar that should motivate the government to set a match to the entire 3,000-page report without any further ado. "When you spoke to the women who were in the various institutions, you got odd snippets of ... You'd get descriptions of their time there," she said. "You got descriptions of, you know, getting women's magazines sent in and letters hidden in the middle. You know, you got bits and pieces like that. You got, you know, some comments on ... I mean one woman said it was like boarding school. We decided not to put that in the report. We thought people would go up in arms over it, but that's actually what she told us."

In effect, what Daly was saying was that the commission censored witnesses' testimonies. This is shocking. It amounts to the suppression of survivors' memories of their own lives, an entirely different matter to the omission of factual assertions that could be contested or attract a threat of legal action. Anyone whose work involves establishing the truth knows it must be told in its entirety, because a half-truth is a lie by another name. You cannot mould the narrative to make it palatable or just because you don't like it. Banishing secrecy and establishing the truth was the paramount purpose of this commission. Daly's admission shows that it has failed abjectly to do that.

We have to ask was anything else altered to suit a subjective value judgment? In February a witness at the confidential committee told this newspaper her testimony published in the report was so twisted that her religious denomination, that of the clergyman involved in her case and of the institution that ran the homes where she was resident were all changed from Protestant to Catholic.

The daughter of Church of Ireland parents, she spent time in the 1980s in two Protestant-run mother and baby homes: Denny House and Miss Carr's. Did the commission consider it too controversial to record that Protestant institutions also behaved abominably towards unmarried females and their children? Was that deemed too unpalatable? Another apt Latin phrase comes to mind: "in absentia lucis, tenebrae vincunt". In the absence of light, darkness prevails.

It is a terrible pity that the commission's final report has been a travesty of justice for survivors. Some of the early work it did was excellent. Among its six interim reports were groundbreaking developments, such as the recommendation to government that survivors of homes who had been excluded from the pre-existing residential institutions redress scheme should qualify for compensation. Its fifth interim report, published in March 2019, dealt with burials of children and women in the homes. It was mammoth in both its significance and disclosures.

At some stage the commission lost its way. Its final report is riddled with contradictions and it cannot be allowed to stand as the official state record.

Roderic O'Gorman, the minister for children, has written to the survivors saying the commission wrongly interpreted its terms of reference when it discounted the testimonies of 550 people who spoke to a confidential committee. Yet he has argued that the report must be accepted in order to allow for a compensation scheme to be established. This is the scheme which, according to the commission, should not be open to anybody who was resident in the homes after the state introduced the unmarried mothers' allowance in 1973. The false assumption underlying that recommendation is that it was money alone that determined if a woman ended up in one of those institutions.

If the government fails to repudiate the commission's final report it will be operating on the same false assumption: that the money is all that matters. Has Ireland learnt nothing from the past three decades of distressing revelations about the institutional abuse of its most vulnerable people? Survivor after survivor after survivor has said that what they want most of all is for the truth to be told and for them to be believed.

By that standard the commission's report has to be disowned by the state. "Beauty is truth; truth beauty," wrote the poet John Keats. But truth is only beautiful when it is told warts and all. Anything less is just platitudes designed to make everyone else feel better.

Vaccine queue-jumping scandals must spring us into action

Vaccine-sharing scandals should be the impetus to tackle social inequality.

The Sunday Times, 4 April 2021

There used to be a programme on RTÉ Radio 1 called *Queuing for a Living* in which the reporter, Paddy O'Gorman, recorded the life stories of people he found waiting in queues. Every week he would take his microphone to dole offices and courthouses and pawn shops, amassing a trove of tales that wove a colourful batik of Irish life, but with one glaring exception. The voices of the rich and the powerful, who otherwise dominate the national airwaves, were never heard. Queues, you see, are not for them. Rather like taxes, waiting in line is for the little people.

Their sort does not queue for buses or prison visits or a bed in a homeless hostel or at methadone clinics or for an operation or at the chipper or for asylum or for a half-price TV in the January sales. Queues have no role in their code of conduct. Their time is much too precious for that. Often, they will pay other people to queue for them. During the Celtic Tiger years, some smart entrepreneurs identified that this reluctance to queue created a gap in the market, and set up a lucrative business offering to queue in the motor taxation office for masters of the universe who had far more important things to be doing with their far more precious time.

This ingrained them-and-us attitude has been exposed once again by the odious cronyism that has gone on with vaccine-sharing between the private Beacon Hospital and St Gerard's private school, and by two consultants in the Coombe Women and Infants University Hospital. It may sound too polite to call this brazen queue-hopping, but that is precisely what it amounts to.

The school has said that the hospital assured it the HSE was fine with vaccines being passed on. But when Beacon Hospital used state-owned vaccines to inoculate some staff at an expensive school attended by the children of the hospital's chief executive, its behaviour was no different to the burly passenger pushing his way past the physically frail to be first on the bus. Actually, it's worse than that, because the consequence was to attain immunity in a pandemic – potentially securing longer, healthier lives for families and cronies. Surely, this is the ultimate in buying time, at the expense of those who cannot afford to do so.

Stories abound about vulnerable people in their eighties and nineties who are still waiting to get their vaccines, while some Twitter users have posted about family members undergoing cancer treatment in Beacon Hospital who are yet to be inoculated. Survey after survey tells us that those worst affected by this public health crisis are women, children, asylum seekers and members of the Traveller and Roma communities. Most anyone would be mortified to be called out for trampling over the elderly, sick and vulnerable to get on the bus first, but these people seem to be devoid of a shame muscle.

Their presumption of privilege is only to be expected. After all, they have attained their positions of influence in a capitalist culture that encourages ruthless ambition and rewards the fittest with survival. Sacking workers to maximise profits and stuffing shareholders' pockets to the detriment of society and the planet is all in a day's work.

F Scott Fitzgerald, an astute chronicler of the wealthy, coined the phrase "the rich are different" in his novelette *The Rich Boy*. "Let me tell you about the very rich. They are different from you and me," the author of *The Great Gatsby* wrote a century ago. "Even when they enter deep into our world or sink below us, they still think that they are better than we are."

You might expect those in charge of a hospital, or the master of a maternity facility, would be the first to deplore others for breaking pandemic rules, having seen the ravages wreaked by Covid-19. Can't you imagine them tut-tutting at hordes congregating in parks and beaches on sunny days, or operating shebeens, or organising student house parties? Yet their moral radar detects no wrong in jumping the queue for vaccines for their own.

I've heard many people say they are mystified that the rich and powerful never seem to learn from their mistakes. Did the people in Beacon Hospital who doled out vaccines to staff in St Gerard's not learn from the preceding controversy over the master of the Coombe giving vaccines to his children? Did they not feel the anger that pulsated throughout the country last August over the Oireachtas Golf Society's dinner in Clifden?

The lesson to be learnt from these scandals is that attitudes will never change until society amends its principles and priorities. As long as inequality is actively encouraged it will thrive, and so will its attendant presumptions. President Michael D Higgins has warned that this pandemic must prompt us to change our ways. "The unaccountable – speculative flows of insatiable capital, a global, unregulated, financialised version of economy – represents the greatest threat to democracy, the greatest source of an inevitable conflict, and the greatest obstacle to us achieving an end to global poverty or achieving sustainability," he told an OECD conference in October.

Mike Ryan, executive director of the WHO's health emergencies programme, has urged the same, with the chilling warning that our species is in danger of exterminating itself by stoking inequality. "We are pushing nature to its limit. We are pushing population to its limit. We're pushing communities to their limits," he said in February, upon receiving an award for his work from Trócaire. "We're stressing the environment. We are creating the conditions in which epidemics flourish. We're forcing and pushing people to migrate away from their homes because of climate stress. We're doing so much and we're doing it in the name of globalisation and some sense of chasing that wonderful thing people call economic growth."

Already, economists and business people are envisaging the post-pandemic economic recovery, speculating about the explosion of pent-up expenditure and demanding that countries be "open for business". So much déjà vu, so little vision for a different future. Naomi Klein coined the term "shock doctrine" to describe how neoliberal capitalists customarily move in for the kill after the people have been softened up by fear following an economic collapse or a natural disaster. The thought of it is horrifying.

Instead of gratuitously excoriating the self-entitlement of the moneyed powerful, better known as the gilded queue-hoppers, let's turn this to our benefit. Venting our spleens about the selfishness demonstrated by Golfgate, and by the behaviour at Beacon Hospital and the Coombe, gets us nowhere, but we should use these scandals as parables to underpin real change. That is the big opportunity this crisis offers us.

The thing is that we all need to buy time – before we run out of it.

Irish history has been shaped by dissenters

Nation's evolution over a century is thanks to
people who dared speak up.

The Sunday Times, 5 December 2021

In the cabinet room at 10 Downing Street 100 years ago tomorrow, five Irish men signed off on the Anglo-Irish Treaty that ended British rule in most of Ireland. Those men would hardly recognise the country nowadays, carpeted as it is with manicured motorways, Michelin-star restaurants and the trophies of Olympian boxers and rowers. Arthur Griffith, who had only eight months left to live when he signed the treaty, might get lost in his native city, between its dockland skyscrapers and its sprawling suburbs. Rising up from the capital's heart, a glittering spire reaches up to the clouds as a symbol of the success of the state that he helped to found.

This is a country it is easy to love. The people are peaceable. The climate is temperate. The seascapes are stunning. There are no tornadoes or recurrent riots or earthquakes or tyrannical dictators or wars to fight. America has Ireland's back. The EU has its hand. The UN has its seat at the table. U2, Riverdance and Ryanair have conquered the world and most of us have food on the table, with a nice bottle of tempranillo at the weekend.

Job well done, one might assure the founding fathers a century after emerging from occupation. But it's not paradise – not yet.

There are those who complain that there is far too much complaining going on. Stop the cavilling, they admonish, and be grateful to the political class that we have such a great little country. But to do so would be to take the road to perdition. For it is criticising that has brought about some of the most attractive features of modern Ireland.

The life of the state is a story of two halves. For the first 50 years, beginning with a vicious civil war, Ireland's lack of confidence as a self-ruler after hundreds of years of foreign rule was manifested in ultra-conservatism. Out of this grew a patriarchal state dominated by one church which advocated large families with their concomitant poverty, discriminated against women, inculcated obsequiousness and cultivated a supine populace. Good Catholics asked no questions.

It was not until the 1970s that the state started to grow up, thanks to the voices of objectors rising from among the oppressed. It is no coincidence that the Irish Women's Liberation Movement was at the forefront of change. The Belfast contraceptive train was soon followed by protesters' sit-ins against nuclear power in Carnsore Point, Co Wexford, and against the destruction of Viking Dublin at Wood Quay. The people had found their voice.

Then the secrets of the past started pouring out, as survivors and whistleblowers insisted they be heard. More than any government, it was the bravery of individuals that made the biggest differences to how the state conducts itself. That roll call includes Christine Buckley, Andrew Madden, Colm O'Gorman,

Catherine Corless, David Norris, Maurice McCabe, Amanda Mellet and Vicky Phelan. If they had not refused to stay silent, it might still be a crime punishable by imprisonment for two people of the same sex to make love or for a woman carrying a fatally ill foetus to have her pregnancy terminated. The abuse of children would have remained a secret, the paternalistic healthcare of women might have gone unchallenged, and reforms would not have been imposed on An Garda Síochána to improve our communal safety.

Long before independence, Ireland had a strong dissenter tradition. While governments have made essential interventions, such as declaring a republic and providing a referendum to allow membership of what was then the European Economic Community (EEC), it is the people of the country who have effected some of the greatest change. Therefore, as long as injustice and inequality persist, criticism is to be encouraged.

There are many people in this country for whom Ireland is no idyll. Those with no homes, members of the Traveller community, families blighted by drug addiction, asylum seekers, people with disabilities, householders who cannot afford to heat their homes, the sick languishing on interminable waiting lists for surgery, parents of children with intellectual needs who cannot get professional help – try telling them to stop their quibbling and be grateful they have such a great little country.

One of the most valuable legacies of colonisation is the enduring democratic engagement by the people. While voter turnout may sometimes be dismally low, as it was in last summer's by-election in Dublin Bay South, other recent exercises in democracy have demonstrated a high level of belief in people power at the ballot box. Remember the throngs of young emigrants returning home to vote in the marriage equality and abortion referendums? Public admiration for Michael D Higgins and his two predecessors as president, Mary Robinson and Mary McAleese, is an endorsement of the people's own choices. That high level of satisfaction dates from 1990, when Robinson's candidacy was unprecedented in offering voters a real alternative to the political establishment of Fianna Fáil or Fine Gael.

Similarly, voters' desire for change has been heard in general elections. The complexion of the Dáil is testament to that. While still abjectly lacking in multiculturalism, the increased numbers of women, independents and left-wing TDs have changed the state's political conversation. Oliver J Flanagan, who famously blamed RTÉ for importing sex to Ireland, would be mortified at Dáil debates about the menopause and period poverty.

The need to "hold the centre" has become the centre's self-promoting anthem, but it is constructive radicalism that has served this state best in the second half of its lifetime. Centrist politicians attribute Ireland's civic peacefulness and economic successes to their policy decisions. What about the people's contribution to those achievements, by debunking the old stereotypes of the drunken, fightin' and lazy Irish? Not only is there a strong work ethic in this country but the people have repeatedly chosen peace over violence. After the International Monetary Fund arrived in 2010, the absence of riots in the streets was a source of marvel among the commentariat. Humour was the weapon of choice when Irish fans attended the 2012 Euros with a flag saying: "Angela Merkel thinks we're at work."

After Michael Collins signed the treaty which split Ireland in two, he foretold that he had signed his own death warrant. The signatories believed that, in time, the island would be reunited. Now, just as objectors within the Republic are told to stop their whingeing, those who share the dream of unification are being told to stop talking about it.

If the treaty negotiators were to ask what was the most valuable lesson learnt by the state that they helped to found, it would be that its people's refusal to stay silent has been the making of it.

UK's rift with Ireland is Johnson's parting gift

His days in office may be numbered but damage could take years to heal.

The Sunday Times, 19 June 2022

So Boris Johnson had an ethics adviser. Well, well, how counter-intuitive is that? Next thing we'll hear is that Donald Trump had his own pope tucked under the bed to hear his lurid nightly confessions in the White House, and Kim Jong-Un has a weapons decommissioner who sneaks out in the middle of the North Korean night to destroy his nuclear arsenal and substitute it with Luke Skywalker's lightsaber.

Actually, the UK prime minister has had not one but two ethics advisers, both of whom have quit his employ in rapid succession. On the positive side, it means the British exchequer no longer has to fund a job that is as superfluous as a conscience to Johnson's requirements. We are, after all, talking about someone who delights in the ethical wasteland of his soul and in demonstrating utter contempt for the laws of both his own land and others'. Nothing is sacred in the fellow's blustering, egomaniacal stride: not the Stormont House agreement or the Northern Irish protocol or the Good Friday agreement; nor the European Convention on Human Rights, the European Court of Justice, the World Trade Organisation or even his own queen, whom he despicably used to unlawfully prorogue the Westminster parliament.

Tedious and unedifying as it may be, it is necessary to keep reminding ourselves of Johnson's untrammeled mendacity. As the SDLP's Claire Hanna said last Monday: "If he told me it was Monday, I wouldn't believe him." There is a slick video of the "life and lies of Boris Johnson" doing the social media rounds. It begins with his auspicious leap from leading-light membership of Oxford's notorious Bullingdon Club, where he described those not as rich as him and his pals as "plebs", to a position of trainee reporter with *The Times* where he was sacked for fabricating a quote in a front-page story. He went on to report from Brussels for *The Daily Telegraph*, lavishly embellishing tales about the bendiness of bananas and an EU ban on prawn-flavoured crisps (not true).

Michael Howard, then his party leader, booted Johnson off the Conservatives' front bench in 2004 for lying about his extramarital activities. That exercise regime now includes having fathered children – while married – with four women who were not his wives at the time of conception.

All of this may be merely banal or, to those with a low giggle threshold, slightly amusing, but they are cautionary tales we need to heed. The British prime minister is not to be trusted. You may think this is stating the obvious but not everyone seems to have grasped that reality yet.

Andrew Bridgen, a Tory backbencher drenched in Brexit-plus testosterone, repeatedly wailed on RTÉ's *Today* with Claire Byrne last week, with all the hurt innocence of a victim: "We trust you but you don't trust us." You don't say, as Byrne didn't say.

Last week, when Johnson's government introduced its bill to crush the guts out of the Northern Irish protocol, the PM brazenly insisted he was motivated by his devotion to protecting the Good Friday agreement. Might this be the same agreement that is predicated upon the principles of the European Convention of Human Rights, which he now wants to jettison too? So deeply does he care about Northern Ireland, his government is passing a so-called legacy bill to deny court trials and inquests for victims of the Troubles, which will conceal British state collusion with loyalist paramilitaries. He is doing this contrary to the will of every political party in Ireland – north and south – and every organisation representing survivors and victims of the Troubles.

It's going down well, though, with Tories who care more for their veterans than for justice, and whose familiarity with Northern Ireland stretches from down-page inside *The Daily Telegraph* to the breaking news ticker tape on *Sky News*. Some of them think the Giant's Causeway is a chapter in *Jack and the Beanstalk*. Bridgen once asserted on BBC Radio 5 that he, and all British citizens, were entitled to Irish passports if they wanted them, but hung up the phone and remained uncontactable when asked to explain that untruth.

Johnson's own knowledge of the top right-hand corner of this island was captured in 2018 when he declared: "It's so small and there are so few firms that actually use that [Irish] border regularly, it's just beyond belief that we're allowing the tail to wag the dog."

It is saddening to watch Johnson's government drag the political Anglo-Irish relationship to the nadir it has reached – "a new low", in the estimation of Micheál Martin, the Taoiseach.

Are we really the same neighbours who held mass love-ins during the reciprocal state visits of Queen Elizabeth to Ireland and President Higgins to England before the Brexit referendum changed everything utterly in 2016? Mutual respect was the leitmotif of those visits, its reiteration by both heads of state painting an oratorical rainbow that promised the sun – now that it had come out – would go on shining.

But that made no allowance for a man called Boris de Pfeffel Johnson, who would lie to Pfeffel to gain an inch for Boris. Respect is not in his lexicon, in any language. When somebody has no values, they value nothing.

The challenge for Ireland is to rise above his low standards, which may sound easy but it gets laborious at around the hundredth time. He goes low, Ireland goes high. The prize will be worth it.

Johnson's days as prime minister are numbered. If he does not willingly slope off the stage soon, his own party will shove him into the orchestra pit to be gobbled up by the coiled tube of a French horn. Then will begin the task of rebuilding relations across the Irish Sea, for the benefit of both countries. One outlandish, fly-by-night prime minister cannot be allowed to rip apart a relationship that took almost a century to repair.

Cop26 showed us it's not easy being green

Consumerism and capitalism are the true causes
of environmental decline.

The Sunday Times, 7 November 2021

The couple watched the mechanical earth-movers smash the hedgerows, and every living thing within them, in an operation to widen the ribbon of country road outside their home. Then, along this crudely made highway, came the steel turbines on gigantic transporters, heading for the nearby hill to mine the Atlantic wind for its energy. After the workers had gone, the ditches lay scattered and dead, and the couple were left to live with the incessant chopping noise of the towering turbines, one just 500m from their house. When the wind comes from the west the sound is so loud that they must shut their windows and front door and retreat inside from their beloved garden.

"What is the countryside for?" ruminates Niall Williams, Ireland's most erroneously undercelebrated novelist, in an exquisite book he has written with his green-fingered wife, Christine Breen. *In Kiltumper*, the memoir named after the west Clare village that has been the couple's home for 35 years, explores a year in the life of their garden – "the year of the turbines" – and one of the great philosophical dilemmas of our time. "How much of the world do we have to spoil in order to save it?" Williams wonders.

Last week something nebulously troubling accompanied the images that appeared nightly on TV news programmes from the Cop26 climate change conference in Glasgow. This was supposed to be a good news story. At last, the world's powers-that-be had woken up to humankind's threatened extinction and were making plans to avert it. So why this knot of worry? Was it the futuristic architecture of the conference centre itself, ablaze with enough electric-light wattage to illuminate a whole village? Or was it what was going on inside its walls as multinational companies sponsored debates and announced lavish funding to save the planet?

The cause of that unease crystallised on Thursday when Jennifer Granholm, America's energy secretary, waxed desirous about the "trillions of dollars" to be eked from a multitude of products yet to be invented and stamped "made in America" – as if the prospect of human survival were not incentive enough. For the political superpowers and their supranational corporate powers, this is war, and only losers waste a good war when there are profits to be made. So US military aircraft will continue to stop off at Kiltumper's neighbouring Shannon airport en route to the lucrative battlefields of the planet.

Many fine words were spoken in Glasgow; not least by Micheál Martin, the Taoiseach, whose speech was welcomed by Friends of the Earth as marking "a step change in political leadership". Despite the absence of China and Russia, agreements reached on reductions in methane emissions and the abolition of coal use have been welcomed internationally.

In Ireland, the new climate action plan that the government

unveiled on Thursday has been hyperbolically hailed as the dawn of a new progressive age. It beggars comprehension how anybody could reach that conclusion when, in reality, the entire kit and caboodle of solutions – global and domestic – amounts to no more than a sticking plaster.

If you had a treatable but chronic and potentially life-threatening illness, would you go to the doctor for a painkiller or for a cure? Well, you would need your head examined if you opted for the painkiller, wouldn't you? Yet none of the proposed remedies for the apocalyptic damage we have inflicted on our environment is designed to tackle the actual cause of it: insatiable consumerism engendered by insatiable capitalism. The hands of the doomsday clock are 100 seconds from midnight, and we are still only addressing the symptoms instead of the cause.

As we enter the season of Black Friday and Cyber Monday, online sales and deliveries will spawn a massive carbon footprint while the acquisition of electronic gadgets will increase electricity demand. These are artificial dates in the modern calendar, designed with the sole purpose of generating mass spending. Then comes Christmas, which will necessitate even more purchasing and a demand for homes and gardens to be festooned with energy-devouring fairy lights.

Much of the €125 billion cost of Ireland's climate action plan will come out of the pockets of individuals and families through retrofitting homes and switching to electric cars. Few deny it is imperative that these changes are made, but there is a sense of the people being left to do it themselves amid a bewildering blizzard of quandaries.

Do we choose air pumps or water pumps for heating our

homes? Where do we get omega-3 for our nervous system and vitamin D for our bones if we shouldn't drink milk or eat fish? How can the government talk with a straight face about expanding our forests when the Department of Agriculture can't even process applications to plant trees? Why do TDs drive to Leinster House while telling the rest of us to take the bus or train? And what is the point of shivering in three sweaters to cut carbon emissions when unimaginably rich multinationals are allowed to build electricity-gobbling data centres? Something has to give.

We have been at this potential turning point before. When some of the globe's richest economies collapsed in 2008 – including Ireland's – acres of rainforest were devoted to analysis of how untrammelled capitalism had precipitated the crisis. Potential solutions were advanced, including the creation of community banks and local business co-ops. It all proved to be pie in the sky.

To rephrase the axiom that "when poverty comes in the door, love flies out the window", in this case, when profits knocked on the boardroom door, the opportunity to make a more equitable and sustainable life on earth flew out the window. The same has happened with the Covid-19 pandemic, when the silencing of road and sky traffic allowed the song birds to be heard in the cleaner air and people thought: "How lovely." Now we are polluting as much as ever again.

A false narrative has been created, portraying a young generation as being angry at those who went before for destroying their world. This version ignores some obvious facts, such as the simpler lives led in the less urbanised past, and the rapacious consumerism of fast fashion, foreign travel and online shopping nowadays. Saving the planet is not a tug of war between old and young, or men and women, or black and white. It is an arm wrestle of ideologies.

Do we fundamentally remake our world as a habitable home where fairness and the beauty of the natural world are more appreciated than commercial assets? Or do we stick to the road we're on, one that ultimately may lead to the conclusion that our species was simply too greedy to save itself?

Transport review puts women in the back seat

Exclusion of female voices shows Leinster
House is asleep at the wheel.

The Sunday Times, 21 March 2021

Have you ever seen a woman on a bus? Yes, I know it's a silly question, but bear with me. Have you ever seen a woman driving a car? Or boarding a plane? Or flying one? Or travelling on a train? Or driving a Luas? Or pedalling a bicycle? Or walking along a footpath?

These are not trick questions – unless you happen to be a politician. In which case, you are liable to get the answers wrong because, in your weird, blinkered little world, women do not exist. Three days before International Women's Day, when the world stopped patting women's bottoms for 24 hours to pat them on the head instead, the joint Oireachtas committee on transport and communications networks published its submission for the review of the €116 billion national development plan.

Have a read – it won't take long. Its 21 pages are short on practical detail while salivating with aspirational clichés about sustainable development and economic connectivity. There are several shout-outs for Shannon airport. The reason why becomes clear when you study the glorious, technicolour parade of the committee's members at the top of the report.

Four of the TDs and senators are from Clare and Limerick, where the airport has long been a political trump card. There is something even more striking and disturbing about that gallery of 13 grinning portraits: there is not a woman among them. And to think these people call themselves "public representatives". More like half-the-public representatives.

Sometimes, Leinster House is so shamelessly antediluvian it makes Middle-earth look positively enlightened. As long as politicians keep their size tens planted in the paternalistic medieval age, they can expect to command zero authority when they purport to espouse gender equality. It is utterly bewildering, frustrating and infuriating that, while taxes paid by women will help fund Ireland's transport plan, the Oireachtas has not even pretended to take women's perspectives, needs and wishes into account in deciding how that money should be spent. If you think that's an overstatement, it gets worse.

In all, ten statements were made by witnesses who met the committee while it was preparing the report. Every one of those witnesses was a man, including the chief executives of Bus Éireann, Cork and Waterford ports, Irish Rail, the National Transport Authority, the secretary general of the Department of Transport, and his minister. Every one of 16 witnesses from Irish Rail, Transport Infrastructure Ireland (TII) and Bus Éireann was male.

"We met with a range of key agencies and stakeholders," declared Kieran, Joe, Michael, Cathal, Timmy, Ned, Duncan, Jerry, Steven, Ruairí, James, Gerard and Darren in their report. No, they did not. They did not meet the women who predominate among passengers on city buses, often lugging shopping, strollers and schoolchildren with them.

They did not meet women who, though they own fewer cars than men, rely more on them and spend more hours in them, according to research. And they certainly did not meet the 55 per cent of women who say they are too frightened to use public transport at night. That finding was contained in a July 2020 report entitled Travelling in a Woman's Shoes, which was commissioned by TII but only circulated last week following the abduction and murder of Sarah Everard in London.

The TII report outlines some of the measures women are genetically programmed to take to protect themselves while using transport, including carrying keys in their hands "as a makeshift weapon". The findings have come as a big surprise to many politicians and journalists, but the biggest surprise for most women is their surprise.

How could you not have known that women often take the longer route to a destination if we consider it safer? Or that we always sit in the back of a taxi in case someone might be lurking there? Or that sweat runs down our spine when we hear footsteps too close behind us on a lonely road at night? You should have known.

When you read court reports of how an aviation executive rugby-tackled a female passer-by and sexually assaulted her on a Dublin footpath in 2010 and, initially, got six months' jail for it, you should have known that would frighten women. When a man led a Spanish student out of Dublin city and raped her over a 21-hour period in 2017, when she feared he would kill her, you should have known.

When a woman was fatally attacked while walking on a

Dublin street near the IFSC on her way home from work earlier this year, you should have known that was every woman's nightmare scenario. And you would have known, if you had listened. It is eight months since Travelling in a Woman's Shoes was compiled.

Until last week, there hadn't been a whisper about it. Even still, the only bits grabbing public attention are the findings about women's fears that took the establishment by surprise. Lads, it's not news. A 2019 report by the Central Statistics Office on crime and victimisation said six in ten women felt unsafe taking the bus and 36 per cent felt in danger walking in their locality at night.

That fell on deaf ears. No wonder the TII report concludes: "As has long been the case, society places the primary responsibility on a woman to keep herself safe, irrespective of the threats she may face ... We see that traditionally male-dominated leadership and management has contributed to an unintended male bias in the design of transport systems, resulting in adverse outcomes for women."

Scant attention has been paid to its recommendation that women should be involved in designing public infrastructure. One can only hope the boys' club that constitutes the Oireachtas transport committee can put down its own riveting report long enough to read this one.

After Sarah Everard was snatched from a London street and horrifically murdered, the city's authorities finally approved funding for extra public lighting. Male columnists have churned out opinion pieces asking "what can we men do?" before proceeding to answer themselves. Switching on the lights and beating your chests will not fix the problem.

It is caused by the sort of exclusion exemplified by the men-only Oireachtas committee. The same committee has begun examining the viability of the post office network and, yes, you've guessed it: they've heard from male representatives of the Irish Postmasters' Union and the Independent Postmasters' Group. Don't women buy stamps?

In his St Patrick's Day meeting with the American vice-president Kamala Harris, the Taoiseach quoted Mary Robinson's determination, upon her 1990 election as president, to write women back into history. Let's start with writing us into the here and now.

Politicians on both sides of the Border have lost control of Ireland's destiny

The political class has gagged unity conversation for too long.

The Irish Times, 7 October 2022

James Nesbitt leaned into the microphone on the stage in Dublin's 3Arena, looked out at the audience that had just given Sinn Féin's leader a standing ovation, and announced: "I'm bloody terrified." After a theatrical pause, the Co Antrimborn, unionist-raised star of television crime dramas, added: "Terrified – not least because, at this stage, I'm probably Northern Ireland's longest-serving police officer."

It was a risky line for the closing speech at last Saturday's gathering of 5,000 people, which was organised by the Ireland's Future civic group and unambiguously themed "Preparing for a New and United Ireland". But it was a risk that won an appreciative laugh and pricked 10,000 ears.

Nesbitt told of his upbringing in Broughshane, a village where about 90 per cent of the residents were Protestants, during the Troubles that barely impinged on the place. "I played in a flute band. I marched," he said, alluding to the influence of the Orange Order. He called himself "an Irishman from the North of Ireland who, in no way, refutes or shies away from my Protestant culture" and said the term "united Ireland" is provocative to people from his background. He prefers "a union of Ireland".

His speech was witty, brave and riveting. Above all, it was respectful in its avoidance of flippancy, soundbites and slogans. The Cold Feet actor had taken the measure of his audience – nestled among them Gerry Adams, the former Sinn Féin president – and talked candidly about the need to respect all opinions. Even those who hate his current television show, *Bloodlands*, are entitled to say so, he asserted – "though that would be rude and bloody ridiculous".

The event was promoted as a platform for 10 political parties to debate Ireland's reunification – and was attended by diplomats from 10 countries – but it was the speakers from unionist and loyalist Northern backgrounds who provided the deepest insights.

Andrew Clarke and Peter Adair, young men from Protestant east Belfast, discussed the North's stultifying stasis in human rights legislation, saying: "The nightmarish thought for me is 20 or 30 more years of this." Rev Karen Sethuraman, a Baptist minister in Belfast, wondered: "Is there something better or is this what we're going to be forever?" Ben Collins, a former Tory government press officer from east Belfast, said: "People say talking about a Border poll is divisive but it's not nearly as divisive as the Border that was imposed 100 years ago."

It took courage for those people to participate in an event in Dublin dedicated to Ireland's reunification. That they were prepared to potentially be branded traitors by their own community demonstrated their desire to be heard. Politicians who have refused to accommodate substantive public debate about a future one-Ireland because they do not want to scare "the unionist community" have, effectively, been gagging these courageous individuals. Equally, Sinn Féin supporters' hostility to unification objectors narrows the debate. What, for instance, do the 300,000 holders of British passports who live south of the Border think about a joined-up Ireland?

Ireland's Future has been the subject of a smear campaign by innuendo that it is, allegedly, a front for Sinn Féin. The claim does not bear scrutiny when its board includes the likes of former SDLP councillor Brian Feeney, novelist Martina Devlin, and Queens University law professor Colin Harvey. However, the party partisanship shown by many in Saturday's audience who gave Mary Lou McDonald a standing ovation not only gave succour to the whispering campaign but will have alienated others who, with some encouragement, may wish to join the debate. As Fine Gael's Neale Richmond observed during his contribution, there were many people in the audience whom he had blocked on Twitter.

No political party owns Ireland's future. None has a monopoly on this State's constitutional aspiration that the island be joined up again. Any party that hijacks an event dedicated to pursuing that ideal damages the cause. If Sinn Féin cannot recognise this cause-and-effect, it is as blind as the DUP. Much of the disaffection expressed on Saturday by those from a unionist culture arose from the intransigence of the biggest unionist party. Its continuing refusal to form an executive at Stormont and its entrenched resistance to liberalising social legislation are causing such disillusionment that former leader Arlene Foster's immediate task under the banner of her new pro-union campaign, Together UK, will be to convince traditional unionists that maintaining the status quo is in their best interests.

There is a sense now that politicians have lost control of Ireland's destiny. Writing in *The Daily Telegraph* last month, Norman Tebbit, a former Tory minister whose wife was severely injured in the IRA's bomb attack on his party's conference in Brighton, said "it looks more likely than not that, in the not too distant future, there will be a united Ireland". His prediction is significant in light of the Good Friday Agreement's failure to specify the circumstances in which Westminster's secretary of state for Northern Ireland should call a Border poll.

There have been rumours in Irish political circles that Leo Varadkar intends adopting a more proactive stance on a united Ireland after he resumes as Taoiseach on December 15th. Yet his party refused to endorse Ian Marshall, a unionist Armagh farmer, for the Seanad in 2020, when Sinn Féin formally backed him. On the 3Arena stage last Saturday, Richmond was asked if his party was doing enough for unity. The Fine Gael TD's reply was short and sweetly received. "No," he said. Jim O'Callaghan, Fianna Fáil's putative leader-in-waiting, was asked if he would accept an invitation to speak at one of Foster's pro-UK events. "I will speak anywhere about a united Ireland," he replied, to applause.

Politicians have read the auguries. Change is inevitable. A nationalist party is the biggest in Stormont. Catholics outnumbered Protestants in the North's 2021 census. Scotland is demanding another independence referendum. Brexit has exposed Westminster's indifference to Northern Ireland's needs. The North's governance structures are in a permanent state of paralysis. Something has to give.

Critics of Ireland's Future demand to see a plan. It's like *Mastermind* for slow united Irelanders. Where's the money?

What colour will the flag be? Name the tune of the new national anthem. But money and emblems are not the priority yet. The first imperative is getting to know each other after a century of being corralled in our binary boxes of nationalist/unionist, republican/loyalist, Catholic/Protestant and North/South. Stories must be told and heard about the effects of partition and why some people want rid of it and others do not. The political class on both sides of the Border has managed to gag that conversation for too long. Only after the people on this island have become acquainted with each other's divided lives can the structural planning begin. For, in this case, Brendan Behan was correct – the first item on the agenda is the split.

The young emigrate yet the golden circle endures

Siteserv report is just the latest iteration of a them-and-us culture in which the ordinary taxpayer must forever stump up.

The Irish Times, 16 September 2022

Four men sat down to dinner at the salubrious In Lain Hotel nestling in the Swiss Alps. One was a billionaire Irish tax exile called Denis O'Brien. Another was his enduring friend and business associate, Paul Connolly. Also at the table was Niall McFadden, a corporate financier whom O'Brien had befriended when the pair became neighbours at the exclusive Mount Juliet golf estate in Co Kilkenny. The billionaire and the financier bonded as boot camp buddies, flying to Kenya and Greece for luxury activity holidays.

By the time of the dinner in Switzerland on January 29th, 2012, McFadden was in a spot of bother to the tune of €30 million worth of court judgments issued against him, after defaulting on debt repayments. With personal bank borrowings of €7 million, he was facing bankruptcy while Siteserv, a utilities company he cofounded in 2004, was insolvent, owing €150 million to the State-owned IBRC, formerly known as Anglo Irish Bank. The company was up for sale. Six parties had bid for it in the first round of the sale process the previous month.

Robert Dix was the fourth man at the dinner table that night. Another business and boot camp buddy of McFadden, he was a non-executive director of Siteserv and chairman of the board's sale subcommittee. Before joining his three fellow ski-holidaymakers downstairs, Dix received a call in his hotel room from Siteserv's financial advisers informing him that the second round of offers had been pared down to just two bids. One of them was from O'Brien. The Commission of Investigation into the sale of Siteserv, chaired by judge Brian Cregan, states in its 1,500-page report, following a seven-year investigation costing the public at least €30 million, that there was "no discussion, or reference, to Siteserv" over dinner that evening in the Swiss Alps.

Cregan also found no evidence of impropriety by O'Brien, whose company, Millington, went on to buy Siteserv for €45.4 million. Effectively, the Irish State was out of pocket by €118 million on the original debt, plus being landed with the colossal bill for Cregan's inquiry. That combined sum could power thousands of Irish homes with electricity and gas for the next year. Yet the monetary loss is not the only startling feature of the Siteserv saga. Most mortals failing to pay their mortgage, for instance, face the prospect of foreclosure and having their home sold without getting any say in the process. Yet here was a company on the rocks and owing €150 million that the bank allowed to manage its own sale. If ever there was proof of one rule for some and another for everybody else, this is it.

Modern Ireland loves to laud itself for being tolerant and equal. The Government is forever bragging about the country's newly minted reputation as one of the most tax-equal states this side of Mars, a claim that deserves closer scrutiny. But what is becoming ever more apparent, as young people pack their emigrant suitcases again in search of somewhere they can afford to live, is that tax equity is merely a sop as long as Ireland's economic preferential culture of golden circles continues untrammeled. Groundhog Day in this land means the taxpayer forever stumping up for the bill as the golden circle waltzes off.

The Swiss dinner took place just 10 months after judge Michael Moriarty published his final report from the tribunal inquiring into payments to politicians. It contained stark and grave findings. One such was that Michael Lowry, the minister for communications in 1995, had "secured the winning" of a State mobile phone licence by O'Brien. Another was that O'Brien had enriched Lowry by more than €1 million. The High Court judge said these two findings were "demonstrably referable". The tribunal cost the public €65.5 million.

Lowry still sits in the Dáil, enjoying all the power and prestige of a Government-supporting TD. The Director of Public Prosecutions has decided not to charge anybody for obstructing the tribunal, despite a formal complaint by Moriarty. A year after the tribunal's findings were made public, the State's bank signed off on a deal with O'Brien, leaving the people of Ireland, who had already paid €34 billion to bail out Anglo Irish Bank, out of pocket yet again. How is any of that fair or equal?

Last December, this newspaper revealed that the wealthy O'Flaherty family who distribute Mercedes-Benz cars in Ireland got €1.8 million in State pandemic subsidies and, at the same time, transferred virtually the same sum in the form of a dividend to an offshore account controlled by the family. They were not alone. Other business families were exposed as having done similar. Not a whisper about any of that since. These revelations coincided with the issuance of State letters to some individual recipients of the €208 weekly pandemic unemployment payment for workers informing them that they wrongly benefited and that the money owed would be automatically deducted from their earnings by Revenue.

Last year, the Davy stockbroker group was fined a measly €4.1 million by the Central Bank over a bond-trading deal involving 16 of its employees, including its former chairman and its chief executive, and a client who was kept oblivious to their involvement. No individual was charged with any wrongdoing, just as nobody in the banks was prosecuted in connection with the tracker mortgage scandal.

Every time a voluminous, expensive and long-overdue report of a State investigation is published, the Government laments the cost, mumbles that there must be a better way of doing things and then shoves the report on to a shelf to gather dust. There is a better way.

Catherine Murphy, the Social Democrats' joint leader whose tenacious questioning in the Dáil helped uncover the torrid Siteserv details, and others are hoarse from advocating the creation of a permanent judicial office to investigate serious matters in the public interest. Not only would it be more efficient and nimble than the current system of commissions of inquiry but such an office would signal a narrowing of the chasm that exists between them and us in Ireland's economic culture. Should it ever come about, tax equity might feel more appreciable.

Sad end of the man who said please and thanks, but little else

Two Christmases came and went without a sign of life in Michael Whiston's cottage on Sallynoggin Road in south Dublin. No lights came on inside. His front door, where he was a familiar sight soaking up the sunshine on summer days, stayed shut.

The Sunday Times, 13 February 2022

A neighbour knocked on the door but got no answer, though that was not unusual as he was a man who "kept to himself". Another neighbour saw a rat outside the house and grew concerned. She phoned Dún Laoghaire–Rathdown county council six times from early 2021, saying she was worried something might have happened to the man who lived in number three, whose name she did not know.

"I was made to feel like an interfering busybody," she said, asking not to be named.

In the autumn, she approached two gardaí on foot patrol in the area and told them about her concerns. On October 15, workers from the council came and broke in Whiston's front door. They replaced it with a brown steel door and affixed a notice to it stating that, if the occupant did not contact the council within a month, his tenancy would be terminated.

All the while, tailbacks of cars and trucks on the road outside the 110-year-old cottage queued to enter a nearby six-exit roundabout. Commuters waited for buses at the stop across the road and pedestrians walked past the single-storey dwelling on the side of the street, oblivious to the growing mystery of what had become of Michael Whiston.

The question was partly answered on February 2 when workers from the council found a hand grenade from the War of Independence while they were clearing out the house.

"Suddenly, it was all guards and flashing lights," said the woman who had repeatedly reported her concerns.

Neighbouring houses were evacuated. The bomb squad came and conducted a controlled explosion in a local park. Only hours later, when the workmen returned to the house, did they find the decomposed remains of 76-year-old Whiston. His body was removed to the Dublin city morgue where a post mortem was performed.

A mystery man in life, mystery now surrounds the circumstances of Whiston's death, though foul play is not suspected. Conflicting rumours abound about who he was and when he might have died. Contrary to one rumour that he had left the house and died in the small back yard while trying to regain entry, his body was found in the back bedroom. He had been a hoarder and when he was found, food, packaging and bottles lay knee-deep in the house.

"I'm very upset to think he was in there all that time," said the woman who reported him missing. "I find it shameful that this could happen in one of the biggest and wealthiest suburbs in Ireland."

The council refused to answer any questions about how long Whiston's rent had been in arrears, when he had last communicated with its officials or if he had any next of kin. "There is a garda investigation. We will not be commenting," a spokeswoman said.

Politicians in the area, who recall that Whiston never answered the door when they called to canvass, say local authorities need to change their practices to avoid the same thing happening to someone else.

"We need some kind of procedure whereby, if rent has not been paid over a period of time that there is an investigation, checking such things as whether the person has been receiving their social welfare and paying utility bills," said Justin Moylan, a Fianna Fáil councillor.

Tom Kivlehan, a Green Party councillor, said: "In former times, there would have been a rent collector and that was a sort of passive surveillance. Now rents are paid by direct debit and pensions go directly into the bank account."

Whiston is thought to have grown up in Monkstown Farm, about half a mile away, and to have never married. Though the electoral register lists a second occupant of the Sallynoggin house, named as Maura Whiston, nobody in the area recalls ever seeing a second occupant.

When he first moved into the house about 14 years ago, Whiston told a local resident that his mother had recently moved into a nursing home and that he had a brother living outside Dublin whom he sometimes visited. He said he was an artist. Records kept by the National Irish Visual Arts Library list 28 items in the name of a Michael Whiston, who appears to have been a student at the National College of Art and Design in the 1960s.

In the Spar shop where he made his routine purchases of

sandwiches, groceries, a half bottle of whiskey and *The Irish Times* newspaper, Whiston is remembered as a "well-spoken" man who always said "please" and "thanks", but not much else. He was a recognisable figure locally because of his distinctive walk which was quick-paced and with one arm bent at the elbow and raised. A neighbour said Whiston used to walk for a couple of hours every day.

"We're the nosiest neighbours you could find," said another, "but we knew nothing about him. He was very private."

Last week, those neighbours left daffodils and tulips on the ground outside Michael Whiston's house and on the ledge of the window, through which strings of cobwebs could be seen entwined with the net curtains.

"It's very sad to think that, at such a busy junction, somebody could have effectively fallen off the face of the earth," said Cormac Devlin, a Dún Laoghaire TD.

What makes a Greek scholar qualified to choose a senator?

Notion only those with an NUI or Trinity degree are capable of selecting people for Seanad is ludicrous.

The Irish Times, 7 April 2023

Remember his name, for he has done his country a significant service. Tomás Heneghan took on the privileged club of Seanad university voters who are presumed exceptionally fit to help shape Ireland, and he won. For more than four years, the young University of Limerick criminal justice and journalism graduate refused to blink as the State threw the kitchen sink and all its silver spoons at him until, finally, the Supreme Court declared: you win.

Where to start with the brazen elitism of a republic that squandered the people's money in a preposterous attempt to keep the upper doors of parliament bolted against a majority? In 1979, more than 90 per cent of those who voted in the referendum for the seventh constitutional amendment supported the proposal to extend academic graduates' voting rights for Seanad Éireann beyond the existing constituencies of the National University of Ireland (NUI) and Trinity College. Politicians thought better, however, and opted to continue reserving the club for the cosy exclusivity of Ireland's poshest universities. In the intervening near half-a-century, successive governments have cocked a snook at the people's wish in a display of sheer contempt.

At present, six of the Seanad's 60 seats are filled by the votes of those preferred graduates with another 43 being elected by TDs, senators and about 900 councillors. Not all of these voters comprise what Samuel Beckett called "the cream of Ireland – rich and thick"; only some. Can anyone explain with an iota of logic why a Greek scholar or, for that matter, Danny Healy-Rae is better able to choose a senator than somebody who drives a train or runs a soup kitchen?

Every few years, when a new batch of senators arrives, it is infuriating to see ushers and support staff in Leinster House, many of whom have no say in the composition of the Seanad, instructing the newcomers in its workings.

It is twice as sickening to watch TDs who have lost their seats in the latest Dáil election swanning into the Seanad chamber for a five-year breather and other aspiring TDs getting an Oireachtas leg-up from their political parties. Their treatment of the Seanad as their property, providing a convenient halfway house for their Dáil candidates, has debased an institution that has much to offer the country.

When Heneghan issued his legal proceedings in December 2018, he claimed that the exclusionary constituencies contravened the Constitution's equality requirements. The State which, with gobsmacking hypocrisy, is currently encouraging school leavers to consider taking up trades as an alternative to academic studies, defended the inequality. Having a better chance of success after losing his case in the High Court, Heneghan confined his appeal in the Supreme Court to asserting his entitlement to vote as a third-level graduate following the 1979 referendum. When six of seven Supreme Court judges ruled that the exclusion of other third-level graduates was inimical to the Constitution, he was happy but not exactly jubilant.

"My preference is universal franchise," Heneghan said. "When I sit down at the family table at Christmas, only one-third of my family around it have a right to vote. I couldn't justify that."

Undoubtedly, the Trinity and NUI panels have produced many fine senators. Not least is David Norris, the longest-serving member in Seanad history. But the ludicrous notion that only people with an NUI or Trinity parchment are capable of selecting senators is contradicted by the extraordinary levels of popularity enjoyed by Ireland's presidents in the past 23 years. Mary Robinson, Mary McAleese and Michael D Higgins were elected by universal suffrage, proving that you don't need a PhD in astrochemistry to be able to pick the ideal person to represent you. Plans are afoot for a referendum to expand the electorate in presidential elections to encompass Irish citizens in Northern Ireland and in the worldwide diaspora. Yet a house of our bicameral parliament is confined to the privileged few.

Even some of the Taoiseach's 11 nominees have, at times, been among the disenfranchised. Maybe you need to be versed in Ovid and the Saturnian meter for it to make sense that someone can be good enough to sit in the Seanad but not good enough to vote for it.

Politicians frequently deride the role of the Seanad in private conversation as an impotent talking shop, which evokes another of Beckett's observations: "There's man all over for you, blaming on his boots the faults of his feet."

The truth is that Seanad debates can be more thoughtful and constructive than the political potshots and written speeches that are customary in the Dáil. Whatever one's view on the merits of the legislation that was planned, the last Seanad's filibustering of the Judicial Appointments Commission Bill into extinction demonstrated the upper chamber's considerable influence. The full electorate implicitly acknowledged that when it voted down Enda Kenny's proposal to abolish the Seanad in the 2013 referendum. In response, the then Taoiseach promised to reform the institution.

A decade later, we're still waiting for that too. At this stage, there have been so many reports on Seanad reform we could carpet a small planet with them. Politicians' shameless cynicism in keeping it for themselves makes one wonder if it was by accident or design that the constitutional amendment resulting from the 1979 referendum was deliberately "incoherent". Judge Gerard Hogan has likened the inserted clause to the "attempted cleaning of an old master by a careless restoration artist who then proceeded to leave an ink-stain on a Rembrandt". Surely not the work of any of the super-smart Trinity and NUI graduates who get to vote for the Seanad.

The Supreme Court has said its finding that the university constituencies are unconstitutional will take effect in July. That means the Government must fix it before the summer recess starts that month. But sticking a Band-Aid on the third-level constituencies to enfranchise about 700,000 graduates will not suffice.

There is a proposal already before the Oireachtas for 28 senators to be elected by all Irish citizens on this island, in addition to the six chosen by graduates. Members of either Houses of the Oireachtas who object to that are unfit to call themselves democrats.

British media was right – Joe Biden's Ireland belongs to Dark Ages

Peter Brookes perfectly captured Irish–America's mythmaking in his *London Times* caricature of three dancing Bidens dressed as leprechauns with pints of stout. The truth hurts.

The Irish Times, 21 April 2023

Sometimes, the old enemy can be a country's best friend, if inadvertently. Loath though any united Irelander bred in the broth of anglophobia may be to admit this, but them-next-door were only stating the obvious when they highlighted US president Joe Biden's paddywhackery homecoming to the old sod.

For four days, Ireland wallowed in a love-in with a thoroughly likable man, unconstrained by any acknowledgment that the planet's most powerful politician had travelled not only 5,500km from Washington DC but about half-a-century back in time too.

It is an uncomfortable truth, indeed, but the Brits were right. Joey's misty-eyed version of Ireland is anchored in its monocultural Dark Age when all its songs were sad, its wars were merry and Brit-bashing was a favourite fireside sport. As he once said: "Irish-Americans think they're more Irish than the Irish, and that's kind of how I was raised." The Scranton native's sincerity about his Irishness is undoubted but it perpetuates a mythical Ireland that prevails in the US of God-fearing, drunken, fightin' inhabitants who, in fact, have long since left that country behind.

On one of the rare occasions when Biden publicly questioned his Irishness, it was on the basis that he is a teetotaler with no relatives in jail. Another time, he announced: "I may be Irish but I'm not stupid." When English people proclaim, as some have, "Ireland, you're welcome to him", it's a valid view.

Peter Brookes perfectly captured Irish-America's mythmaking about the Emerald Isle in his *London Times* caricature of three dancing Bidens dressed as leprechauns swinging pints of stout. Inevitably, that cartoon triggered high dudgeon in Ireland. The truth hurts. It hurts especially when you have convinced yourself that the arrival of your very important guest is tantamount to the second coming of John F Kennedy, which took place when Biden's Ireland was still the real Ireland.

There is no greater comfort than in the turning of a blind eye. Why spoil a presidential jolly by pointing out that your esteemed visitor has strayed into the wrong country? Being Olympian diplomats, we Irish chose tactful silence. The code was "don't mention the war", whether cultural wars or American wars, and just surrender to the heart-warming nostalgia of it all. What a lovely man, went the chorus in a voice quavering with the frightful memory of his Oval Office predecessor. Any country would be proud to claim him as one of their own.

Clearly, the British would like to make him theirs but five-eighths-Irish Joey is not so keen. He has recounted how his mother slept on a hotel floor after being told that the British Queen had previously stayed in the same room and how his

Aunt Gertie told him: "Your father is not a bad man. He's just English." If an Irish politician were to broadcast such fond family anecdotes, Whitehall would summon the Irish Ambassador and the DUP would demand an immediate boycott of Dublin Bay prawns. Before Biden made his foreshortened appearance in Northern Ireland for the Belfast Agreement's 25th anniversary, the DUP's former leader, Arlene Foster, who has an indelicate way with words, declared that the US president "hates" the UK.

It was an ill-timed and ugly intervention, but its truth is hard to deny. The president, whose ancestors fled Ireland during Famine times, seldom resists an opportunity to spurn his British DNA. On the US election campaign three years ago, a reporter called out to him: "Mr Biden, a quick word for the BBC?" The candidate responded: "BBC? I'm Irish." As non-sequiters go, it was a clanger.

After Foster's accusation, Biden might have been expected to demonstrate some of the dignity he kept espousing during his Irish trip. He might even have taken Oscar Wilde's advice to "always forgive your enemies – nothing annoys them so much". Instead, in his Leinster House address, the US president implicitly scolded the British government for not doing enough to help its Irish counterpart maintain peace on this island. The remark was unhelpful.

In an ongoing peace process that has been painstakingly built by participants swallowing their prejudices, one-upmanship is detrimental. While it is true that Brexit and the galumphing premierships of Boris Johnson and Liz Truss wilted Anglo–Irish relations like lettuce in yesterday's salad, it would have been constructive had Biden acknowledged that the relationship has perked up somewhat since Rishi Sunak unpacked his bags in Number 10. That would have assured London that the powers that be in Dublin were not bad-mouthing them to the superpower's president behind their backs.

The orgy of mutual admiration that unfolded as Biden reiterated, in his single transferable speech, the values that he claimed bind him to Ireland was utterly seductive. What a nice fuzzy feeling to watch this kindly grandfather eulogise truth, respect and dignity; to hear the stories of his forebears recounted as parables; to witness the emotion of a man unexpectedly encountering the priest who had anointed his deceased son on the other side of the ocean; to understand that the joy in his face was genuine as he preached goodness outside the cathedral in Ballina. At times, it felt more like a papal visit than a presidential one.

What made it extra special was the likelihood that this was the last hurrah for the greening of the White House. That realisation added greater impetus to the céad míle fáilte. Ireland's access to the epicentre of global political power is what turns London green with envy, and now more so than ever. Having amputated their own arm of fraternity with their European partners, it must have been galling for many Britons to watch the American president come dance in Ireland. Their reaction did not spring from base jealousy of a neighbour but from the indignation of Brexiteers who had wrongly presumed they would get a quick trade agreement with Uncle Sam, regardless of what their little neighbour thought.

None of this makes them wrong when they question Biden's brand of Irishness; only hypocritical. While Joey's big hug in the Emerald Isle infuriated Britannia, the media there turned a blind eye to the queue of its own people who have borrowed from the same heritage to obtain Irish passports in order to hasten their post-Brexit passage through airports in Nice and Alicante.

In the new multicultural, outward-looking, self-confident Ireland, Irishness is whatever you're having yourself. Sure, isn't it what we bottle and sell?

The €15.90 chicken wrap that proves Michael D Higgins has a point

We have nurtured an economy hostile to solidarity. Why is the Government allowing rip-off culture to flourish?

The Irish Times, 5 May 2023

Expect to see a new dish of the day on a menu near you very soon – the goose that laid the golden egg, basted and battered. Ever since the Government caved into the hospitality sector's intensive lobbying to retain its emergency VAT rate of 9 per cent, the cost of eating out, or even sipping a cup of tea, has reached staggering heights.

One of the most indigestible greedflation examples I recently spotted was €15.90 for a Caesar chicken wrap in a retail park daytime restaurant. Chips on the side cost extra. There must have been 24-carat gold filings blended into the mix of chicken bits, cheese, lettuce and "crispy bacon", otherwise known as a fried rasher, to warrant that price. Even more galling was that, in another restaurant immediately next door in the same retail park, an identical wrap was priced at €8.50. How can one outlet charge almost double the price of the other's when, presumably, both pay roughly the same rent and appeared to employ a similar complement of staff?

Before restaurant representatives dash to pen furious letters to the editor protesting that this particular case of wraponomics is an exception rather than the rule, let it be said that this reflects a surging trend in rip-off-pricing that cannot be justified by increased energy and food costs. Other examples on a postcard, please.

As people still delight in shaking off the cabin fever of Covid lockdown, there are as many reasons to be cheerful as there are to suspect that the human need to get out and reconnect with others is being exploited for commercial profit. The appetite for an astronomically-priced sandwich you could rustle up at home for a couple of euro is superseded by the hunger for human contact. The thirst for a cappuccino costing €4.20 – yes, really, and €4.90 when it comes with a sprinkling of turmeric – turns some customers into collaborators willing to pay prices reminiscent of the Celtic Tiger economy, before it crashed in flames.

Just because you can afford it doesn't mean you should pay a ludicrous price. If we all walked out and went next door, the message might sink in that, actually, we're people, not patsies. This is the essence of what President Michael D Higgins was talking about in his address at a Tasc think-tank event in Áras an Uachtaráin last Friday, but it got lost in the cacophony of indignant economists hitting their keyboards with self-righteous gusto. Speaking in the context of climate change, the President espoused economic solidarity and a departure from the profit-is-king school of thought, warning against the prevailing "emphasis on insatiable consumption and wealth accumulation".

The contrasting economic policies the Government applies to the hospitality sector and the home rental sector show a microcosm of the growth-obsession that Higgins ventilated.

With one hand, the Cabinet extended the special 9 per cent VAT rate for hotels and restaurants and, with the other, it terminated the eviction ban at the height of a severe homelessness crisis. Its rationale in dropping the VAT rate by 4.5 per cent was to mitigate inflationary market forces, while its interventions in housing are historically predicated on the theory of letting the market set the price.

There is an ever-deepening impression that the State would pawn the Rock of Cashel to prop up business while happily letting the citizens defend their own interests. After it was reported on Tuesday that food inflation had eased by 0.2 per cent in April, the money ministers, Michael McGrath and Paschal Donohoe, politely suggested that companies might pass any price reductions on to their customers. They might as well have asked them to replace the zeros in their bottom line with love 'Xs'. Despite congratulating itself on having an Arcadian bounty of prime beef, cheese, milk, butter, pork, lamb, prawns, salmon, strawberries, blackberries and various libations, this country has the second-highest food prices in the EU. Why is there no Government intervention in that market?

The last time Ireland let loose its rip-off-republic id, the minister for enterprise, trade and employment at the time, Mary Harney, was condemned for advising people to "shop around" for value, yet the same principle still applies. State regulation on behalf of the buying public is paltry. Bills for groceries, home repairs, medicines, mortgage repayments and home heating have got so big they barely squeeze through the letter box.

There are, of course, excellent restaurants and hotels in Ireland and many great-value cafés and pubs but spiralling prices have reached the point in Dublin where it is increasingly difficult to get a cup of tea and a sandwich for less than €10. The capital is pricing itself out of existence. In March, a couple visiting from South Africa for St Patrick's week were so shocked by the cost of everything that they decided to buy nothing beyond their essential needs during their stay. Considering that the hospitality sector's lobbying pitch was that the low VAT rate would generate increased tourism revenue, could there be a better metaphor for biting the hand that feeds you?

We live in a country where we are constantly reminded that the Swanee is only waiting to wash us away the day the multinational behemoths pack their bags and leave. That refrain consistently undermines the peoples' contribution, as evidenced by the exchequer returns for the month of April alone showing income tax accounted for €3.1bn compared to €308 million worth of corporation tax. As President Higgins said in his Tasc speech: "Let us not forget that this surplus has been made possible by an educated and hard-working population as well as by foreign direct investment." Unfortunately, that insight, too, got lost in the economists' outcry.

The OECD has reported that real earnings have been pushed down by inflation in Ireland and still a culture of price gouging is allowed to flourish. Hotels do it without shame or censure to cash in on big cultural and sports events. Under the gaze of a passive State, solo travellers are still sometimes penalised with single supplements; domestic customers continue to be charged inflated energy prices; banks, insurance and utility companies discriminate against anyone without access to or adeptness with technology. There is little doubt that we have nurtured an economy hostile to the ethos of solidarity.

Last weekend, a man arriving in Dublin from London was charged €82 for a 37-kilometre journey from the airport to Foxrock Church in Deansgrange, a drive which the AA estimates as costing €4.63. How can people switch to public transport and leave their cars at home when a short taxi drive costs the equivalent of a flight to a sunny island off Africa?

If the Government wants the people to help save the planet, it must help the people. Allowing a rip-off culture to flourish under its nose is no way to do that.

At last, women are getting their revenge on Donald Trump

A handful of strong women are proving his biggest obstacle to getting back into the White House. Let's hope the women who voted for him follow their lead.

The Irish Times, 12 May 2023

Donald Trump is correct – E Jean Carroll is not his type. The woman is way out of his league. For one thing, she takes inspiration from literary classics. She named her poodle Lewis, so that its full name was Lewis Carroll. She called her Toyota Prius car Miss Bingley after a protagonist in Jane Austen's *Pride and Prejudice* and borrowed from Dean Swift for the title of her book, *What Do We Need Men For? A Modest Proposal*. She has written for the political satire programme *Saturday Night Live* and for 80,000 readers as an advice columnist with *Elle* magazine. When her feminist book was published to critical acclaim in 2019, *The Atlantic* magazine described her as a "beloved and famous writer".

After an excerpt from it containing the Trump rape allegation was published, he protested that he didn't even know who she was. Enough said about his lowbrow range. How chilling it is to recall that, at the time of those initial denials, his groping fingers were hovering over the nuclear levers in the White House.

Then there is the way Carroll comports herself. It is easy to imagine how her aura of dignity might test the ego of a crass bonehead who once boasted that his own daughter was so "hot" he would date her himself.

The contrails of the former US president's private jet, complete with its 24-carat gold fixtures, had barely evaporated from Ireland's sky after his flash visit last week when a New York jury determined that he had sexually abused the now 79-year-old writer about 30 years ago in a changing room at the Bergdorf Goodman store in Manhattan.

The six male and three female jurors also deemed that Trump, who was commonly known in the 1990s as The Donald, defamed Carroll by rubbishing her allegation that he raped her as "a con job" and a ploy to boost sales of her book. She was the 22nd of 26 women to accuse the big sulky orange man with the not-fooling-anybody comb-over of sexual misconduct.

During his fleeting stop over at his golf club in Doonbeg, Co Clare, where he was entertained by a troupe of child dancers, Trump said he was going back to America to face down Carroll in the courtroom. He didn't, the coward. Perhaps his lawyers swore "over my dead body", because everyone knows their client is a liar, and not a deft one either. In his book, *Fear: Trump in the White House*, Bob Woodward quotes the former and would-be-again president as saying: "You've got to deny, deny, deny and push back on these women."

A lovely man I know found a neatly folded piece of paper in his father's wallet while sorting his belongings after his funeral. On it, his father had typed the legend that women would only ever be truly equal when they could walk down the street fat, bald, and ugly, and thinking they were irresistible.

Those words never fail to conjure up an image of skin-deep Trump who once decreed that Angelina Jolie's celebrated looks were "not beauty, by any stretch of the imagination", that Heidi Klum "sadly, [is] no longer a 10", that Jessica Chastain was "certainly not hot", that Rosie O'Donnell was "a big, fat pig", and that Arianna Huffington was so "unattractive" he could "understand why her former husband left her". What those women have in common are stellar accomplishments, independent means and DNA etched "not your type, Mr Trump".

Many people around the world felt an enormous sense of relief when the former reality TV host was compelled to pack his bags and leave the White House after the 2020 presidential election, following a lethal riot in Washington unleashed on his behalf. After four years of holding our breath, it was as if we could breathe again.

Were he not threatening a repeat performance in the Oval Office, we might still be laughing and saying thanks for the buffoon memories. Alas, Trump-watching is back on the box.

There is a difference this time, though. In 2016, large numbers of female voters in America watched the *Access Hollywood* tape in which the republican candidate bragged that he, as "a star", was implicitly licensed to sexually assault women by grabbing their genitalia, and then they went out and voted for him. This time, it is women who are presenting the biggest obstacle to his White House comeback. In America's criminal courts, fraud charges arising from claims made by a former porn actress, Stormy Daniels, could prove to be a bridge too far for the Republican Party.

In New York's civil court, Carroll was able to sue Trump

under the Adult Survivors Act, a law signed only last year by governor Kathy Hochul. Carroll's case was strengthened by corroborating evidence given by her female friends during the trial, which the plaintiff has described as the achievement of her septuagenarian self and her five-foot-three-inch attorney, Roberta Kaplan. When gender equality closes in on critical mass, the world can be made a better place.

There has been speculation that Carroll's triumph will not damage Trump's fortunes in the ballot box. I beg to differ, if only because it highlights what a relict of a bygone age he is, with his ugly sexism and offensive misogyny. The era when it was considered admirable for men to objectify women is dead. It's with Benny Hill in the grave. Trump's antiquated attitude makes his octogenarian rival Joe Biden look like a teenager.

In the aftermath of the Carroll case, Trump-watching has assumed the compellability of the fall of the Borgias, with Alec Baldwin replacing Jeremy Irons in the lead role. What is unfolding is not confined to the undoing of one obnoxious male chauvinist. This is about the end of a world order where men such as Trump and Harvey Weinstein made careers out of crushing women's self-esteem and women suffered them in solitary, isolated silence.

After the trial this week, Carroll said her triumph was for "every woman who has suffered because she was not believed". Let's hope its legacy will be that women who voted for Trump the last time will believe in their multifaceted selves the next time. Maybe they will leave their Women for Trump outfits in the wardrobe and march to the polling stations in T-shirts emblazoned: "Not his type".

What part of branding refugees as potential rapists is not racist?

Unconscious bias must be checked when words such as 'unvetted' drip from our mouths with scorn.

The Irish Times, 26 May 2023

Anyone expecting sympathy for being accused of racism while protesting against foreigners moving to their neighbourhood has a warped opinion of themselves. What part of branding groups of men who are fleeing other countries as potential rapists and paedophiles does not constitute racism?

Besides, aren't there little racists lurking inside most of us?

"Your racecard has been declined, do you have another argument?" challenged a protester's placard outside a warehouse in Santry, north Dublin, which has been earmarked to accommodate some international protection applicants. If that is a question, the answer is yes.

There is an old joke about a nightclub bouncer asking a would-be patron at the entrance to identify himself. "Give me a mirror and I will," goes the punchline. To simply look in the mirror and declare oneself "not a racist" does not constitute case closed, especially when the evidence includes demands for prior consultation before international protection applicants are given accommodation in your midst and claims that no woman or child will be safe if the applicants are allowed in.

We all need to check our unconscious bias when we hear words such as "undocumented", "influx" or "unvetted" dripping from our mouths with scorn. One man protesting in Santry this week claimed that, if 30 male asylum seekers moved into the industrial estate, local women would not be able to walk around the place in safety. As if they ever could. Do we need reminding that most murders of women are committed by men known to them?

The dire scenarios being depicted by the anti-migrant bandwagon have all the hallmarks of phobias, also known as irrational fears. They are being stoked by agitators who fancy themselves as Irish patriots. They puff out their macho chests on social media with quaint proclamations that they are "protecting our women and children". No, they are not. They are using women and children as disingenuous arguments to drag Ireland back to the insular, dictatorial, patriarchal, cruel and judgmental country it used to be and where they ruled the roost; a place where children were abused in open secret and women were consigned to second-class citizenry.

In truth, many so-called nationalists who are fomenting the protests detest the Ireland they claim to love – this new Ireland of solidarity and live-and-let-live – and they are exploiting social inequality for their own agenda.

Xenophobia is a tried-and-tested tool. Most people have racist instincts to some degree. Unlike pregnancy, it is, actually, possible to be a bit racist. There are echoes of Ireland's history of discrimination against the Traveller community in what is going on now as entire groups of people get tarred with one brush. Because some Traveller members engaged in crime, all members got tagged thus and were barred from hotels and pubs and, in effect, from the nexus of Irish life. Yet, the same does not happen when members of the settled community form a disorderly procession through the courts.

The Saylat (Say Anything You Like About Travellers) is the Nimby's first cousin. Peter Casey, a businessman who contested the 2018 presidential election, benefited from this bias when he described Travellers as "basically people camping in someone else's land [who are] ... not paying their fair share of taxes in society". Tellingly, he came second, after Michael D Higgins, in the election.

These days, unfounded rumours are spread about asylum seekers sexually assaulting women, with the intention of ghettoising yet another group of people and, even when these rumours are established as lies, the mud still sticks.

Prejudice is an emboldening human condition, at least until it is called out. Its early manifestation is observable in the schoolyard, where certain children decide they don't like the look of certain other children and bar them from joining the gang. Prejudice is seductive because it makes us feel superior. Tuppence ha'penny never felt better than when it was looking down on tuppence.

James Comey, the former director of the Federal Bureau of Investigation (FBI), talked about the universal susceptibility to racism in a speech he gave at Georgetown University in 2015 following incidents of police brutality against African-American citizens. While in no way excusing them, he said police officers had human instincts and, when they had dealt with incidents involving citizens from a particular socio-economic demographic, they developed prejudices. As a descendant of Irish emigrants, he recalled how American society had once viewed the Irish as "drunks, ruffians and criminals". That's how the "paddy-wagon" got its name.

How quickly we forget. Xenophobia comes in many guises. In this country, Brit-bashing has been a national sport for more than 100 years. Anglo-Irish history sowed the seeds and a long wallow in an inferiority complex has watered and fed it. In a similar vein, how often have you heard natives on a Dublin bus moan "they're back", when some raucous Spanish students appear as predictably as the swallows each summer? Like it or not, that is prejudice.

Politicians have a special duty to guard against stirring up these feelings. During the blockade of a property in Inch, Co Clare designated to accommodate asylum seekers, some national politicians seemed to give them validity by criticising the State for not "consulting" the community in advance. Holly Cairns, the Social Democrats leader, has clarified that, when she called for "engagement" with locals, she wrongly implied that they should have a veto over who gets to live among them.

A further inference that is widely drawn by protesters is that the accommodation of international protection applicants somehow deprives Irish nationals of homes and State benefits. The fallaciousness of this claim is self-evident. Hands up, how many Irish people want to live in a warehouse or on a floatel in a storm? Contrary to the protesters' mantra, Ireland is not full. It's just full of empty spaces and a generous scattering of Nimbys.

This week's news that the numbers of protests against accommodating asylum seekers have declined, in contrast with international trends, shows that, if Ireland is closed to anything it is to closed minds. Now, that's a country to love.

Judge Deirdre Murphy's warning on our broken legal system must not be ignored

Her assertion about legal fees has an ear-splitting ring of plausibility, and a disgusting stench of scandal.

The Irish Times, 23 June 2023

When Nuala O'Faolain was dying, she told Marian Finucane in one of the most riveting interviews ever broadcast by RTÉ that she dreaded all the knowledge she had accumulated during her lifetime dying with her. Her intimacy with classical music and literature, the understanding of life and human relationships the journalist and author had gleaned, was all going to vanish in a puff with her final breath; all come to naught, she grieved.

Something similar, though less heart-rending, occurs when senior judges retire. After careers spent microscopically inspecting humankind and adjudicating on its conflicts, they climb down from the bench one last time, pack their briefcases with the unique insights they have acquired, and head for the horizon. Traditionally, they maintain a dignified public silence forever after. All that wisdom is buried by the spade of propriety.

So, when one of their number decides to break ranks and share what she has learned from her judicial experience, the rest of us ought to pay heed. In a candid and quite radical interview on Monday with Mary Carolan, this newspaper's legal affairs correspondent, retired High Court judge Deirdre Murphy urged the State to stop using the law courts to grind down those of its citizens whom it has badly served. To paraphrase, she said the State's job is to help the people, not hound them all the way to the steps of the courthouse before grudgingly accepting its liability.

"If it's wrong, it's wrong," she said. "If you take the line that this is going to cost a fortune, then you should have done it right in the first place and you wouldn't have exposed the State to paying a fortune. When you know there is a problem, deal with it. Don't let it fester, and then say the State cannot afford to pay for a problem it has actually created."

She called for the adoption of a policy known as the model litigant obligation, whereby the State effectively acts as a disinterested litigant obliged to uphold everybody's rights. On Wednesday, a set of non-binding principles for State litigation was published, echoing this model, following Cabinet approval.

Murphy diagnosed that Ireland's litigation system is "broken" and warned that the public's access to justice is shrinking evermore because of the dominance of "a small number of huge" law firms. Civil servants, she observed, can be less cost-conscious when agreeing to pay the public's money than if they were spending their own funds.

In a startling disclosure – one which some of her erstwhile colleagues at the bar may consider a betrayal of a professional secret – Judge Murphy recalled being told when she was a senior counsel being offered a brief by one of the major solicitors' firms that she did not charge a handsome enough fee. "The bigger firms want to brief somebody who will charge a fortune so that they can justify charging a fortune," she said. Considering that legal costs are customarily calculated on the basis that the solicitors' bill amounts, roughly, to two-and-a-half times counsels' fees, Murphy's assertion has an ear-splitting ring of plausibility, and a disgusting stench of scandal.

What her anecdote illustrates is something akin to a cosy cartel operating in plain sight, predicated on a caste system. It is the same big law firms that keep getting the bulk of State work and keep briefing their favourite counsel. Massively lucrative litigation is jealously kept within this club while the numerous small firms around the country seldom get a look in. As any consumer watchdog will attest, this blatant disregard for competition is bad for those who must pay the bill.

"We're talking about the people's money," Murphy said. "A fair and equitable distribution of State work will make the system better because work will be distributed among those capable of doing it and not just the favourites of particular people."

When it comes to the law, the State's foremost obligation is to provide equal access to the dispensary of justice. But, by maintaining a club culture that fattens the big firms' coffers, it is colluding in a culture of exorbitant costs that prohibit many citizens from ever darkening a courthouse door in pursuit of fairness. As gold-star graduates of the Law Library that serves as the judiciary's nursery, senior judges know this. Frank Clarke, the last chief justice, publicly denounced Ireland's astronomical legal costs. His remarks were met with uncharacteristic silence from the oratorical bar.

On Tuesday, another retired High Court judge, Bernard

Barton, warned the Joint Oireachtas Justice Committee in Leinster House that the proposed abolition of juries in defamation trials would have "very serious consequences" for citizens' legal rights. That is arguable in a jurisdiction where almost all other civil law cases are heard by judges in the absence of juries, but what is inarguable is that there are many more immediate obstacles to people gaining access to justice. Top of the list is the expense.

As Judge Murphy tells it, this is ratcheted up by an attitude within the Civil Service that complaints are often best ignored, until they can no longer be ignored. Answer that letter, she suggests. Take that phone call. If State respondents, such as prison governors, replied substantively to the first letter of complaint, she said, many trips made to the courts could have been avoided.

"If you just send a letter and it's all deny, deny, deny, they bring a judicial review."

What she says makes sense but, in her experience, it is not common. Ireland is an exceptionally litigious country with prohibitive costs that have turned the civil law courts into the domain of the State and wealthy individuals, at the expense of most citizens.

Murphy said at the end of her interview that she wants to "be of more service". A role should be created for her to oversee the implementation of the State's new litigation principles. To allow the insights she has gained as a judge – and which she has had the courage to share with us – to wither and die would be a terrible loss to this country.

Tubridy is paying a high price for not exposing RTÉ's deceit

Folly of judging somebody's worth by size of their remuneration is lesson Ireland has repeatedly been taught, yet never seems to learn.

The Irish Times, 30 June 2023

Ryan Tubridy has a lovely home. It is a mirror of its owner – congenial with no excess bulk. This I know because I interviewed the broadcaster there at his invitation in 2021 and he proudly showed me around it. Before our meeting, the RTÉ press office ordered that his house was not to be identified and required a written undertaking in advance that there would be no questions about the Montrose star's "private life". The day after the interview, another diktat arrived. This one said there was to be no mention of "who appears in photographs, paintings or specific book titles in his house". I checked the calendar to see if it was April Fools' Day.

At that time *The Late Late Show* presenter's published salary from RTÉ was €495,000. Last week, the rest of us great unwashed found out that the public service station was paying him an extra €75,000-a-year, camouflaged as "consultancy" fees and paid through a British company. When I had broached the subject of his lavish remuneration, RTÉ's highest-paid presenter had replied that his lifestyle was not expensive, as epitomised by the 14-year-old car he drove. "I think if I was to end up working in a bookshop tomorrow I would downsize comfortably because my needs are not outrageous," he said.

I believe he meant it sincerely. So why did he feel the need to extract more than half-a-million-euro annually from his impoverished employer?

Ego may be a big chunk of the reason. According to the crude calculations of the capitalist market, a person's worth is measured by the number of zeros in their pay cheque. Fame, pampering and fans may attest to popularity, but it's your salary that positions you at the top of the heap. Being in the public eye can make an ego fragile. Tubridy hinted thus when discussing critics-in-the-street he had encountered. "It's a pity because the neediness of this job means you don't want to elicit that reaction from someone," he said in the interview, "and you nearly want to go to all the people who don't really rate you or like you and say, 'Can we have a cup of coffee because, honestly, I'm not that bad? In real life, I'm even a bit nicer'."

The folly of judging somebody's worth by the size of their remuneration is a lesson Ireland has repeatedly been taught, yet never seems to learn. In fact, the Government might check its own integrity when it denounces RTÉ's arrangement with Tubridy. Its deal with Robert Watt when he became the secretary general of the Department of Health with an €81,000 pay rise was equally inexplicable. In both cases, the organisations where Watt and Tubridy reign supremely-paid are blighted by under-resourcing and held together by workers dedicated to the public service they provide.

Paying the chosen ones huge salaries is a guaranteed way for hubris to flourish; the sort of hubris that made Watt think it acceptable to arrange a professorship for his colleague, the former chief medical officer Tony Holohan, at a potential cost to the public of €20 million.

It echoes the self-entitlement that led bankers on bonkers bonuses to, in the immortal words of Anglo's David Drumm, pick extortionate numbers out of their arses and collapse the economy.

Tubridy is paying an excruciating price now. Overnight, he has been re-cast from hero to zero. While he is blameworthy for not exposing RTÉ's deceit about his pay, he is less the cause and more the symptom of something amiss in our financial culture.

Instead of asking why he needed so much money, the question that needs to be most urgently answered by RTÉ is why it felt the need to pay it. The explanation that he was a flight-risk from Montrose to a rival station is unconvincing. Where would he have gone in Ireland? RTÉ was his brand. When I interviewed him he said the BBC had not offered him a job but that he could have moved there, except he was too much of a home bird to leave Ireland. He quoted his late father having once said: "Poor Ryan, he'd get homesick in Greystones."

One of the trademarks of Tubridy's *Late Late Show* chat style was his incessant declarations of his love for Ireland. So frequent were these professions of patriotism that some people speculated he might be a candidate in the next presidential election. Did his paymasters ever watch the show, and ponder how unlikely he was to abscond to foreign shores, or wonder if he might concede in his contract negotiations that his service to his homeland could compensate for some shaving of his salary?

The other explanation often given for his bloated pay

package was the benefit to RTÉ of advertising revenue generated by *The Late Late Show*. There is no doubt that Tubridy is a fine entertainer and brilliant with children on *The Toy Show*, but he was presenting the world's longest-surviving chatshow in television's weekly prime time slot. How did those who approved his remuneration separate the dancer from the dance?

As he finds himself at odds with RTÉ about the legal status of his contract, Tubridy is discovering the lonely reality of the maxim that everyone is dispensable. Pat Kenny, whom RTÉ was paying over €950,000 at one stage, knows it well. When he switched to Newstalk in 2013, there were dire predictions that his old RTÉ radio slot would crumble and die. It did quite the opposite. The audience actually grew when Seán O'Rourke took over as presenter.

Politicians have been asking RTÉ bosses at Oireachtas committee meetings why Tubridy's extra payments were concealed. The answer is obvious. Had it been known he was getting more than €500,000, other presenters, with some justification, would have demanded more in their pockets too. Until a pay cap is imposed in RTÉ, including on management, celebrity agents will continue to negotiate big bucks to bolster their clients' self-esteem. Because, as we ought to know by now, that's the way the money goes.

Acknowledgements

My thanks to the inestimable Miriam Lord for sprinkling her word magic in the foreword.

This book would not be what it is without the high standards politely but insistently required by its publisher and editor, Ciara Considine.

While it has been a happy labour, the book was started and completed amid chaos in my life, while I was selling my house and building a new one. Without the love and support of my sisters, Adrienne and Gina, and my brothers-in-law, Ronald and Patrick, it would never have happened. They gave me a place to sleep and work, fed and spoilt me, tided me over financially and propped me up whenever I faltered.

Thanks are due to the staff in the National Library for their gracious assistance during the weeks I spent researching its newspaper archive.

I could not have produced the journalism in this book without the trust of strangers who allowed me to tell their stories. Everything here is testament to their resilience and courage. From the bottom of my heart, thank you for taking a chance with me.